MEN AND DEPRESSION

Clinical and Empirical Perspectives

MEN AND DEPRESSION
Clinical and Empirical Perspectives

Sam V. Cochran
University of Iowa
Iowa City, Iowa

Fredric E. Rabinowitz
University of Redlands
Redlands, California

Academic Press

San Diego London Boston New York Syndney Tokyo Toronto

This book is printed on acid-free paper.

Academic Press
A Division of Harcourt, Inc.
525 B Street, Suite 1900, San Diego, California 92101-4495, USA
http://www.apnet.com

Academic Press
24-28 Oval Road, London NW1 7DX
http://www.hbuk.co.uk/ap/

Library of Congress Cataloging Card Number: 99-64636

International Standard Book Number: 0-12-177540-2

PRINTED IN THE UNITED STATES OF AMERICA
99 00 01 02 03 04 MM 9 8 7 6 5 4 3 2 1

Acknowledgment

Many persons have contributed in many ways to this volume. First and foremost, our patients, the men with whom we have worked over the past twenty years, have taught us the most about depression in men. Without their willingness to open their hearts and minds and let us accompany them in their struggles with depression we would never have been able to conceive of this book much less write it. We will be forever grateful.

A number of colleagues have contributed support, advice, and suggestions. We want to acknowledge the support of our friends in the Society for the Psychological Study of Men and Masculinity of the American Psychological Association. In particular, Glenn Good, Ph.D. and William Pollack, Ph.D. have provided important encouragement of our efforts. Scott Stuart, M.D. and James Levenson, M.D. offered suggestions for references and assisted in our sifting of the literature. Dr. Stuart contributed an important chapter to the volume.

Our editor at Academic Press, George Zimmar, Ph.D., and his colleagues Michael Leuci and Traci John all provided the necessary technical advice and expertise along the way. George in particular had great faith in the contribution this volume would make, and we are grateful to him for his perseverance and support.

Finally, without the support and love of our families this book could never have been completed. Thanks, Lucy, Kate, Janet, Karina, and Jared.

Sam V. Cochran, Ph.D.
Fredric E. Rabinowitz, Ph.D.

Contents

* University of Iowa, Iowa City, Iowa

8 *Reflections on Theorizing, Diagnosing, and Treating Male Depression*   *165*

Preface

There was a time in the not-too-distant past when disclosure by a man that he had suffered from and been treated for depression was enough to disqualify him in the public eye for electoral office. Today, a number of prominent men have "gone public" with their struggles with depression. Mike Wallace, Rod Steiger, Andrew Solomon, and William Styron, to name a few, have all shared their experiences with depression. Styron's *Darkness Visible* (1990) is a moving memoir of his struggle with and recovery from depression. Terrence Real's (1997) recent popular book *I Don't Want to Talk About It* opens the door wider on this neglected topic. Popular literature and film portray men with mood problems openly and sympathetically. Perhaps the tide is shifting, the pendulum swinging a bit. Maybe it is becoming easier for men to acknowledge depressed feelings. Are we beginning to see a change in how men view their emotions; a shift from hiding and suppressing their emotions to a more open, accepting, and affirming posture with respect to the emotional aspects of their lives?

It has been 20 years since we each began treating men in psychotherapy. Looking back on our experiences, many of the men we have seen and treated were suffering from some form of depressive disorder. A broken relationship, a failed marriage, a lost job, a death of a friend; these experiences were the keys that opened the door to a vast emotional landscape with which most of these men were unfamiliar and that frightened them. Since that time, an increasing number of scholars and authors have written about the psychological problems of men and have speculated about the best ways to treat men who come to therapists for assistance in their problems with living, including problems with moods.

Within this emerging discourse on the psychology of men, some voices have been devoted to articulating the problem of unrecognized and untreated depression in men. There is an emerging consensus that the male gender role in our culture is problematic. Aspects of the male gender role, as traditionally constructed, discourage both awareness and expression of psychic pain. At the same time, these traditional gender roles actually contribute to such pain by prompting men to follow a path that rewards emotional restriction and denial of psychological pain. Increasing sophistication in research on the psychology of men and the theory-building that utilizes a gender-sensitive lens have advanced our understanding of the problems men struggle with and how we might respond to these men. We have, indeed, come a long way in the past twenty years.

So why a book on men and depression? In spite of these advancements in the study of men and their problems in the past two to three decades, it has been both puzzling and sobering to read the research on gender and mental disorders. Men are conspicuously underrepresented in the tally of most of the common psychiatric disorders, particularly the mood disorders and the anxiety disorders. On the other hand, many more men than women suffer from alcoholism, drug abuse and dependencies, and a number of the more severe personality disorders (Golomb, Fava, Abraham, & Rosenbaum, 1995; Robins & Reiger, 1991). Although data amply document these imbalances, findings of most large-scale epidemiological studies confirm that the frequency of all mental disorders is quite evenly distributed between men and women. In one of the most widely cited studies, men are actually slightly overrepresented in all classes of disorders compared to women by a margin of 36 to 30% (Robins & Reiger, 1991). Nonetheless, in the category of mood disorders, men are dramatically underrepresented. Major depression and dysthymia are two of the conditions in which men appear to be outnumbered by women by a ratio of approximately two to one (Nolen-Hoeksema, 1990). This ratio has been remarkably consistent across time and cultures (Culbertson, 1997). On the other hand, with regard to bipolar affective disorder, manifest in both manic and depressive states, the discrepancy between men and women is closed, with each sex represented at approximately the same frequency (Weissman, Bruce, Leaf, Florio, & Holzer, 1991). Why are men so underrepresented in what are called the unipolar depressive conditions? What might account for this discrepancy? Should we not expect this same underrepresentation in the other mood disorders such as bipolar disorder? Is it the case that half as many men actually suffer from depression? Clinical experience and discussions with our colleagues have caused us to wonder where the men whom we treat are hiding in these numbers.

Findings regarding who seeks psychotherapeutic treatment are similarly skewed. Most empirical investigations find that half as many men as women seek psychotherapy. This is another ratio that has remained remarkably consistent across time (Vessey & Howard, 1993). Whatever the barriers might be that prevent men from seeking treatment from mental health professionals, they seem to have existed for a number of years, and seem to persist in spite of our increasing sensitivity to gender differences in psychological conditions and treatment approaches. Considering the finding that somewhat more men compared with women may actually be afflicted with psychiatric conditions, why are not more men seeking treatment? What forces keep men from seeking help in larger numbers? Why are there two women in the consulting office for every man who walks through the door?

Finally, and perhaps most compelling, the data on suicide cause us to wonder where the depressed men might be hiding. Men complete suicide at least three and up to six to eight times more frequently than women, depending upon age (Anderson, Kochanek, & Murphy, 1997). Even though women appear to make suicide gestures or attempts more often than men, the numbers are unmistakable here. Men are killing themselves in alarming numbers, especially as they get older. These findings would cause any reasonable person to conclude that there are clearly many men who are depressed and who are at risk for killing themselves. Where might these men be represented in the numbers on mood disorders? Are they included in the epidemiological findings? What might we make of this consistent sex reversal in the statistics on who commits suicide?

These scientifically derived findings and the various explanations offered for them often mask the day-to-day realities of the many men who struggle with economic hardship, family commitments, substance abuse disorders, frustrations, and unnamed or unmet expectations. One wonders why there are not more men in the numbers on mood disorders. A recent news story, reported in a local newspaper and, perhaps, sadly familiar to all of us, illustrates the real dangers in these often unrecognized and frequently untreated forces in men's lives. One day a local firefighter who, according to neighbors and coworkers, had been "stressed out" and "depressed," and was not sleeping well, came home after a night of drinking. He grabbed one of the many guns he collected, took his spouse and two daughters hostage in their own home, and finally murdered them before killing himself. In spite of several hours spent attempting to convince him to come out and seek help, negotiators and crisis personnel were unable to persuade him to surrender. All who offered a comment on this incident were mystified at what would cause such a "good" and "responsible" man to suddenly break like this. As the news story unfolded over the next few days, though, this firefighter had been sanctioned at his place of employment for exhibiting emotional outbursts that many considered threatening. He had been referred for alcohol treatment but refused to go. He had been observed crying alone and nervously pacing, both at work and in his neighborhood. Many neighbors acknowledged he appeared troubled. The human price of such a desperate act is incalculable; yet such a man is unmistakably depressed. In spite of the fact that such dramatic stories sell newspapers and magazines, this story is almost archetypal in its haunting and tragic familiarity. The vast majority of perpetrators of violence are men (Hastings & Hamberger, 1997). Indeed, more than 90% of homicide/suicide offenders are men, and a similar percentage of their victims are women (Felthous & Hempel, 1995). How many men who are desperately depressed ultimately end their pain and shame in such a fashion? Too many do.

In light of the mood problems men struggle with and their consistent underutilization of mental health services in general, efforts that might diminish the barriers men encounter when seeking mental health treatment are warranted. The purpose of this book is to examine the literature in the area of mood disorders with an eye toward what we can learn about men and their moods. How are men represented in this literature? What might be some of the reasons that men are underrepresented in the epidemiological findings? What can we learn about men and how men manage their moods? What attempts have been made to understand the male–female imbalances in the statistics on mood disorders? What treatments work best for men's mood disorders? What research might further our understanding of men's mood disorders? These are only some of the questions we will raise as we make our way through this largely uncharted territory.

In the past 20 years, a number of men and women working in the behavioral and social sciences have developed what has become known as a "New Psychology of Men" (Levant, 1996). Early workers in the field, including Pleck and Sawyer (1974), Farrell (1975), Fasteau (1974), and Goldberg (1976) took up the challenge to traditional masculine values that feminists had made and began to examine the negative and oppressive aspects of traditionally constructed gender roles. These efforts included an examination of the psychologically restrictive nature of most of the cultural conditioning little boys and men experience. Pleck (1981), in his seminal critique of male gender identity ideology, introduced the concept of male gender role strain and conflict. This conceptualization resulted in a paradigm shift for workers in the area of the psychology of men. Emphasis was no longer only on the individual, intrapsychic determinants of gender. Now, we looked at how culture and social factors interacted with internal dynamics to produce a more complex but more accurate representation of how gender is experienced by men and women. This shift has led to research and theory-building efforts that are now grouped under the broad rubric of a "New Psychology of Men." Levant and Pollack (1995) collected a number of papers into a volume devoted to the articulation of this perspective. This new psychology of men begins with the feminist critique of our traditionally constructed gender roles and asks how these roles impact men and shape men's behavior and emotional lives. This has led to reexamination of the traditionally constructed male gender role and the detrimental impact that strict and rigid adherence to its norms and values has upon men's lives. We view our work as consistent with this tradition and hope it will advance our understanding of mood disorders in men. It is our hope that by viewing this topic through a lens informed by the new psychology of men, we will be better equipped to assess and treat men who suffer from the major mood disorders.

Although this book is devoted to an examination of men and depression, it is in no way intended to ignore, minimize, or discount the great numbers of women who suffer from depression and who are represented in large numbers in the epidemiological studies on mood disorders that we will review. We are indebted to the significant research that has occurred in the past 20 years on women and depression (e.g., McGrath, Keita, Strickland, & Russo, 1990). It is only through careful examination of this literature that we have begun to ask questions about men and depression. We hope to advance our understanding of men and their moods, not to diminish or discount the struggles a large number of women have had over the years.

This book is intended for the practitioner and the researcher interested in increasing her or his knowledge base about mood disorders in men. Even though there is a large body of knowledge pertaining to mood disorders in women, there is a relatively sparse knowledge base that looks at these phenomena and asks what we might learn about men. We want to know what we can learn about men—how to understand mood disorders in men, how to better assess these problems, and how to offer effective treatments for these mood problems in men.

Our approach will combine empirical and clinical perspectives. We began working in this area primarily as clinicians. Moving back and forth between our clinical experience and the literature on men, gender, and depression, we have come to appreciate the clinical insights that many writers have developed by working with men. In addition to this clinical literature, we have also come to appreciate the hard work involved in the design and execution of quality empirical research on both mood disorders and psychotherapy treatment. We will look at the literature from psychiatric epidemiology that defines mood disorders and attempts to understand their occurrence in the population in general and in the sexes in particular. There have been great strides made in the last 20 years in the standardization of description and diagnosis of these disorders. These advances have led to highly sophisticated epidemiological investigations that have yielded greatly improved data on the incidence and prevalence of mental disorders. What can we learn about men when we look carefully at this literature?

We will examine some of the hypothesized reasons for the discrepancies between men and women with regard to the development and existence of mood disorders. What factors account for the consistent two-to-one ratio of women to men found in studies that examine the diagnosis and treatment rates for some mood disorders? Are there any divergences from these findings? If so, what might they tell us about the differences between the sexes?

We will look at some of the specific models and theories that have been put forward to account for men's relative underrepresentation in these numbers. Do men become alcoholic and women become depressed? Do men hide or "mask" their depressive moods in ways that are not detected in our formal diagnostic or assessment schemes? Are men more likely to engage in behaviors designed to distract them from their painful affective states? Are there other factors that might account for men's relative underrepresentation in the numbers on mood disorders? How do these various models stand up under empirical scrutiny?

We will consider how men might express their depressed moods through atypical means such as reckless or antisocial behavior, interpersonal avoidance, aggression, or outbursts of anger. Are these means by which men mask their depressed moods? Is this a more legitimate expression of feelings in men? How do men's experiences of loss, trauma, and grief play a part in their vulnerability to depression? What implications might this have for our assessment and treatment of men?

We will examine treatment approaches for working with mood disorders in general, and look at the literature on treatment effectiveness—what works, with whom, and under what conditions. In this area, as in the epidemiological studies, great scientific advances have occurred in the past twenty years in terms of how clinicians view effective treatments for mood disorders. We will examine how this literature might inform therapists' thinking about treating men, and how there are similarities and differences that therapists might encounter when working with men and women.

With any examination of mood disorders, depression, and men, it is important to examine the issue of suicide; since men do actually commit suicide at three to six times the rate that women commit suicide. The data on suicide alone should make us wonder what would account for this male preponderance in the act of suicide, when men are so obviously absent in data on studies of other categories of mood disorders. What might account for this dramatic reversal in the gender split typically seen in most studies of mood disorders? Is it possible that there are many men who are depressed and who we might not be identifying and counting in the "up-front" assessment of these problems? Does this sex difference in suicide rates indicate that there is clearly a significant number of men who suffer from severe depression? How might the gender roles men and women play in our culture figure in this ratio?

Finally, we will speculate about what the future might hold for clinicians treating men, as well as for researchers who will be looking into these and other related topics. In spite of the large literature on mood disorders, we are just beginning to understand some of the ways that sex and gender play a part in both the development and maintenance of these disorders and in the effective treatment of these conditions. It is an exciting time to be working in this area. We are beginning to articulate the conditions and perspectives that may ultimately lead more men to seek help for their mood problems.

A comment is warranted about terminology we have chosen to use throughout this volume. Unless otherwise indicated, depression in our volume refers to major depression or unipolar depression as defined in the *Diagnostic and Statistical Manual of Mental Disorders* of the American Psychiatric Association (1994). In addition to this specific form of depression, some authors also refer to depression by using the term "affective disorder." The term "affective disorder" encompasses more than major depression. It includes bipolar disorder in addition to the unipolar depressive conditions on which we will focus. There are a number of unresolved nomenclature-related debates in the literature that we will not address in this book. For example, a number of scientists are attempting to carve out the boundaries of subclinical depressive conditions. Some of these conditions share a border with dysthymia, and some include various subclinical syndromes composed of fewer diagnostic criteria compared with a major depressive episode but warranting clinical attention nevertheless. We do not attempt to include the specifics of these and other debates in our treatment of this subject.

A book that examines distress and depression in men may be seen by some as politically provocative. Our intention is not to be provocative. Our intention is to raise awareness in clinicians and researchers of the problem of undiagnosed and untreated depression in men. The cost of ignoring these problems is great. As mentioned, we owe a great debt to the researchers and clinicians who have taken the psychiatric and psychological establishments to task regarding the condition and treatment of women. Many insights and initiatives have come from this hard work. Nonetheless, it is remarkable, and disconcerting, that so little attention has been devoted to men's suffering from depression. When sorting through the hundreds of books and the thousands of journal articles and monographs on depression, there is but a scant handful that specifically address the topic of male depression. The acceptance and production of such a volume is encouraging. The tide is indeed turning. We owe the men in our consulting rooms and our lives nothing less than our best possible efforts to understand and help them in their journeys. It is our greatest hope that this volume will help researchers to better understand the complexities of male depression and will equip clinicians to more effectively treat the men who seek them out for help.

CHAPTER 1

Figuring Depression in Men: Defining the Terms of Depression

A lot of questions about the woods can't be answered by staying all the time in the woods—and it also works the other way, a lot of the deep inner questions get no answer unless you go for a walk in the woods.

Norman Maclean

Defining Mood Disorders
Depression: A Disorder of Mood
Epidemiology of Mood Disorders
The Epidemiological Catchment Area Study
The National Comorbidity Survey
Depressed Men: Cultural and Social Considerations
Depressed Men: Course of Depressive Disorders
Summary

Any clinician working with men will soon notice a discrepancy between the officially reported statistics on the incidence and prevalence of mood disorders and his or her cumulative clinical experience. Official statistics consistently tell us that men suffer from and are diagnosed with depression about half as frequently as women. Clinical experience soon bears out the reality that men do get depressed. Many men suffer from longstanding and unremitting depression. Men experience depression in myriad ways. Far too many depressed men ultimately succumb to the most tragic risk associated with depression—suicide. Indeed, when we consider suicide, the murder of the self, the official statistics are reversed. In general, two to three times as many men as women actually commit

Young Men and Fire (pp. 104)

suicide. This number rises dramatically with advancing age, particularly for men over age 65. This statistical finding alone should be enough to raise our curiosity about mood disorders in men. But what of the many men we might never see in our consulting rooms who suffer in lives of quiet desperation? How many men, as a result of our culture's prohibition on men's showing weakness or emotionality, avoid seeking help? Would these men not be included in the official numbers on mood disorders were we to somehow capture them and get them to talk to us? How do they experience and express their moods? Do men have a different vocabulary for the expression of depressed moods that renders them both inaccessible to most helping efforts and invisible to most questionnaires and assessment instruments in use to establish the statistics on mood disorders?

Clinician Query—"Sad and all alone"

Steven was a 28-year-old single man who was employed as a custodian in a hotel. He was referred for evaluation and possible psychotherapy by the psychiatrist with whom he had been working for approximately one year. His psychiatrist had treated him for depression with a trial of fluoxetine that Steven felt had not really helped that much and that he discontinued on his own. At the time of the initial consultation with the psychotherapist, Steven had quit a second medication trial of imipramine, feeling that it had too many unpleasant side-effects. Steven was tall and lanky, but walked slowly and had difficulty organizing his thoughts and articulating them to the therapist with whom he was consulting. Steven clearly exhibited many signs and symptoms of depression in his initial interview. He reported that he was "following through" with his psychiatrist's suggestion that he "get some therapy."

As he and the consulting therapist talked about his current situation, he stated that he felt depressed, frustrated with his job, and was oversleeping quite a bit. His job shift was from 3 p.m. until 12 midnight. After getting off work, he would come home, go to sleep, and often sleep until noon or 1 p.m. the next day. Then he would get up, go back to work, and repeat the cycle. Weekends were mostly devoted to sleeping and watching television. He had few friends, did not have, and had never had, an intimate relationship, and felt that his life was basically "a dead end." He captured the tone of his existence by stating that he was "sad and all alone."

Steven was the youngest of eight children. Both parents were in their 40s when Steven was born. His father died when Steven was 5-years-old. His mother worked hard to provide for the children. But, according to Steven, she herself had struggled with depression after the death of her husband. Two sisters had been treated for depression, and one brother had an alcohol problem. Another brother was in prison.

Long pauses were characteristic of the interaction with the consulting therapist. Steven would appear to be in reflection as he considered his responses to the consultant's questions.

"We've covered a lot of territory today, Steven. What do you think would help?" the therapist asked as a means of directing the initial consultation interview to a conclusion and beginning the process of formulating a possible treatment plan.

"I don't know. I just have never really had much interest in working or doing much of anything. Maybe if I had more of an interesting job or something. It took me eight years to finish college."

"You sound as if you feel that is longer than it should have taken," the therapist followed. "What happened?"

"Well, I started out in pharmacy, but switched to psychology. Then, my mother died when I was starting my junior year, and I basically just dropped out that semester. I just quit going to classes and flunked all my courses. I never really got over that—her death. It was a real setback."

"Sounds like it was a really difficult time. You never really got over it?" the therapist asked, following up on Steven's obvious emotional reaction to this topic.

"Yeah," Steven replied, with a sigh. Tears slowly welled up in his eyes. The therapist waited for him to continue. He did not say anything else on the subject. "It just seems like nothing has gone right for me since then. No, really, nothing has ever gone right. I basically got by in high school, but didn't ever really work very hard. Nothing interested me. I didn't have any friends. I still don't. I've probably been depressed at least since mom died. But I think it even goes back further than that. Probably to high school, maybe even junior high. I don't know."

- How is depression manifest in men?

- How many men are at risk for developing a depressive disorder at some time in their lives?

DEFINING MOOD DISORDERS

Depression, as we know it, has most likely existed since before recorded history and has been recognized by authors and scientists for thousands of years (Jackson, 1986). Over these years, physicians and clinicians have observed how some people behave in obvious and distinctly different ways from what would be considered normal at the time. In reading accounts of the pioneers in medical and psychological science, from Hippocrates to Kraeplin and Freud, it is obvious that they all recognized and attempted to characterize what we today would call depression. Early descriptions of depression, or melancholia, as it was often termed, are remarkably similar to our current diagnostic descriptions. Hippocrates clearly recognized the existence, in what he called melancholia, of a condition that would today be considered major depression. According to him, this mood disturbance was caused by an excess of one of the four body humors—"black bile." The buildup of this substance in the body was thought to produce the disturbances of thought and mood that characterize depression. The influence of this perspective has been enormous, and Hippocrates' conceptualization of melancholia represents one of the earliest attempts to formulate a biological or somatic explanation for depression.

This early identification and description of what was clearly depression was an important step in our understanding of the mood disorders. Emil Kraeplin (1921) proposed what was to be an enduring distinction between what he called "dementia praecox" (schizophrenia, in today's nomenclature) and manic–depressive psychosis (bipolar disorder). He suggested a terminology that separated mania from depression, noting that, in depression, the individual manifested a "sad or anxious mood, retardation or sluggishness of thought and behavior." Mania, on the other hand, was characterized by Kraeplin as consisting of flight of ideas, exalted mood, and pressured activity. These observations regarding the distinction between mania and depression have stood the test of time. Today, they form the basis of one of the main distinctions between the two broad classes of mood disorders—the depressive disorders and the bipolar disorders.

In 1917, Freud (1917/1957), in his classic paper "Mourning and Melancholia," identified and described normal (mourning) and pathological (melancholia) mood states and drew a sharp and, in many ways, still relevant distinction between the two. As characterized by Freud, mourning was a normal, albeit painful, mood. It was a grief reaction, most often triggered by a loss of someone near and dear to the person. Melancholia was the term Freud chose to describe the more morbid mood characterized by symptoms that one would associate today with clinical depression. Freud thought this mood state was related to normal mourning, but was manifest in more extremes of thought and mood, and often appeared without an apparent loss. One aspect of the extreme nature of this reaction was the consistent and seemingly uncharacteristic self-criticism or self-reproach manifested by the melancholic person.

Because mourning, as Freud termed it, was triggered "in reaction to" a real or imagined loss, it became associated over the years with syndromes characterized as "reactive" or "psychogenic" depressive disorders. Melancholia, on the other hand, became understood as an endogenous or "psychotic" mood disturbance. It could be triggered by a loss, but persisted beyond the bounds of what was normally expected in bereavement.

In this early distinction, Freud clearly marked out the boundaries of depressive disorders that have endured to the present. The early *Diagnostic and Statistical Manuals* published by the American Psychiatric Association emphasized, as did Freud, the distinction between the psychogenic or reactive depressions that Freud would have considered mourning and the physical or endogenous depressions that Freud would have considered melancholia (Silverman, 1968). Such a distinction continues to this day, as researchers and clinicians attempt to differentiate those mood disturbances that might be driven primarily by biological forces from those triggered by psychosocial stressors or events in the person's life. Indeed, one of the key considerations in the assessment and diagnosis of a mood disorder is whether the disturbance has been precipitated by a recent stressor of some kind, such as the death of a loved one or some other actual or symbolic loss. The existence of specific and identifiable stressors in the individual's life often has both diagnostic and treatment implications.

The distinction described here between the psychologically driven depressive states and the biologically driven states has had profound implications for research endeavors, theory building, and treatment approaches. Early psychoanalytic thinkers such as Abraham

(1911/1948), Freud (1917/1957), and Bibring (1953) explored the psychological aspects of depression and helped advance our understanding of the psychodynamic aspects of both the causes and the effective treatment of depression (see Gaylin, 1983). More recently, biologically oriented investigators such as Snyder (1980) and Winokur (1991) have advanced our understanding of the neurochemical substrates of depressive disorders, the hereditary aspects of these disorders, and effective pharmacological agents to treat these disorders. Sometimes, these approaches to understanding and treating mood disorders have not appeared to be compatible, but each has advanced our understanding in significant ways, and each continues to be a significant force in the work on understanding and treating these disorders today.

Depression: A Disorder of Mood

Depression is considered a disorder of mood (sometimes called an affective disorder, signifying the disturbance of "affect") in all widely used classification and diagnostic schemes. In general, a mood disorder represents a departure from what we might consider to be a typical mood state experienced by most persons most days of their lives. Depressive disorders are characterized by sad, guilty, remorseful, tired, withdrawn, moods and the influence of these moods on a person's day-to-day behavior. Depression, as we know it, is sometimes called unipolar depression when not accompanied by the mania of bipolar disorder. Depression itself is a misnomer. Some scientists think what we usually consider depression may be better characterized as a syndrome rather than a discrete or specific disorder since a syndrome may have many causes that result in what appears to be the same constellation of symptoms (Winokur, 1997).

Bipolar or manic–depressive disorders are characterized by both the depressed aspect of mood and a manic component of mood. Mania refers to an elated, expansive, or elevated mood that is frequently accompanied by restlessness, increases in motor behavior, distractibility, racing thoughts, and irritability. This component of mood disorder, too, is thought by some to be better characterized as a syndrome than a specific disorder.

Psychiatric nomenclature and diagnostic schemes have advanced dramatically in the past 50 years. Diagnostic criteria for mood disorders have become progressively more specific, particularly with the coordination of the World Health Organization's decennial *International Classifi-*

cation of Diseases (I.C.D.) and the American Psychiatric Association's official *Diagnostic and Statistical Manuals of Mental Disorders* (Gold, 1990). Current diagnostic and descriptive nomenclature codified in the fourth edition of the American Psychiatric Association's (1994) *Diagnostic and Statistical Manual of Mental Disorders (DSM-IV)* defines two classes of mood disorders in adults: depressive disorders and bipolar disorders. Included within the category of depressive disorders are major depressive disorder, dysthymic disorder, and depressive disorder not otherwise specified. The depressed mood disturbance that characterizes these disorders is often called unipolar depression. The bipolar disorder category is comprised of bipolar type I and bipolar type II disorder, cyclothymic disorder, and bipolar disorder not otherwise specified. Bipolar disorder is only diagnosed when mania appears, or has appeared in the past, in the clinical picture. Sometimes, what appears to be a unipolar depression at one point in time will later appear as a bipolar disorder due to the emergence of a manic episode. In addition to these definitions of mood disorders, the *DSM-IV* also includes mood disorder due to a medical condition, substance-induced mood disorder, and mood disorder not otherwise specified.

Depression is diagnosed based on the extent to which a person endorses various criteria or symptoms of a depressive episode. According to the *DSM-IV,* a major depressive episode (see Table 1-1) consists of at least five of the following symptoms which have been present for at least a two week period of time and that represent a change in the individual's typical level of function. These symptoms include depressed mood, diminished interest in all or most all activities most of the day, weight loss or change in appetite, insomnia or hypersomnia, psychomotor agitation or retardation, loss of energy, feelings of worthlessness or inappropriate guilt, decreased concentration, and thoughts of death or suicide. Since men and women suffer from the bipolar disorders in approximately the same ratio (in contrast to the consistent two-to-one female-to-male ratio in the major depressive disorder or unipolar depression category), the criteria for a manic episode are listed in Table 1-2. In addition to both depressive episodes and manic episodes, the *DSM-IV* also describes a mixed episode and a hypomanic episode. In a mixed episode, the criteria for both a manic episode and a depressive episode are met. In a hypomanic episode, an individual must meet the same criteria as for a manic episode but the symptoms need be present only for four days or longer and need not impair to quite the same extent the individual's occupational or social functioning.

TABLE 1-1 *DSM-IV* Diagnostic Criteria for Major Depressive Episode

---

Major depressive episode

A. Five (or more) of the following symptoms have been present during the same 2-week period and represent a change from previous functioning; at least one of the symptoms is either (1) depressed mood or (2) loss of interest or pleasure. (*Note:* do not include symptoms that are clearly due to a general medical condition, or mood-incongruent delusions or hallucinations)

1. depressed mood most of the day, nearly every day, as indicated by either subjective report (e.g., feels sad or empty) or observation made by others (e.g., appears tearful). *Note:* In children and adolescents, can be irritable mood.

2. markedly diminished interest or pleasure in all, or almost all, activities, most of the day, nearly every day (as indicated by either subjective account or observation made by others).

3. significant weight loss when not dieting or weight gain (e.g., a change of more that 5% of body weight in a month), or decrease or increase in appetite nearly every day. *Note:* In children, consider failure to make expected weight gains.

4. insomnia or hypersomnia nearly every day.

5. psychomotor agitation or retardation nearly every day (observable by others, not merely subjective feelings of restlessness or being slowed down)

6. fatigue or loss of energy nearly every day.

7. feelings of worthlessness or excessive or inappropriate guilt (which may be delusional) nearly every day (not merely self-reproach or guilt about being sick).

8. diminished ability to think or concentrate, or indecisiveness, nearly every day (either by subjective account or as observed by others).

9. recurrent thoughts of death (not just fear of dying), recurrent suicidal ideation, without a specific plan, or a suicide attempt or a specific plan for committing suicide.

B. The symptoms do not meet criteria for a Mixed Episode (both mania and depression).

C. The symptoms cause clinically significant distress or impairment in social, occupational, or other important areas of functioning.

D. The symptoms are not due to the direct physiological effects of a substance (e.g., a drug of abuse, a medication) or a general medical condition (e.g., hypothyroidism).

E. The symptoms are not better accounted for by Bereavement, i.e., after the loss of a loved one, the symptoms persist for longer that 2 months or are characterized by marked functional impairment, morbid preoccupation with worthlessness, suicidal ideation, psychotic symptoms, or psychomotor retardation.

Reprinted with permission from the *Diagnostic and Statistical Manual of Mental Disorders,* 4th Edition. Copyright 1994 American Psychiatric Association.

Clinician Query—"I can't work. I can't eat. I can't sleep."

L. J., a 29-year old married man, was admitted to the emergency treatment center one night after his spouse, Donna, and brother, Cecil, found him passed out in the

TABLE 1-2   *DSM-IV* Diagnostic Criteria for Manic Episode

Manic episode

A. A distinct period of abnormally and persistently elevated, expansive, or irritable mood, lasting at least 1 week (or any duration if hospitalization is necessary).

B. During the period of mood disturbance, three (or more) of the following symptoms have persisted (four if the mood is only irritable) and have been present to a significant degree:

  1. inflated self-esteem or grandiosity

  2. decreased need for sleep (e.g., feels rested after only 3 hours of sleep)

  3. more talkative than usual or pressure to keep talking

  4. flight of ideas or subjective experience that thoughts are racing

  5. distractibility (i.e., attention too easily drawn to unimportant or irrelevant external stimuli)

  6. increase in goal-directed activity (either socially, at work or school, or sexually) or psychomotor agitation

  7. excessive involvement in pleasurable activities that have a high potential for painful consequences (e.g., engaging in unrestrained buying sprees, sexual indiscretions, or foolish business investments).

C. The symptoms do not meet criteria for a Mixed Episode.

D. The mood disturbance is sufficiently severe to cause marked impairment in occupational functioning or in usual social activities or relationships with others, or to necessitate hospitalization to prevent harm to self or others, or there are psychotic features.

E. The symptoms are not due to the direct physiological effects of a substance (e.g., a drug of abuse, a medication, or other treatment) or a general medical condition (e.g., hyperthyroidism).

Reprinted with permission from the *Diagnostic and Statistical Manual of Mental Disorders,* 4th Edition. Copyright 1994 American Psychiatric Association.

kitchen of his apartment. He had rented a small efficiency apartment at the urging of his spouse because she had become frustrated with his efforts to stop drinking. In addition, she was considering divorce and had recently informed L. J. of this.

Donna had become concerned after she was unable to contact L. J. over the phone. She had gone to her brother's house and enlisted him to accompany her as she checked on L. J. to see what might be happening. When they arrived, there was no answer at the door, but they could see him through the window lying on the floor of the kitchen. The door was open, and they entered. L. J. could not be roused, and they called an ambulance.

"What are you doing here?" L. J. demanded to know, regaining consciousness and struggling to get to his feet. He pushed Donna away as she attempted to help him.

"We tried to call you, but there was no answer. I got worried," Donna replied.

"Yeah, let's just take it easy," Cecil said, attempting to calm L. J.

At this point, the paramedics arrived and assessed the situation. They could see that L. J. was distraught and intoxicated. There was a quart bottle of vodka on the kitchen counter that was almost empty.

The paramedics convinced L. J. that he might need to be examined by a physician and transported him to the emergency room. There he was evaluated by a physician and interviewed by the on-call intake worker for the hospital's alcohol treatment center.

"Everybody thinks I've got a problem. Donna. Cecil. You, too, I guess. My only problem is that she kicked me out," L. J. lamented to the intake worker. "I don't know what I'm going to do."

"Don't know what you're going to do?" the intake worker responded, attempting to track L. J.

"I can't work. I can't eat. I can't sleep. I just want to roll over and die," L. J. responded.

"It sounds like you might be depressed. You can't eat. You can't sleep. You can't work. You just want to die. That sounds like depression to me. And you're just drinking yourself deeper and deeper into a hole," the intake worker responded. "Come on, L. J., what are you going to do? You can't keep going on like this."

This confrontation took hold of L. J., and he looked up at the intake worker. At this point, L. J. began crying and got up and paced around the examining room. "Yeah. Yeah. What am I going to do? Everything's wrong. Everything's wrong. Everything's wrong."

"You sound like you might be a little scared, too."

L. J. didn't respond directly, but sat back down and put his hands on his head and leaned over, looking at the floor. He was crying and sniffling. "I don't know what to do. I can't deal with this. I just can't deal with it."

- In what ways does depression manifest itself in men in addition to the traditional symptoms designated in the *Diagnostic and Statistical Manual?*
- How much overlap is there between alcoholism and depression in men?

EPIDEMIOLOGY OF MOOD DISORDERS

Epidemiological inquiry attempts to establish the distribution and determinants of disease phenomena in the general population (Zahner, Hsieh, & Fleming, 1995). Psychiatric epidemiology has developed in parallel with the advancements in description and codification of mental disorders in the United States (Kaelber, Moul, & Farmer, 1995). Yet in spite of efforts to clearly and unequivocally define a case of any specific disorder, psychiatric conditions remain relatively "fuzzy." There are at least two reasons for this. First, psychiatric disorders are not typically causally associated with specific disease-causing pathogens characteristic of most medical disorders. Indeed, much epidemiological inquiry involves identification of and tracing the route of transmission of disease-causing pathogens. Second, the symptoms of psychiatric disorders require an individual to identify and endorse emotional states often considered subjective. These descriptions are fraught with the nuances and inaccuracies encountered when asking an individual to identify and report emotional states. Such difficulties further complicate the case for mood disorders, since there is unresolved debate as to whether the entity we formally designate as unipolar depression is a syndrome characteristic of a homogeneous or heterogeneous disorder (Winokur, 1997) and whether depression exists as a discrete diagnostic entity or is manifest along a continuum with varying degrees of severity and symptomatology (Flett, Vredenberg, & Krames, 1997).

In spite of these potential difficulties in defining and studying psychiatric disorders, many investigators have taken up the challenge. One of the most consistent findings in the epidemiological study of mood disorders over the past 50 years in the United States is that women suffer from depression at approximately twice the rate of men. This finding has been replicated in a number of different populations and set-

tings, lending support to the assertion that this represents a true difference in the natural rate of the disorder as opposed to an artifact of
sampling or case-finding methodology (Nolen-Hoeksema, 1990,
1987).

Early data on the epidemiology of psychiatric disorders were derived
mainly by studying patients in psychiatric hospitals and by examining
admission rates to mental institutions. Typical findings from this era of
epidemiological studies indicate that the female-to-male imbalance in
what were then called affective reactions paralleled rates found in pre-
sent-day studies. First admission rates reported from the 1950s ranged
from 2.4 to 11.1 per 100,000 for men and from 4.6 to 18.6 per 100,000
for women. These rates yield a range of female-to-male ratios from 1.35
for men and women over age 65 to 2.7 for men and women in the
25–34 age group (Silverman, 1968).

Nolen-Hoeksema (1995) reported rates for persons treated for affective disorders in the United States in 1980. Rates for women were
greater than for men in all age groups, with a range of female-to-male
ratios from 1.23 (age 18–24) to 1.78 (age 45–64). These admission and
treatment rates provided early empirical evidence of the sex-split in
affective disorders. Of course, the obvious confounding variable with
such data is the fact, now well documented, that considerably fewer men
sought treatment for psychological or psychiatric problems as well as for
medical problems and that these data would be skewed by the inclusion
of greater numbers of women.

The Epidemiological Catchment Area Study

With the increasing sophistication of methodology and assessment
instruments, epidemiological studies with greater reliability and validity
have been conducted (Dohrenwend, 1995). Limitations of the studies
that reported information gleaned only from current psychiatric patients
or from admissions rates to psychiatric hospitals were recognized. One
recent effort to establish community base rates of psychiatric disorders is
the Epidemiological Catchment Area study, sponsored in part by the
National Institute of Mental Health and reported by Robins and Reiger
(1991). This large-scale investigation used trained interviewers to survey
samples from five population centers in the United States (New Haven,
Connecticut; Baltimore, Maryland; Raleigh–Durham, North Carolina;
St. Louis, Missouri, and Los Angeles, California). A total of 19,182 per-

sons were interviewed in the first wave of data collection. The survey instrument used to establish diagnoses of mental disorders in this study, the Diagnostic Interview Schedule (Robins, Helzer, Croughan, & Ratcliff, 1981), was designed to be used by lay interviewers to assess a number of signs and symptoms of mental disturbance. Table 1-3 summarizes the lifetime prevalence estimates, reported by sex, of the various disorders examined in this study.

The findings summarized in Table 1-3 have been cited in support of the assertion that approximately twice as many women as men suffer from depression. This appears to be the case for major depressive episode, major depression, and, to a slightly lesser extent, dysthymia. However, when the bipolar disorders are examined, the gap between men and women closes somewhat, with the resulting ratio much closer to one. Interestingly, men outnumber women in alcohol-related disorders, drug-related use and disorders, antisocial personality, and any psychiatric condition. The large numbers of men in the alcohol abuse and dependence categories elevate the "any condition" category to the point where men actually outnumber women. Additionally, the sex imbalance in these male-dominated disorders raises the question of how many men

TABLE 1-3   Lifetime Prevalence Estimates (Percent) of Psychiatric Disorders by Gender

Category (for all ages)	Male (%) ($n = 8311$)	Female (%) ($n = 10,971$)	F : M Ratio
Any psychiatric disorder	36	30	0.83
Affective disorders	5.2	10.2	1.96
Major depressive episode	3.6	8.7	2.41
Manic episode	0.7	0.9	1.28
Major depression	2.6	7.0	2.69
Bipolar I	0.7	0.9	1.28
Bipolar II	0.4	0.5	1.25
Dysthymia	2.2	4.1	1.86
Alcohol abuse/dependence	23.8	4.6	.19
Illicit drug use	36.1	25.4	.70
Drug abuse/dependence	7.7	4.8	.62
Generalized anxiety disorder	2.40	4.95	2.06
Obsessive–compulsive disorder	2.03	3.04	1.49
Somatization disorder	.02	.23	11.5
Antisocial personality disorder	4.5	.80	.17

Summarized from Robins and Reiger (1991).

who might be "depressed" are manifesting their depression in these categories or through other undocumented syndromes.

The National Comorbidity Survey

A second large-scale inquiry into the incidence and prevalence of mental disorders that was designed, in part, to minimize gender bias in the reporting of symptoms of mental disorders, including depression, was the National Comorbidity Survey reported by Kessler, McGonagle, Zhao, Nelson, Hughes, Eshelman, Wittchen, & Kendler (1994). This investigation used an instrument known as the Composite International Diagnostic Interview (Robins, Wing, Wittchen, Helzer, Babor, Burke, Farmer, Jablenski, Pickens, Reiger, Sartorins, & Towle, 1988) to assess a stratified probabilistic sample of 8098 men and women between the ages of 15 and 54. Lifetime prevalence rates of all disorders assessed in this investigation are summarized by sex in Table 1-4.

TABLE 1-4   Lifetime Prevalence Rates (%) for Diagnoses Reported in the National Comorbidity Survey

Category (for all ages)	Male (%) (n = 4009)	Female (%) (n = 4089)	F : M Ratio
Any NCS disorder	48.7	47.3	0.97
Major depressive episode	12.7	21.3	1.69
Dysthymia	4.8	8.0	1.66
Manic episode	1.6	1.7	1.06
Any affective disorder	14.7	23.9	1.62
Panic disorder	2.0	5.0	2.5
Agoraphobia	3.5	7.0	2.0
Social phobia	11.1	15.5	1.40
Simple phobia	6.7	15.7	2.34
Generalized anxiety disorder	3.6	6.6	1.83
Any anxiety disorder	19.2	30.5	1.58
Alcohol abuse	12.5	6.4	0.51
Alcohol dependence	20.1	8.2	0.40
Drug abuse	5.4	3.5	0.65
Drug dependence	9.2	5.9	0.64
Any abuse or dependence	35.4	17.9	0.50
Antisocial personality disorder	5.8	1.2	0.20

Summarized from Kessler, McGonagle, Zhao et al. (1994).

These results parallel the Epidemiological Catchment Area study in that men are proportionally underrepresented in the mood disorders categories. However, two interesting trends are apparent when comparing findings from these two investigations. The lifetime prevalence estimates reported in the National Comorbidity Survey are greater than those reported for the Epidemiological Catchment Area study in the area of mood disorders. Second, the female to male ratio is noticeably narrowed in the National Comorbidity Survey. These two trends are thought to be a result of instructions given to the interviewers that were intended to counteract the hypothesized tendency of men to forget or underreport their symptoms. If men tend to forget or underreport symptoms, the implications for case-finding are significant. This will result in fewer men being included in the categories studied, thus skewing the reported sex ratios. The National Cormorbidity Survey findings also parallel findings of other investigators who have found that men are substantially overrepresented in alcohol and drug abuse and dependence categories by large proportions (e.g., Hanna & Grant, 1997).

Findings from both the Epidemiological Catchment Area Study and the National Comorbidity Survey support the assertion that men suffer from depression in fewer numbers than women. In fact, follow-up studies of subjects in both of these studies indicated that differences in the prevalence of major depression remained relatively constant for each sex (Eaton, Anthony, Gallo, Cai, Tien, Romanoski, Lyketsos, & Chen, 1997; Kessler, McGonagle, Nelson, Hughes, Swartz, & Blazes, 1994). In consideration of these findings, we must conclude that men appear to be at reduced risk when compared with women for development of major depression in the populations sampled. However, in both the Epidemiological Catchment Area study and the National Comorbidity Survey, men far outnumber women in the alcohol abuse and dependence category, the drug abuse and dependence category, and the antisocial personality disorder category—conditions which, as we will see, have significant comorbidity with depression. In light of the significant comorbidity of mood disorders, alcoholism, and substance abuse, could these findings imply that men merely self-medicate their depressive moods with alcohol and other mood-altering substances? Indeed, as Pollack (1998a) has pointed out, when percentages for alcohol abuse, depression, and antisocial personality disorder for men and percentages for depression and anxiety disorders for women derived from epidemiological surveys are combined, the results are very comparable.

In summarizing findings from the National Comorbidity Survey, Kessler McGonagle, Nelson *et al.* (1994) concluded that women were more likely to report major depressive episodes. However, there were no sex differences in either the chronicity or recurrence of depressive disorders, suggesting that the higher prevalence of depression among women was due to women's having a higher lifetime risk of first onset than do men. This similarity between men and women regarding the characteristics of depression has been confirmed in additional investigations examining course and chronicity of depressive disorders (e.g., Simpson, Nee, & Endicott, 1997; Zlotnick, Shea, Pilkonis, Elkin, & Ryan, 1996).

Clinician Query—"I'm having a lot of losses
to deal with all at once."

Bob was a 48-year-old man who was referred for consultation by a physician who had been working with him and his spouse at an *in vitro* fertilization clinic. Their efforts had failed to produce a viable pregnancy, and Bob, his spouse, and the attending physician had decided it was time to begin talking about the possibility that they would be unable to conceive. This failure, combined with recent job stresses and a host of new physical maladies in Bob's life, had caused him to withdraw from his spouse, Sandy, and act depressed at home. He would frequently spend time in his workshop alone.

Bob was a successful, well-known and well-liked businessman who worked in both insurance and real estate. He had married in his early 30s to Sandy, whom he had dated for five years. They had tried unsuccessfully for three years to conceive a child. Feeling the tick of the biological clock, they had both been evaluated for infertility and had been participating in an *in vitro* fertilization program for two years, also without success. Bob's sperm count was quite low and, combined with Sandy's advancing age, they had simply been unable to conceive. In addition to this, Bob had recently experienced a prostate enlargement that required a minor outpatient surgical procedure. When he met with the therapist, Bob was gregarious and open. He shook hands with confidence and warmth and sat down to begin.

"What brings us together today?" the therapist asked Bob to open their interview.

"Dr. Jones referred me. I guess I'm having a difficult time coping with the idea that we can't get pregnant," Bob replied in a rather matter-of-fact manner.

He proceeded to tell his story as his therapist listened carefully. He gave no obvious indications of depressed mood or that he was having any particular difficulty dealing with his situation. His mood appeared upbeat.

"What makes you say you're having a difficult time coping with this?" the therapist asked.

"Well, I guess I just seem to think about it all the time. You know, not being able to get pregnant. It's a real blow to Sandy. And I get real sad thinking about the fact that I'm not going to be a father and what that means. It really bothers me. I've been able to do just about anything I've wanted in my life, and now this…" Bob's eyes glanced downward.

"And now this?" his therapist queried.

Tears filled Bob's eyes. "Yeah. It's hard to deal with. I find myself restless at night, not getting a good night's sleep. I'm spaced. I'm tired a lot. I don't concentrate well at work. I don't seem to be all here. Sandy keeps checking in with me, wanting to know what's going on with me. It just doesn't make sense to me." Bob sighed and paused. "As I said, I've been able to do just about whatever I set my mind to, but this is just too much. I've worked hard to get where I am businesswise, but as Sandy and I have been going through this fertilization stuff, it has made me realize how much I want to be a dad. Then, on top of it all, this damn prostate situation. That really scared me, but after the surgery, I feel a lot better, and things are working a lot better now, if you know what I mean. It just seems like I'm having a lot of losses to deal with all at once."

As the interview unfolds, Bob expresses the sadness and sense of loss he feels in dealing with the failure at the *in vitro* fertilization clinic and the possibility he might not get a chance to father a child. He also expressed fears and sadness at his health difficulties. He revealed that he feels tired a lot of the time. He gets frustrated easily. At times, he lashes out at Sandy and his coworkers, although he also says that this is very uncharacteristic of him. He has been isolating himself at home more and more. He has been devoting himself more to his work, and he openly wonders if this might be a means of escape for him.

- How do cultural stereotypes and gender-role strain contribute to the development of depression in men?
- What cultural strains are most likely to contribute to depression in men?

DEPRESSED MEN: CULTURAL AND SOCIAL CONSIDERATIONS

Although there is a consistent and robust literature that documents the prevalence of depression in men at rates approximately half that of women, there is an increasing number of investigations that diverge from this finding. These studies document the importance of cultural and social factors related to the eventual development and reporting of depressive symptoms in both men and women. Although the incidence and prevalence of depression has been accepted by researchers and clinicians to be half as great for men as for women, divergent findings that introduce culture and social factors as mediating variables compel us to consider possible reasons for this divergence. Culture as a mediating variable and the convergence of gender as an important facet of culture are significant determinants of depression in an increasing number of population samples.

Perhaps one of the most interesting studies to first call attention to the importance of culture in the epidemiology of mental disorders was the study of the Old Order Amish of Lancaster County in Pennsylvania by Egeland & Hostetter (1983). This study ascertained rates of affective disorders in a relatively self-contained sample of Amish adults in Pennsylvania. Findings revealed approximately equal rates of disorders between men and women for all psychiatric illnesses identified (55% of males identified; 57% of females identified), including affective disorders. Of 38 persons identified with bipolar disorder, 58% were men while only 42% were women. In the unipolar depression category, 49% of persons identified were men while 51% were women. This finding is clearly at odds with the typically reported two-to-one ratio of women to men for affective disorders, particularly unipolar depression. One explanation offered by the investigators was that alcohol abuse as well as sociopathy are relatively uncommon or unreported in this population, and therefore did not mask the expression or identification of depression among the males. Although the case-finding methods used in this study are different from those used in the major epidemiological studies, the importance of cultural considerations in the ultimate emergence and documentation of mental disorders cannot be ignored.

Murphy, Sobol, Neff, Olivier, and Leighton (1984) sampled a general population drawn from Atlantic Canada and demonstrated that when more "gender-fair" stems are used in questionnaires to assess depression and anxiety disorders, the sex discrepancy in rates of mood disorder narrows substantially. This study reported prevalence rates for depression of 4.7% for men and 6.0% for women in a 1952 cohort, and 5.7% for men and 5.6% for women in a 1970 cohort. When incidence rates of depression were examined for differences at age of onset, the gap between men and women narrowed further. The incidence rate of depression for men under 40 years of age was found to be 2.6%, while for women it was found to be .9%. This gap broadened to 2.9% for men versus 3.6% for women between the ages of 40 and 49. For men over 50, the incidence was 1.4%, while for women in this age group the incidence was 2.9%. Overall incidence for men was 2.1%, while for women the overall incidence was 2.5%. This investigation demonstrates that, in addition to cultural factors, age emerges as a salient confounding variable in the measurement of prevalence rates of depression.

In another study that took into consideration the culturally mediated aspects of mental disorders, Loewenthal, Goldblatt, Gorton, Lubitsch, Bickness, Fellowes, and Sowden (1995) examined rates of depression in a sample of 339 (157 men and 182 women) Jews affiliated with orthodox synagogues in London. They found no statistically significant sex differences in cases of depression when using a mood questionnaire combined with symptom stems from the "Bedford College" list that is similar to the *DSM-III* major depressive disorder. This study found rates of 13% for women compared with 10% for men when examining all cases of depression; and 6% for women compared with 4% for men when examining 12-month prevalence of depressive disorder). This study again demonstrated that, for specific cultural groups, the commonly reported two-to-one male to female prevalence rate of depression is not always found to hold true.

Wilhelm and Parker (1989) initially found no differences between men and women in lifetime rates of depression when initially examining a group of 380 postgraduate teacher training students from New Zealand. However, as they followed this cohort over 5- and 10-year follow-up, assessments revealed an emerging discrepancy in the rates of depression at 10-year follow-up that were more consistent with the typically reported two-to-one sex ratio. These differences were found to be a result of variability in the "case" definitions used in the study. The authors questioned the presumption of gender inequality in depressive disorders, especially when case definition and social class are controlled.

An examination of 1747 Chinese American adults living in Los Angeles by Takeuchi, Chung, Lin, Shen, Kurasake, Chun, and Sue (1998) found that there were no sex differences in rates of depressive episode, dysthymia, and depression with dysthymia between men and women. Significantly, when acculturation was introduced as a variable in the analyses of these data, women who were more acculturated (to United States culture) were found to be more depressed than the men who were more acculturated. In the comparable groups where there was low acculturation, no sex differences in rates of depression were found. This is perhaps one of the more compelling examples of the importance of how culture intersects with sex differences in the determination of the sex-ratios in incidence and prevalence of depressive disorders.

Finally, in a sample of the very elderly (subjects over 75 years of age), Girling, Barkley, Paykel, Gehlhaar, Brayne, Gill, Mathewson and Huppert (1995) found that the rates for depression in this cohort were greater for men than women (4.4% of men contrasted with 2.3% of women). This finding is consistent with rates reported by Bebbington, Dunn, Jenkins, Lewis, Brigha, Farrell, and Leltzer (1998), who found that

TABLE 1-5   Studies Reporting Variance in Usual Prevalence Rates of Depression in Men and Women

Study	Author(s)	Female : Male Ratio
Old Amish Study	Egeland & Hostetter (1983)	1 : 1
Sterling County Study	Murphy *et al.* (1984)	1 : 0.78 (1952)
		1 : 1 (1970)
		1 : 2.8 (under age 40)
Anglo Jewry Study	Lowenthal *et al.* (1995)	1 : 0.95
New Zealand teachers	Wilhelm & Parker (1989)	1 : 1
Chinese Americans	Takeuchi *et al.* (1998)	1 : 1 (nonacculturated)
		2 : 1 (acculturated)
Elderly	Girling *et al.* (1995)	1 : 1.9
	Bebbington *et al.* (1998)	1 : 1.8

in a sample of British citizens aged 16–54, the female overrepresentation in depression was confirmed (2.7 versus 1.7%). However, this ratio was substantially altered when examining subjects aged 55–64 (1.1% for women compared with 2.0% for men).

These divergent findings, summarized in Table 1-5, strongly suggest that the influence of specific demographic (e.g., age), societal (e.g., social class composition), and cultural (e.g., race, ethnicity, and religious background) factors on both the diagnosis and reporting of depression is considerable. Within large scale, heterogenous, community-based samples typical of investigations such as the Epidemiological Catchment Area Study or the National Comorbidity Survey, the ratio of prevalence rates between men and women with regard to mood disorders is in the range of 1.5 to 2.0 to 1.0. However, the divergent findings reported above force us to conclude that there exist samples in which social and cultural norms alter these ratios and result in a much more even distribution of rates between men and women.

What is it about the men in these samples that might account for the results reported in these studies? There are several possible explanations for these divergent findings. First, the variable distribution of alcohol and other substance abuse disorders in selected population samples compared with the general population may result in fewer depressed men being counted in these or similar diagnostic categories. Second, the suppression of sociopathic or antisocial behavior patterns that often serve to mask depression will increase the likelihood that depressed mood will be manifest in a more direct and accessible manner in more narrowly selected populations. Third, the variable effect of specific cultural norms on the expression of depressed mood among men in these selected populations may result in variations in recognition, expression, or suppression of depressive symptoms.

The cultural construction of gender-related norms and the suppressing effect such norms may exert on the identification and expression of specific emotional states is one conclusion such findings suggest. Indeed, as previous theorists have speculated about the impact of internal and culturally constructed prohibitions on the expression of certain affective states in women (e.g., Lerner, 1980), a number of investigators are beginning to examine parallel effects for men (e.g., O'Neil, 1981; O'Neil, Good, & Holmes, 1995). The findings on prevalence of depression summarized here that diverge from the usual two-to-one women-to-men prevalence ratios strongly suggest that cultural variations plays a crucial role in our understanding of depression.

DEPRESSED MEN: COURSE OF DEPRESSIVE DISORDERS

Studies that examine the nature of depression itself challenge many conclusions regarding sex-related differences in the nature of depression. A number of investigations have examined sex differences in the eventual development, chronicity, course of disorder, rate of recovery, and rate of recurrence for depressive disorders and have failed to identify any compelling differences between men and women.

Coryell, Endicott, and Keller (1992) examined risk factors for first onset of major depression in a nonclinical sample. They confirmed the two-to-one ratio for risk of first onset of depressive disorder between men and women (15.3 vs 7.6%). However, they found few other significant differences between men and women, including no differences in the mean number of symptoms per episode, clinician-rated global assessment scale, percentage of subjects with suicide attempts, the year in which they reported their first episode, or the proportion who received treatment. Women were somewhat more likely to have had more than one episode of a depressive disorder.

Simpson, Nee, and Endicott (1997) examined gender differences in the course of depressive disorders. Their results showed that men and women did not differ in time to recovery from their initial depressive disorder, the time to their first recurrence of a depressive disorder, or in the number or severity of subsequent depressive episodes. These findings were consistent with previous findings reported by Frank, Carpenter, and Kupfer (1988), in which no sex differences were found in age of onset of depression, number of prior episodes of depression, or the duration of the initial episode of depression. In addition, Frank, Carpenter, and Kupfer (1988) did not find any differences in clinician-rated severity of depression, although they did find that women tended to score higher on two self-report scales used in their study (the Beck Depression Inventory and the Symptom Checklist-90).

In a follow-up of patients treated in the National Institute of Mental Health Treatment of Depression Collaborative Research Program, Zlotnick, Shea, Pilkonis, Elkin, and Ryan (1996) found that gender did not predict type of treatment the individual had received, severity of depressive symptoms at follow-up, or dysfunctional attitudes. Stressful life events and social support system availability, however, were related to the level of depression for both men and women.

In all studies on the actual clinical features of unipolar depression, including the types and number of symptoms, the chronicity of the disorder, the tendency of the disorder to recur, and duration of depressive epidodes, there are few consistent differences between men and women reported. Is the actual disorder itself the same for both men and women? If so, how are we to make sense of the persistent underrepresentation of men in investigations that examine large-scale populations? Perhaps these large, heterogeneous population samples simply disperse the men throughout a number of discrete diagnostic categories and do not accurately portray the reality of depression in men.

SUMMARY

Depression is a disorder that has been studied through recorded history. Hippocrates was one of the first physicians to document the phenomenon of depression and to speculate about the causes of depression. In the Middle Ages, persons suffering from depression were thought to be possessed, or to be witches or devils. Even today, our cultural norms make it more difficult for some persons to admit to depressive symptoms than others.

The scientific study of depression has grown significantly with recent improvements in the validity and reliability of diagnostic schemes and epidemiological inquiry. Two large-scale studies of mental disorders, the Epidemiological Catchment Area study and the National Comorbidity Survey, have established accepted base-rates of depression in the general population. Findings from both of these studies indicate that men suffer from depression about half as much as women suffer. However, an increasing number of investigations diverge from this accepted ratio, finding that, in some population samples, men and women suffer from depression in approximately equal rates, and in others, men actually exceed women in rates of depression. These studies highlight the importance of within-group as well as between-group differences in phenomena including incidence and prevalence rates of mental disorders. They also signify the important effect various culturally defined dimensions of emotional expressiveness are likely to have on the measurement of rates of depression.

In addition to these divergences in findings regarding the rates of depression, the general characteristics of depression and the eventual course of the disorder appear to be remarkably similar between the sexes. The numbers of symptoms reported, the length of time between recurrences of episodes of depression, the severity of the symptoms and the level of impairment all appear to be substantially equal between the sexes. These findings are interpreted to signify that the actual disorder—depression—does not differ between men and women. Men suffer from depression in much the same ways as women suffer from depression. Once depression has developed, the nature of the disorder, except for a very few characteristics, does not differ at all.

CHAPTER 2

Relating Traditional Models of Depression to Male Depression

To prove himself a man, a boy must first prove himself not a woman. His definition of self is always comparative and contrary. It is in opposition to something—but something that is inescapably within him. He will forever feel threatened in his gut, in his essential identity, by anything that reminds him of feminine behavior and the early feminine identification from which he can never escape.

Willard Gaylin, M.D.

Biologically Based Theories of Depression in Men
    Sex Hormones and Mood
    Genetic and Family Studies of Mood Disorders
Psychological Models of Depression
    Cognitive Models of Depression
    Interpersonal Models of Depression
    Psychoanalytical Models of Depression
Gender-Role Models of Depression
Explaining Depression in Men

Since studies utilizing large, heterogeneous population samples have found that there appear to be fewer men who suffer from depression than women, it has been less common to attempt to parcel out the possible etiologies for depression in men. In discussions of the differences between men and women with regard to the incidence and prevalence

From *The Male Ego* (p. 26), by Willard Gaylin, M.D. Copyright © 1992 by Willard Gaylin, M.D. Used by permission of Viking Penguin, a division of Penguin Putnam, Inc.

of depressive disorders, various explanations have been constructed using biological, psychological, and social theories. Empirical support for these various perspectives is summarized in a number of references (e.g., Beckham & Leber, 1995; Gotlib & Hammen, 1992; Nolen-Hoeksema, 1990; Wolman & Stricker, 1990; Mann, 1989). Primarily, the discussions have been devoted to attempts to explain the female preponderance of depression and have not attempted to explain the comparatively low proportion of men represented in many of these studies. This chapter will review traditional explanations of depression through a lens designed to illuminate what these explanations tell us about male depression. Might other hypotheses be warranted if traditional models are inadequate to account for male depression?

The explanations constructed for the causes of depression and the differences between men and women have paralleled historical trends in the social and behavioral sciences. The physicians from antiquity, Hippocrates and Galen, emphasized disturbance in body humors as pathognomic and believed that an excess of black bile caused melancholy. This earliest biological construction has evolved into present theories emphasizing the role played by brain structure and function and the underlying physiochemical processes in the brain and central nervous system. Early psychological explanations found their fullest expression in the psychoanalytic perspectives of Freud, Abraham, and other psychoanalytic pioneers. Current psychological constructions represent both the evolution of psychoanalytic thinking in areas such as attachment theory, object-relations theory, and self-psychology as well as in the more empirically based perspectives of cognitive theory, personality theory, and explanatory style theory. Social and culturally anchored perspectives on depression and its treatment have roots in the work of Dix and other pioneers in social treatment that emphasized social conditions and the cultural aspects of mental disturbance. Recent advancements in feminist-informed theory and scientific inquiry have emphasized the cultural contributions to the causes of mental disorders. These advances have led to new and innovative approaches to psychotherapeutic practice that combine elements of traditional, empirically verified treatments with contributions that emphasize the culturally constructed aspects of men's and women's gender roles. What aspects of these explanations help in our efforts to understand depression in men? In what way do these explanations fail to account for the findings related to male depression?

Clinician Query—"I think I'm developing a depression."

John was a 20-year-old undergraduate engineering major who consulted his campus psychological service for help with depression. He was in the second semester of his second year of college, and was becoming increasingly unhappy. He was not attending his classes and was withdrawing from his typical social activities. He had called home and talked to his mother, and she had encouraged him to seek help. She had been treated for depression on several occasions, and was on a maintenance regimen of fluoxetine to help stabilize her own mood. John met with a psychologist at the campus counseling service and discussed his troubles.

"I just don't feel like doing anything. I've been really tired, and just feel like sleeping most of the time. I get up late, and just sit around the apartment and watch TV most of the day. I don't really like my classes."

"And you think you might be depressed?" the psychologist asked.

"Yeah. My mom suggested I come in and get checked. She has been depressed off and on for a long time. As long as I can remember. I think I'm developing a depression like her."

"Well, let's see. You're sleeping a lot. You aren't going to any of your classes. You aren't going out with friends. How is your mood? Do you feel depressed?"

"Well, mostly I feel kinda self-conscious and guilty for wasting my parent's money. I'm just blowing everything off."

"O. K. So you feel guilty and self-conscious. How about your eating and appetite? Any changes there?"

"I don't really have much of an appetite. I've probably lost 10 pounds in the past month."

"Have you had any suicidal thoughts while this has been happening? Have you thought of killing yourself?"

"No. Not really. I guess sometimes I just think how much easier things would be if I just disappeared or something. Or maybe I think about how I just wish a bus would hit me. But nothing really serious. I had an uncle who killed himself. That really sucked, for our whole family. I don't think I would ever really do that."

"O.K. Now I know you said you called your mom, and she was the one who suggested you come in to talk. But I'm wondering, is there anything in particular that you think might have triggered this depression? Did anything happen recently that caused you to be depressed?"

"Well, I don't think so. Hmm. No, not really. Ever since I came back from break and the semester started back up, I have just been sliding into this depression. I guess I was having some doubts last semester about coming back to school, but things were better over break. Now, thought, I just feel really down."

"So, let's see. You're sleeping more than usual. You have lost weight and don't have much of an appetite. You don't really like your classes and have stopped going to them. You feel guilty for wasting your parents' money. You've had some thoughts of how things would be easier if you just died, or if you just got hit by a bus. These are all pretty typical symptoms of depression, John. I'm glad you decided to come in. Why don't we talk about what we should do to address this depression?"

- What theories have been advanced to explain depression in men?
- How does a family history of depression influence the eventual development of depression in men?

BIOLOGICALLY BASED THEORIES
OF DEPRESSION IN MEN

Biologically explanations of the differences between men and women with regard to the incidence, prevalence, and expression of depression have received a great deal of attention. With roots in Hippocrates' body humor theory of melancholy, biological explanations of depression have been at the forefront throughout history. In recent years, as more effective pharmacological agents have been discovered to treat depression, interest in the biological substrates of mood disorders has increased even more. Although there are many aspects of human biology that may have bearing on mood states, ranging from nutritional and dietary aspects of human behavior to the subtle interplay of our hormone and neurotransmitter systems, two lines of investigation in the search to understand depression have relevance for advancing our understanding of depression in men. These two aspects of explanation relate to the influence of sex hormones on mood states and to the findings from family and genetic studies of affective disorders.

Sex Hormones and Mood

The role of the sex hormones in the regulation of mood has received much attention. Since women have been thought to be particularly vulnerable to mood swings during the premenstrual period, postpartum period, and in conjunction with the changes that accompany menopause, the idea that hormonal factors play a role in influencing mood states has gained considerable popularity. Kornstein (1997) summarizes a number of references to the possible trigger effect of female hormones in the precipitation of depressive episodes in women. Hormonal triggering may account for apparent increases in vulnerability to depressive episodes during premenstrual periods, as well as for the phenomenon of postpartum depression. Might there be a parallel male sex hormone influence on male mood states? After reviewing the literature pertaining to hormonal influences on female depression, Nolen-Hoeksema (1990) concluded that there was no consistent compelling evidence to support the role of female sex hormones in their contribution to women's depression. Is it possible that male sex hormones would influence male mood states? Since sex differences in depressed mood emerge during adolescence (Nolen-Hoeksema & Girgus, 1994) and are maintained through adulthood, an examination of the influence of male sex hormones in the manifestation of depression in boys and men is warranted.

The influence of the male sex hormone androgen begins to be manifest as early as the sixth week of fetal development. At this time, undifferentiated tissues that are predecessors of sexual organs begin to differentiate, based on the presence or absence of androgen produced by the fetal testes. The influence of fetal androgen, driven by the presence of fetal testes, causes the differentiation of wolffian ducts into parts of the male reproductive tract. After birth, the function of the male sex hormones is relatively subtle until around age 10. Coinciding with the onset of puberty, secretions of gonadotropin stimulate increased production of estrogen and progesterone in young women and testosterone in young men. Secretion of testosterone in young men results in the lowering of the voice, an increase in facial and body hair, and the development of the secondary sexual characteristics that are associated with sexual maturity in our culture. Could it also be that this increase in the production of testosterone has some protective influence with respect to the mood states of boys, resulting in the apparent decrease in levels of depression at adolescence that continues through adulthood? In light of the fact that the persistent sex differences in rates of depression emerge with puberty and adolescence, testosterone certainly could be implicated in this phenomenon as it pertains to young men.

One avenue for understanding the role testosterone plays in male depression is to examine the relationship of levels of testosterone to depression in adult men. Sternbach (1998) reviewed the literature on the natural decline of testosterone in men as men grow older and found a distinct relationship between lowered levels of testosterone and various manifestations of mood disturbances, including increased depression, anxiety, sexual difficulties, and irritability. These natural consequences of the lowering of testosterone may mimic a mood disorder in normally aging men. Such a relationship provides indirect support for a link between levels of testosterone and depression in men.

Studies that examine the role of testosterone levels in adult depressed men have yielded mixed results. Yesavage, Davidson, Widrov, and Berger (1985) examined testosterone levels in depressed men and found a modest inverse relationship between the severity of depression and testosterone levels when severity of depression was controlled. Steiger, von Bardeleben, Wiedemann, and Holsboer (1991) compared cortisol and testosterone levels in depressed men before and after treatment for endogenous depression. Their findings indicated that testosterone level increased after remission while cortisol levels decreased. In spite of modest support for the testosterone–depression connection in men, both of these studies have limitations in terms of small numbers of subjects as well as inconsistencies in criteria used to define depression in the subjects included in the studies. Nonetheless, in both studies, the expected relationship between levels of testosterone and levels of depression was found.

In contrast to these studies, a number of investigators found no differences in testosterone levels between depressed men and matched controls. Rubin, Poland, and Lesser (1989) assessed testosterone concentrations in 16 adult males with endogenous depression and compared these levels with 16 matched control subjects and found no differences in testosterone levels. Similarly, Levitt and Joffe (1988) found no differences in either free or total testosterone between 12 depressed men and

12 age-matched normal volunteers. Davies, Harris, Thomas, Cook, Read, and Riad-Fahmy (1992) examined free plasma testosterone levels obtained from saliva samples and found no differences between 11 men with major depression and 10 age-matched controls. They did, however, find a relationship between increased severity of depression and lowered testosterone level in the depressed men. Cooper, Finlayson, Velamoor, Magnus, and Cernovsky (1989) found no relationship between pre- and post-electroconvulsive therapy treatment, severity of depression, and levels of testosterone measured 15 min prior to treatments and 15 min after treatment. The general trend in these studies is that there are no consistent or reliable differences in testosterone levels between depressed men and nondepressed control groups. In addition, these studies provide more compelling evidence that there is no testosterone–depression connection because they incorporate use of matched control groups for comparisons.

A second line of research that has bearing on the role of testosterone in depression in men is based on the use of testosterone replacement therapy in the treatment of depressed men. Several investigations (Wagner, Rabkin, & Rabkin, 1998; Wagner & Rabkin, 1998; Rabkin, Wagner, & Rabkin, 1996) have reported positive results when testosterone replacement therapy is used to treat symptomatic depressed men with human immunodefiency virus (HIV) infection and acquired immunodefiency syndrome (AIDS). In addition to these studies, Seidman & Rabkin (1998) report a finding that biweekly testosterone replacement therapy for five depressed men who had not responded to selective serotonin reuptake inhibitor therapy resulted in a rapid recovery from major depression. They also found that subjects who discontinued the testosterone treatment began to relapse rapidly. Summarizing the efficacy of standard and alternative antidepressant treatments in depressed HIV men, Wagner, Rabkin, & Rabkin (1996) concluded that testosterone replacement had a high favorable response rate, somewhat higher (81% for testosterone compared with 70% for standard antidepressant medications), when used to treat depression in patients with HIV.

Although it may be appealing to look for a hormonally based biological substrate to explain the level and rates of depression in men, there is no consistent evidence that testosterone plays anything other than a mediating role in the severity or levels of depression in men. Treatment studies indicating this are conducted with medically fragile men, some of whom are also suffering from major depression. It is difficult to draw general conclusions from these research reports about the role of testosterone in depression. It does appear that elevation of testosterone levels as a result of replacement therapy does have a significant impact on the patient's mood states. However, studies that have examined directly the testosterone levels in depressed men have been mainly inconclusive and contradictory.

Genetic and Family Studies of Mood Disorders

Genetic studies have found inherited vulnerabilities and risks for various mood disorders. Twin and adoption studies have consistently demonstrated a genetic linkage in bipolar disorder and, to a somewhat lesser extent, unipolar depression. Rates for concordance of bipolar disorder in monozygotic twins (twins that share identical genetic information) are estimated to be between 50 and 95%. Rates for dizygotic twins (twins that share only half their genetic information) are estimated to be between 0 and 40% (Sevy, Mendlewicz, & Mendelbaum, 1995). In addition, family studies have shown an increased risk for bipolar disorder in first-degree relatives of individuals who have been diagnosed with bipolar disorder. This risk has been estimated to be around 20% for both parents and siblings of persons diagnosed with bipolar disorder. Second-degree relatives typically show a decreased morbidity risk, which would be expected in a genetically transmitted vulnerability.

Maier, Lichtermann, and Merikangas (1993) reviewed the genetics of unipolar depression and its associated comorbid conditions. Paralleling the findings in studies of bipolar disorder, there is a significant increase in the likelihood of unipolar depression in relatives of probands diagnosed with unipolar depression. In addition to this increased risk, there is also an increased likelihood of panic disorder in first-degree relatives of subjects with unipolar depression. An investigation of 3790 twin pairs found heritability of major depression to be the same in men and women, with 39% of variance in concordance rates being accounted for through genetic factors (Kendler & Prescott, 1999), a rate consistent with previously reported rates.

In addition to studies that examine the genetic loading of affective disorders, a number of investigators have studied the co-occurrence of affective disorders, including unipolar depression, with anxiety disorders and alcoholism. Results from a number of these investigations (e.g., Kendler, Neale, & Kessler, 1992; Merikangas, Risch, & Weissman, 1994) indicate that there exists an increased risk for panic disorder in persons who suffer from unipolar depression, and vice versa. In these studies, associations between unipolar depression and alcoholism are not as strong, possibly due to the confounding of increased unipolar depression in women and increased alcoholism in men (Reiger, Farmer, Rae, Locke, Keitn, Judd & Goodwin, 1990). Other studies, however, have found higher comorbidity of alcoholism and unipolar depression in men (Kornstein, Schatzberg, Yonkers, Thase, Keitner, Ryan, & Schlager, 1996) as well as greater frequencies of concurrent and secondary depression in men, compared with women, with alcohol use disorders (Hanna & Grant, 1997).

Wesner and Winokur (1990) summarize twin, adoption, family, and genetically related biological marker studies and conclude that there is ample evidence to support the contention that unipolar depression has a strong genetic component. However, complications that arise due to the apparent heterogeneity of unipolar depression make it difficult to accurately parcel out contributions associated with each sex. It appears, though, that there are more similarities than differences between men and women at the genetic and family-pedigree level of analysis. In summarizing research on family studies of affective disorders, Winokur (1997) concludes that unipolar depression is mainly a homogeneous disorder or syndrome with many different etiologies that is produced via various pathways which result in a common set of symptoms. Probably, some of these pathways differ from men to women, but the common final outcome, unipolar depression, appears to be very similar.

One aspect of the genetic analysis of affective disorders that deserves special attention due to its implications for understanding the complicated role of sex in the various affective disorders is the depressive spectrum disease conceptualization (Winokur, 1997, 1979, 1972; Winokur, Behar, & Van Valkenburg, 1978). Initial reports indicated that investigators were able to correlate familial characteristics of depressed subjects by separating depressed patients into early-onset and later-onset depressive disorder. For patients with early-onset of depression (i.e., before age 40), investigators found a much higher rate of familial alcoholism and antisocial personality, especially in the males. In these early-onset subjects, there was an increased risk of depression among the female relatives compared with male relatives. In late-onset subjects (i.e., after age 40), there was no difference in risk of depression between male and female family members. Is it possible that, in the early-onset subjects' families, the men, rather than overtly manifesting depression, were manifesting a "depressive spectrum disease" variant through alcoholism or antisocial personality?

The current spectrum disease classification of affective disorders specifies three subtypes of unipolar depression (Winokur, 1997). One subtype, reactive depression, is often secondary to bereavement or medical illness, or is associated with a natural catastrophe. A second subtype, familial pure depressive disease, is characterized by family histories of depression only and an absence of antisocial personality and alcoholism in relatives of persons identified with the depressive disorder. A third subtype, depressive spectrum disease, is associated with greater emotional instability in the person with depression and is more consistently associated with anxiety disorders, alcoholism, substance abuse, and personality disorders in relatives. This third subtype of depressive disorder may explain the finding of smaller numbers of men in most studies of incidence and prevalence of unipolar depression since many more men than women are diagnosed with alcoholism and antisocial personality disorder. The importance of this model in understanding the smaller numbers of men in epidemiological studies of affective disorders and the large numbers of men in the alcoholism, substance abuse, and personality disorder categories has not been fully explored. Nonetheless, as a model that may account for some of the observed discrepancies in the data on affective disorders and substance abuse disorders, it appears to have great merit. It also points to an important component of the assessment of depression in men, namely, the roles that alcoholism and substance abuse play in many men's expressions of mood disturbance (e.g., Hanna & Grant, 1997; Heifner, 1997; Powell, Penick, Nickel, Liskow, Riesenmy, Campion & Brown, 1992).

The two most obvious biologically based models of male depression have demonstrated only modest validity. The relationship of testosterone to depression in men is ambiguous. Most controlled studies find no differences between depressed men and normal controls in terms of their levels of testosterone. However, therapies that utilize testosterone to treat depression have demonstrated a relationship between increased testosterone levels and decreased levels of depression. The genetic studies that have uncovered relationships between subtypes of unipolar depression and familial characteristics may ultimately prove to be of greater value in understanding male depression. The depressive spectrum disease conceptualization of depression may help us understand how men might be underrepresented in the traditional categories of depression, and how they might be counted in the alcohol and other drug abuse and personality disorder categories. Findings that are based on this model appear promising but have not yet been widely accepted. More research that is based on this model of affective disorders is warranted as we seek to better understand the many possible manifestations of male depression.

Clinician Query—"She was all I had."

George was a 73-year-old man referred for psychotherapy by his personal physician 6 months after the death of his wife of 52 years. George, who described himself as a "health nut," was in good shape for a man of his years. He appeared to be growing a beard and looked as if he had not had a haircut in several months. He wore jeans and a workshirt and had a dull look in his eyes. George said that he used to run every day, at least a mile. In the past month, he had stopped running and had been spending most of his days sitting in his apartment feeling like he had nothing meaningful to do.

George and his wife had been best friends. Since retirement 10 years ago, they had taken trips around the world and continued to enjoy a vigorous sexual relationship. His wife was diagnosed with uterine cancer about a year ago. He took care of her throughout her illness, providing her with unwavering emotional support. He was at her side when she finally passed away. George's two daughters took turns staying with him for the month after their mother's death, providing each other with support as they provided support for George. When they left, George had told them not to worry. He was strong, and Linda, his wife, would have wanted him to go on and live his life.

In recent days, George had been to his longtime physician several times to be checked for illness. He believed that he might have cancer, but all tests were negative. His physician insisted, against his protests, that he speak with a therapist.

"I really don't know why I'm here. I know what I have to do," George opened an early session with his therapist. "Linda would have wanted me to move on. I carry her with me in my heart, and I know she would want me to live fully."

"So what is keeping you from doing this?" the therapist queried.

"I don't know. I just stopped everything I enjoy doing. I stopped running. I stopped getting up early. I don't feel like shaving. I don't care about anything," George replied.

"Do you connect this to Linda's death by any chance?"

"That was six months ago. I should be able to keep going. Don't you think? Maybe I have cancer or something," George responded.

"You got that checked out and you didn't have any signs of it. Is it possible that you are still grieving the loss of Linda?"

"I don't know. It just feels like there is something wrong with me."

"What would Linda have said to you if you were saying this to her?" his therapist probed.

"She would tell me not to feel sorry for myself. I want to believe her but I feel like I've never felt before in my whole life. Is this what depression feels like?"

"It's not uncommon for a man who has lost his partner of 50 years to feel a sense of despair. After all, you two were very close and connected."

"I wish she was still here," George commented with sadness.

"It's o.k. to feel your grief whatever way it comes out. For you, it may be that your body is saying it doesn't want to run. Maybe it is telling you to slow down and spend some time feeling the loss."

"You are probably right, but I don't like this feeling," George responded. "It makes me feel old and weak."

"As long as Linda was around, you didn't have to worry so much about mortality. Maybe she buffered you against this reality," George's therapist suggested.

"You know, I feel like I just work up to reality. I'm just beginning to realize how much I didn't have to be aware of with her in my life."

"It seems like quite a shock. How do your friends help out here?"

"Most of our friends were Linda's friends. They are nice to me, but it's not like we're real close. I have lost touch with a lot of my male friends," George lamented.

"The loss of Linda makes you realize that you have lost a lot, a way of seeing and living life. It will be a lot like starting over in many ways," his therapist reflected.

"I'm not sure I have the energy for this," George responded with a sad look on his face.

"Yes. It's hard to imagine having to recreate your life when you are feeling this kind of heaviness."

- What effect does loss of a spouse or partner have on depression in men?
- How does social and personal support for men who are grieving protect them from depression?

PSYCHOLOGICAL MODELS OF DEPRESSION

Since depression is a disorder in which psychologists have both a clinical and a research interest, psychological models to account for the sex differences in depression have received considerable attention. Theoreticians and researchers have proposed models for depression that draw from cognitive, interpersonal, and psychodynamic conceptualizations. Historically, many of these psychological models of depression have been examined in light of how they contribute to our understanding of the preponderance of women who suffer from unipolar depression. However, several of these models also have great potential to contribute to our understanding of how depression is manifest in men, how men experience depression, and how men respond to treatments for depression.

Cognitive Models of Depression

Cognitive models of depressive disorders have been both descriptive and explanatory. These models have led to many advances in understanding depression, as well as to effective treatments for depression. Beck and his colleagues (Beck, 1976; Beck, Rush, Shaw, & Emery, 1979; Newman & Beck, 1990) have been prominent in formulating cognitive models of depression. In this model, a set of information processing biases or internal mental representations are believed to determine how a person sees the self, his or her life circumstances, and the future. These information processing biases are called schemas. In depressed individuals, Beck and his colleagues propose that a "cognitive triad" of schemas exists that produces negative views of the self, the person's personal world, and the person's beliefs about the future. These schemas related to self, world, and future are consistently present in depressed individuals and contribute to the development and maintenance of depressed mood. The significance of altering these negative cognitions and the impact on mood and behavior has also been documented in studies of the impact of cognitive psychotherapy. The cognitive model of depression has also led to an expansion of research on cognitive mediated models of affective disorder and depression (e.g., Gotlib & Hammen, 1992).

This cognitive perspective on mental functioning and the influence of thinking on mood has spawned a number of theories about depression. An important development in this area is the study of the way individuals explain to themselves the circumstances and events of their lives. Seligman and his colleagues originally formulated a learned helplessness model of depression that was based on behavioral animal studies (Seligman, 1975). Later elaborations of this model included a cognitive component, the attribution reformulation (Peterson & Seligman, 1984). In this model, the attributions or explanations that an individual constructs are related directly to beliefs about her or his capacity to control life events. Increasing evidence supports this model and its usefulness in our study of depression (e.g., Bruder-Mattson & Hovanitz, 1990) and has led to findings of sex and gender differences in attributions for depression (e.g., Boggiano & Barrett, 1991; Handal, Gist, & Wiener, 1987).

A related model that has yielded useful insights into the sex differences found in the incidence and prevalence data on depression is the response style model of depression formulated by Nolen-Hoeksema (1990, 1987). In this model, a distinction between a ruminative response style and a distracting response style as two means of dealing with mood states is made. In the ruminative response style, an individual focuses on her or his negative moods and explanations for these moods at the expense of more positive efforts to deal with problems. This style of responding to negative mood states quite frequently leads to prolonged periods of depressed mood and ineffective or inadequate efforts to relieve the depressed mood (Nolen-Hoeksema, Morrow, & Fredrickson, 1993). Examples of a ruminative response style include thoughts that focus on individual shortcomings that an individual believes might have caused a depressed mood, a selective focus on dysphoric mood states combined with attempts to explain these states, and withdrawal from both interpersonal support and constructive, instrumental coping. In contrast, the distracting response style is one in which the individual copes with negative mood states by thinking about other things, by not focusing on the negative elements of the mood or other personal difficulties. Examples of a distracting response style include benign means of coping with a negative mood such as participation in a hobby or exercising. Other distracting response styles may be more dangerous or self-destructive, such as reckless driving or engaging in personally risky behavior. Many distracting response styles are found to relieve depression in the short run but may actually exacerbate longer term improvements in mood due to ineffective efforts at solving the problems which have led to the depressed mood (Nolen-Hoeksema, 1991).

The response style model of coping with depressed mood has been quite fruitful in uncovering differences between men and women in how each deals with depressed mood states. In addition to the gender differences in ruminative response styles reviewed by Nolen-Hoeksema (1990), Butler and Nolen-Hoeksema (1994) and Nolen-Hoeksema, Morrow, and Fredrickson (1993) found that college women were much more likely to enlist a ruminative style in response to depressed mood than were college men. A ruminative response style has also been associated with more prolonged periods of depression and with more severe depression when used as a means for coping with bereavement, specifically when used by men (Nolen-Hoeksema, McBride, & Larson, 1997; Nolen-Hoeksema, Parker, & Larson, 1994).

The response style model of managing depressed mood suggests that men may employ a distraction response style in dealing with depressed moods, as opposed to the ruminative response style that appears to be favored by women. Such a response style might cause men to underidentify and underreport negative moods, and this may result in fewer men being counted in typical studies of the incidence and prevalence of depressive disorder. However, recent findings (e.g., Nolen-Hoeksema, Morrow, & Fredrickson, 1993) indicate that women are more likely to utilize a ruminative response style and that there are actually no sex differences in utilization of the distraction response style.

Levit (1991) and Gjerde, Block, and Block (1988) found that young men tended to utilize externalizing, outwardly directed response styles and defense mechanisms in coping with depressed mood. Such differences are consistent with the distracting response style identified by Nolen-Hoeksema and may offer another avenue by which to investigate the manner in which men choose to cope with depressed mood states. If it is true that men tend to utilize externalizing, distracting response styles, then men might also tend to deflect focus away from their negative mood states, resulting in a tendency to underidentify and underreport such states. In fact, Kessler, Brown and Browman (1981) found that men tended to inhibit problem recognition compared with women, a finding that would be consistent with men's tendency to utilize a distraction style of coping with unpleasant or depressed moods.

These response style and defense mechanism findings are consistent with speculations on the impact of cultural conditioning on coping patterns. Women tend to adopt patterns of coping that emphasize or highlight self-blame, resulting in decreases in self-esteem and, ultimately, increases in depression (Kaplan, 1977). Men, who tend to avoid such coping patterns, may benefit from this cultural conditioning to the extent that such conditioning may encourage them to externalize blame and focus on instrumental problem-solving when faced with depressed mood. In such instances, an action-oriented coping style may actually protect men from experiencing depression.

The response style approach to studying depression has yielded useful findings in our efforts to understand the sex differences in level and extent of depression. However, there are a number of possible questions that arise from this approach, including the extent to which men's utilization of distraction or externalizing coping styles might suppress their identification and reporting of depressive symptoms and depressed mood. Since men are more likely to utilize an externalizing style of coping, the distraction hypothesis is consistent. Further exploration of this important dimension of managing depressed mood will lead to additional insights into our understanding of male depression.

Interpersonal Models of Depression

A second influential model of depression is the interpersonal model (Klerman, 1989). The interpersonal model of depression emphasizes the importance of attachment in human development, the detrimental impact of the disruption of important interpersonal relationships, and the relationship of these events to the development of depression. The interpersonal model of depression described by Klerman, Weissman, Rounsaville, and Chevron (1984) has roots in the psychoanalytic perspectives of the interpersonal school of psychiatry as well as in the attachment theories of the British object-relations theorists. This approach to understanding depression emphasizes the centrality of interpersonal relations in the development and maintenance of psychological and psychiatric disorders, including affective disorders.

One critical feature of this model is the important role of attachment in psychological growth and development. Spitz's findings (Spitz &

Wolf, 1946) relating to the detrimental impact of disruptions of the parental bonds demonstrate the negative effects on children of the loss of these attachments to close caretakers. In these findings, young children, when separated from their mothers, react with typical and predictable responses that begin with anxiety, develop into protest at the mother's absence, and later coalesce into withdrawal, depression, and sadness. Bowlby (1980) recognized the similarity of such a reaction to the processes of mourning, and emphasized the connection between mourning and depression. Recent investigations have found significant relationships between various kinds of adversity experienced in childhood and the eventual development of depression in children and adults. Kessler and Magee (1993) found that negative events in childhood, such as parental divorce, marital problems, violence in the family, and drinking in the family, were all related to the incidence of major depression in adults. Children of depressed parents also show an increased risk for depression themselves (Weissman, Gammon, John, Merikangas, Warner, Prusoff, & Sholomskas, 1987). These findings suggest that disruptions in the positive relational milieu of the family, due to such factors as parental depression, marital problems, violence, or drinking, are directly related to the development of depression in both children and adults.

Another important aspect of the interpersonal model of depressive disorders is its contribution to understanding the relationship of marital and close interpersonal relationships with depressive disorders in men and women (Beach, Sandeen, & O'Leary, 1990). Several investigations have demonstrated the important role the nature of the marital relationship plays in depressive disorders in both men and women (e.g., Beach, Arias, & O'Leary, 1987; Beach & O'Leary, 1986; Beach, Jouriles, & O'Leary, 1985). In a sample of depressed, married inpatients, compared with a matched sample of nondepressed nonpatients, Merikangas, Prusoff, Kupfer, and Frank (1985) found that marital adjustment was significantly lower in the patient group than in the nonpatient group. The depressed patients reported much more dissatisfaction with their marriage than did the nondepressed control group. In addition, other investigations have shown that sex differences in depression are more pronounced in married versus nonmarried samples and that marriage or a close interpersonal relationship offers protection against depression for men (Ali & Toner, 1996; Wu & DeMaris, 1996).

In general, interpersonal models of depression underscore the consistent finding that disruptions in interpersonal attachments have a close relationship to the development of depression. In addition, research within this tradition has demonstrated that interpersonal support at times of stress may serve as a prophylactic to the development of depressive disorders and that the social support networks of depressed persons tend to be more restricted than those of nondepressed counterparts.

Psychoanalytical Models of Depression

Early psychoanalytical models of depression were rooted in Abraham's and Freud's conceptualizations of depression, first advanced in Abraham's paper "Notes on the Psycho-analytical Investigation and Treatment of Manic–Depressive Insanity and Allied Conditions" (Abraham, 1911/1948) and in Freud's paper "Mourning and Melancholia" (Freud, 1917/1957). These early conceptualizations provided the groundwork for the later object-loss theorists by underscoring the close connection between the grief of normal mourning processes and its abnormal expression in the pathology of melancholia. Abraham emphasized unconscious hostility toward the lost object that was internalized and directed against the self. Freud also noted the importance of unconscious hostility and aggression in both mourning and melancholia. He proposed that the ego becomes "divided against itself," with a part of the ego manifesting the unconscious hostility towards itself. This anticipated the function that the superego plays in depression and the development of this idea by subsequent psychoanalysts including Rado (1951, 1928), Jacobson (1954), and Bibring (1953).

The British object-relations theorists focused less on the internal, structural aspects of depressive states and more on the role that external relationship conditions play in depression. Roy (1987, 1981) examined the impact of parental loss on men's risk for depression and found that parental death before age 17 was one of three vulnerability factors in a sample of 71 depressed men. Patten (1991) confirmed the relationship between the death of the mother before age 11 and depression in adult women. Such findings are consistent with the object-relations theorists' proposal of a link between object-loss and the development of depression. These findings also confirm the clinical experience of many therapists treating depressed individuals; namely, that there is a common theme of early parental loss that continues to exert a depressing effect beyond the time of the actual loss.

More recent psychoanalytic models of development have greater relevance for understanding depression in men. Chodorow (1989, 1978) has explored the importance of culturally sanctioned child rearing practices on male and female personality development. Her acknowledgment of the differential, culturally driven, impact that child-rearing practices can have on the development of boys and girls has given rise to a number of discoveries. Findings related to sex differences in moral reasoning (Gilligan, 1982), emotional expression (Lerner, 1980), and psychotherapy relationships (Carlson, 1987; Pollack, 1990, 1992) have been based on features of this perspective on human development. Her identification of the divergent developmental pathways that little boys and little girls traverse has resulted in a number of important insights and hypotheses regarding the cultural derivation of many observed sex differences.

Another perspective on understanding the development of healthy self-esteem, the self-in-relation model of women's development, outlines a new way of thinking about women's development (Jordan, Kaplan, Miller, Stiver, & Surrey, 1991). Integrating feminist analysis with psychoanalytic insights, this model critiques the separation–individuation paradigms characteristic of traditional psychoanalytic thinking and emphasizes the interpersonal, relational basis of emotional growth and well-being. Bergman (1995) has extended this perspective in an effort to conceptualize men's development. The distinctive features such a perspective contributes to our understanding of depression in women have been formulated by Kaplan (1986) and Jack (1991), and are prominent in Pollack's (1998b) views of understanding depression in boys and men. Little boys, like little girls, are endowed with an innate capacity for interpersonal connection. Early experiences of relational affirmation and empowerment, usually provided by the parents, have a profound and long-term effect on the development of a healthy sense of self and self-esteem. The self-in-relation conceptualization of women's depression views women's depression as a natural reaction to our culture's devaluing of women's natural relational orientation. Since little boys are often discouraged, via these same cultural norms and expectations, from fully benefiting from experiences of relational empowerment, they are frequently left with an emotional vulnerability when confronted with relational disconnection. In much the same way as we might view a woman's depression, a man's depression is his natural reaction to our culture's insistence on his devaluing and denying his own important needs for connection and affirmation in important relationships. In this model, we might find an explanation for the protection from depression afforded many men who are married or involved in an intimate personal relationship.

Pollack (1995b) has proposed a model of male development that draws upon Chodorow's cultural–psychoanalytic analysis of the effect of child-rearing practices on the development of self, the self-in-relation model of development, and Kohut's (1977) ideas about the development of healthy self-esteem. The central feature of this model is that, for most little boys, our cultural practices that encourage autonomy and separation in boys effect a premature dislocation from the emotionally secure attachment of the mother's care and love. This "traumatic abrogation" of the earliest holding environment is thought to be a psychological event of dramatic and everlasting proportion. This abrogation causes little boys to defensively armor themselves against painful affect and creates in them a specific vulnerability to mood disturbances based on this early object loss. Unresolved grief and feelings of loss are carried into adulthood and are manifest in a tendency toward disconnection in interpersonal relationships and an avoidance of emotional states linked to depressive affect. In this model of male development, depression is a common theme in many men's psychological struggles with identity, self-assertion, and interpersonal relationships.

Psychoanalytic models of depressive conditions have been rich with theoretical speculation regarding conditions that contribute to depressive states. They have also provided useful clinical and applied perspectives. More recent psychoanalytic ideas that have been modified using a feminist viewpoint have shown the greatest potential for advancing our understanding of sex differences in depressive conditions in both men and women.

> *Clinician Query*— "Cancer. I never thought
> it would happen to me."
> Dan is a 66-year-old married man, recently retired from
> his position as a university professor. His ruddy complexion
> and white hair give him the look of a man who has seen a
> lot in his life. His blue eyes shine with intensity and reflect
> his engagement with his life—intellectually, aesthetically,
> physically. Dan has three grown children with whom he
> maintains close contact, even though they live several thou-
> sand miles away. He plays golf daily, writes poetry, paints in
> watercolors, and enjoys spending time with his wife. He has

an active social life with a variety of friends he met and had gotten to know through his work.

Dan's diagnosis with prostate cancer was quite a shock to him. He was accustomed to a clean bill of health from his yearly physicals. Dan came to therapy at the recommendation of one of his friends from the university community who had become concerned about how he way handling himself after receiving this bad news.

"Why me? I know that sounds so elementary and naive. Of course, I know cancer can happen to anyone. But I can't help but think that maybe I did something to bring it on," Dan announced at the beginning of an early therapy session.

"It's hard for you to accept that maybe you didn't have control over this," his therapist responded.

"Well, I know I should accept it, but some part of me is fighting this all the way. The question has been haunting me. Why me?"

"What's your answer?" Dan's therapist followed.

"My guts say that I let down too much after I retired. It's almost like I'm soft, not keeping myself disciplined like I did when I was working full time."

"I think you are stretching. How does cancer relate to being disciplined? I wonder if you're not just plain scared of dying and you really don't want to face how out of your control this really feels."

"Intellectually, you are correct, of course. I'm scared of dying. Wouldn't you be?" Dan responded.

"That doesn't sound like an intellectual statement but rather a very real emotional fear."

"Yeah, it is. I'm scared," Dan said after hesitating for several seconds. He looked down as if he was taking in the reality of his fear fully for the first time.

"It's normal to be scared. Death is scary."

"It's not normal for me," Dan replied, having obvious trouble staying with his therapist's suggestion at this point.

"I'm here to help you deal with the fear so you can make your best run at living. We'll do our best in the face of this unhappy news."

"I know. Cancer. I never thought it would happen to me."

- How does the loss, or threat of loss, of physical functioning impact a man's sense of self and create vulnerability to depression?
- How does the male gender role affect how a man deals with a serious health crisis like cancer?

GENDER-ROLE MODELS OF DEPRESSION

Social constructions that have been developed to account for sex differences in depression have emphasized the effects of gender roles on various aspects of behavior, the negative psychological effects of strict adherence to traditional gender roles, and the effects of interpersonal and societal oppression. This gender-role analysis explanation proposes that rigid adherence to gender roles, by both men and women, creates a strain that is experienced as psychological distress. A number of investigations of depression-related phenomena have found predictable culturally related sex differences. For example, Chevron, Quinlan, and Blatt (1978) identified sex differences in the experience of depression which were consistent with what they viewed as societal sex-role expectations. Men in this study tended to have higher levels of depression in relation to issues of self-criticism. Depression in women tended to be related to issues of dependency. Oliver and Toner (1990) found gender-role differences on Beck Depression Inventory responses, with male subjects endorsing more withdrawal and somatic symptoms than women. This is consistent with Nolan and Willson's (1994) findings that Beck Depression Inventory items related to self-criticism and disappointment in self discriminated between depressed undergraduate men and women. Vredenburg, Krames, and Flett (1986) also found that depressed males tended to be more likely to report sex-role appropriate symptoms, such as work problems and somatic concerns.

With the revolution ushered in by feminist viewpoints in psychology, many aspects of the psychology of men were reviewed and revised. The new psychology of men has advanced our understanding of both the cultural impact of the male role and the internal dynamics of the male experience. Pleck's (1995, 1981) gender-role strain paradigm proposes a way to conceptualize the cultural and social contributions to men's depression. This paradigm offers a new way to think about the impact of socially constructed norms and behavioral roles on individual men. As men attempt to conform to gender roles, they frequently experience strain that results in psychologically maladaptive symptoms and behaviors that include depression.

Efforts directed toward empirical verification of this perspective have been an important feature of the psychological study of men. O'Neil (1981) developed a model of men's gender-role conflict that emphasizes men's culturally conditioned fear of femininity and the role that culturally sanctioned, institutionalized sexism plays in men's lives. For O'Neil, both the fear of femininity and institutionalized sexism create powerful forces in men that contribute to psychological strain and distress. Originally, six aspects of gender-role strain were proposed. These included restrictive emotionality; homophobia; health concerns and negative health behaviors; competition, power, and control; obsession with success and achievement; and restrictive affectionate behavior between men. The Gender Role Conflict Scale (O'Neil, Helms, Gable, David, & Wrightsman, 1986) was developed to assess these aspects of men's gender-role conflict. Subsequent factor analytic investigation of the Gender Role Conflict Scale found that the scale was actually comprised of four subscales—success, power, and competition; restrictive emotionality; restrictive affectionate behavior between men; and conflicts between work and family relations. O'Neil, Good, and Holmes (1995) reviewed the development of the Gender Role Conflict Scale and research that has been conducted using the Gender Role Conflict Scale.

The Gender Role Conflict Scale has been particularly useful in examining men's psychological distress in general and has offered insights into aspects of male gender-role conflict related to male depression. Good and Mintz (1990) found correlations between depression as measured by the Center for Epidemiological Studies Depression Scale and gender-role conflict measured by the Gender Role Conflict Scale. The highest correlation of gender-role conflict with levels of depression in their sample of young college men was found with the "conflicts between work and family relations" subscale. In a subsequent investigation, Good and Wood (1995) confirmed this strong relationship between the gender-role conflict and depression in college men. In this study, a relationship between gender-role conflict and negative attitudes toward seeking professional help, as measured by the Attitudes Toward Seeking Professional Counseling Services scale, was also uncovered. The highest correlation between gender-role conflict and depression was also reported on the conflicts between work and family subscale of the Gender Role Conflict Scale. Good, Robertson, Fitzgerald, Stevens, and Bartels (1996) also found a relationship between both gender-role conflict and general psychological distress using the Symptom Checklist-90 (SCL-90) and the Gender Role Conflict Scale. This investigation, consistent with the other investigations, found the highest correlation with depression measured by the SCL-90 to be with the conflict between work and family subscale of the Gender Role Conflict Scale.

Heifner (1997) confirmed the impact of rigid, traditional gender-role expectations and the effect these expectations have on depression in men. In her investigation, all but one of the men interviewed in a qualitative examination of men's experience of depression reported strong, well-defined traditional and stereotypical gender-role identities. These included expectations of the self as strong, successful, in control, capable of handling problems without help, and hiding emotions. To have problems, struggle with one's mood, or to show vulnerability was to be weak and considered to be a taboo. Such expectations of self, when unmet, provide fertile breeding ground for depression in men.

The cultural analysis of gender-role strain and conflict has proven useful both in specifying aspects of masculine gender-role strain that are related to psychological distress and relating these aspects of gender-role strain to depression in men. A strong relationship exists between depression in young men and the conflict between work and family subscale of the Gender Role Conflict Scale, underscoring the negative impact that rigid adherence to culturally prescribed gender roles has on men.

EXPLAINING DEPRESSION IN MEN

After consideration of the biological, psychological, and gender-role models that have been developed to account for the findings on depression in men and women, several conclusions are warranted. First, there are no consistent empirical findings that draw on biological models to explain many aspects of depression in men. Testosterone may mediate depressive symptoms and mood in some patients, but, in general, there is no consistent relationship between levels of testosterone and depression in either nonclinical or clinical samples.

Psychological theories that account for the differences between men and women in prevalence of depression as well as the means used for coping with depression have been more promising. Object-relations theories have been developed to describe the influence of early parental relationships on the developmental trajectories of little boys and little girls. These trajectories often take differing forms. For little boys, our culture stresses suppression of emotions, relational hardening, defensive autonomy, and utilization of anger and aggression as a primary means of emotional expression. Other psychological explanations of depression have offered insights into the manner in which men and women cope with depressed mood and the gender-bifurcated correlates of depressive risk factors. Rumination and distraction as response styles are consistent with our gender stereotypes of the inwardly focused, brooding woman and the outwardly focused, instrumental man. To what extent are these differences in response styles related directly to the sex differences in depression that we find in studies of depression? How can these differences be used in planning effective treatments that are sex-specific and gender sensitive?

Social and cultural theories have provided useful insights into the effect of gender-role strain on psychological health in men. These male gender-role identifications and strains influence psychological health in general and male depression in particular. As we have discovered, culture has been an important mediating variable in a number of epidemiological studies of depression. A common theme underlying a number of these studies is the important relationship between culture and the effect of cultural norms on the identification, endorsement, and reporting of depressive symptoms. To the extent that our culture's construction of gender roles has a strong influence on the experience and expression of emotional states in both men and women, we will find these roles shaping our understanding of depression in men and women.

CHAPTER 3

Loss, Trauma, Grief, and Masked Depression in Men

*Much obviously remains to be learned (and a great deal will doubtless con-
tinue to be a mystery, owing to the disease's idiopathic nature, its constant
interchangeability of factors), but certainly one psychological element has
been established beyond reasonable doubt, and that is the concept of loss.
Loss in all of its manifestations is the touchstone of depression—in the
progress of the disease and, most likely, in its origin.*

William Styron

Normative Loss Across the Life Span
Trauma and Depression
Grief and Depression
Manifestations of Covert Depression in Men
Summary

Many men may not exhibit classical symptoms of depression as directly
as women. Unlike men, women are afforded culturally sanctioned permission to express emotional pain overtly. For many men, an insidious
and covert depressive syndrome may exist that is much less apparent to
the outside observer but may have significant deleterious effects.
Depressive syndromes that are not manifest through the classic constellation of depressive symptomatology have been variously described as a
"depressive equivalent" or "masked depression" (Fisch, 1987; Lesse,
1983; Pichot & Hassan, 1973). This syndrome is thought to manifest
itself in a variety of behaviors that seem incompatible with depression,
including alcohol abuse, delinquency, reckless behavior, anger, and

Darkness Visible: A Memoir of Madness (p. 56)

Men and Depression: Clinical and Empirical Perspectives
Copyright © 2000 by Academic Press. All rights of reproduction in any form reserved.

somatic complaints. Might men express their depression through these outlets, many of which are more culturally acceptable?

While the *DSM-IV* distinguishes major depression from uncomplicated bereavement, in which there has been a tangible loss to the individual, the overlap and timing of these two conditions has not been fully specified. Early psychoanalysts noted the close relationship between bereavement and melancholia or depression (e.g., Abraham, 1911/1948; Freud, 1917/1957). Personal and cultural variability in the mourning process makes it difficult to connect depressive symptomology to loss (Manson, 1995; Wortman & Silver, 1989).

For many men, there may appear little correlation between experiences of trauma, loss, and the onset of depressive symptomology. Men are less likely than women to show obvious symptoms of depression initially following a traumatic loss experience. In studies comparing the grief response of widows and widowers, males were significantly more depressed than their female counterparts after two to four years (Umberson, Wortman, & Kessler, 1992). This finding was especially prominent when comparing widows and widowers living alone. Men who did not address their grief in therapy following the death of a spouse tended to be more depressed later in their bereavement than were widowers who took this action (Stroebe, 1998). Recently bereaved men were more likely to be diagnosed with an alcohol problem than an affective disorder (Cramer, 1993) and more likely to develop a serious physical illness (Ferraro, Multran, & Barresi, 1984), commit suicide (Li, 1995), or die prematurely when compared to bereaved women (Parkes, Benjamin, & Fitzgerald, 1969). Taken together, these studies suggest that men tend to have difficulty expressing their grief directly and may be more prone to long-term mental and physical health problems as a consequence of their culturally derived tendency to truncate normative grief processes. Men who have experienced both active and passive trauma may be susceptible to delayed or covert grief reactions, and these delayed or covert reactions often include significant depressive components.

Instead of overtly expressing the emotional impact of loss, men are prone to outwardly diminish its significance in order to maintain some semblance of control over their lives. Men are more likely to rely on externalization-based defenses and coping styles that often serve to detach them from their emotions (Levit, 1991). Traditional male cultural training has stressed emotional stoicism, control, denial of weakness, and logical thinking in the face of emotional chaos (Brannon, 1976; O'Neil, 1981). While this may be an effective short-term strategy, it is a poor long-term one for most men. The losses of life that accumulate for many men may result in unforeseen consequences, such as unexplained depression, identity crises, and bouts of severe anxiety at middle age (Cochran & Rabinowitz, 1996; Levinson, Darrow, Klein, Levinson, & McKee, 1978; Kernberg, 1985). For older men who have relied solely on a spouse or significant other to buffer them against the effects of life's tragedies, the loss of this person multiplies their exposure to psychological and physical health risks (Fitzpatrick, 1998).

In this chapter, the interplay of depression with loss, trauma, and grief that men experience at various points across the life span will be explored. We will see that men are vulnerable to loss and grief in distinctly masculine ways. How does this vulnerability relate to depression in men? Loss will be defined as the separation or dissolution of a man's way of self-identification. Trauma will be defined as active and passive experiences of physical or psychological pain originating from outside the person. Bereavement will be defined as the permanent loss of a significant other. Grief is the affective state accompanying bereavement and loss. Attention will be paid to the unique ways that men experience these emotionally charged states.

Clinician Query—"I just want to get back to work."

Adam sought consultation after having been arrested for "creating a disturbance" at his ex-girlfriend's apartment one night. He was home by himself, had drunk a number of beers, began feeling sad and lonely, and decided to visit her in hopes of renewing their long-term relationship that she had abruptly ended two days ago. He arrived at the apartment and began pounding on the door, pleading that she let him in so they could talk. She responded by informing him that if he didn't leave she would call the police. He continued to pound away, and she called the police. Before they arrived, he broke a fire-extinguisher container in the corridor and cut himself in a number of places on his arms. When the police arrived, he was transported to the emergency room. There, the attending physician determined that he was intoxicated but at minimal risk for serious harm to himself or to his ex-girlfriend. He was arrested and transported to jail.

The following day, he visited a therapist for consultation. His attorney advised him that this might help in his efforts to obtain a deferred sentence since he had no other criminal record or history of this kind of behavior. He was composed and articulate, and appeared embarrassed at his behavior as he discussed the previous evening. His appearance did not seem consistent with the story that preceded him. He was short and slightly overweight, with a roly-poly appearance, a sheepish grin, and an easygoing, self-effacing demeanor. He presented himself as polite and easy going.

"I just couldn't believe she really meant it. I still can't believe it's over," he lamented in response to a question about what had happened the previous evening. Then, he quickly changed the topic of conversation. "I have a lot of accounts to work up and a lot of territory to cover. I just need to get myself focused on my work. That will make things better. I just want to get back to work."

"You seemed pretty bent on creating quite a scene," his therapist queried in an effort to direct Adam's attention back to the problems that had brought them together. "What with the emergency room visit and winding up in jail. Quite an evening of it, I would say, wouldn't you?"

"I was just at the end of my rope. I didn't know what to do. Why would I do such a thing? I've never acted like this before! I feel so embarrassed and ashamed of myself," Adam responded with sincerity.

"That's a good question. Why would you do such a thing? What do you think? Do you have any theories?" his therapist probed.

"The breakup, and the way Angie has been behaving towards me, have just been too much for me to handle, I guess," Adam replied.

"Too much to handle? In what way?"

"I've been really depressed, just not myself. I'm way off my pace at work, I just don't feel like doing anything. It's only been a couple of days, but I feel like I can't live without her. And she has just cut me off. She won't talk to me or answer my phone calls. It's really frustrating. I just get really fed up with the whole situation. I just can't handle it."

- To what extent is male depression related to vulnerability to emotional abandonment and relationship dissolution?
- How do men behave when faced with the challenge of coping with feelings of abandonment, loss, and shame when a close relationship ends?

NORMATIVE LOSS ACROSS THE LIFE SPAN

A number of psychoanalytically informed theorists, including Chodorow (1978, 1989) and Gilligan (1982), have pointed out the gender-bifurcated impact of our culture's child-rearing practices. In these conceptualizations, little boys must traverse an emotionally challenging and problematic developmental trajectory. This trajectory requires them to prematurely seek connection outside the maternal emotional holding environment in order to conform to our culture's prevailing conceptions of masculinity. For little girls, this cultural script is played out developmentally via connection to the mother, who is experienced "like me." In our maternally based child-rearing culture, identity and relatedness become fundamentally connected for little girls. Little boys, on the other hand, must negotiate their construction of gender in a process that is based on separation and distancing from the mother as well as the culturally sanctioned push away from the mother's relational holding environment. In this process, a little boy's conception of himself becomes intertwined with separation from others and autonomous emotional functioning.

Greenson (1968), Tyson (1982, 1986), and Pollack (1995a) identify this breaking away from the maternal bond early in life as an important one in male development. Pollack (1995b) has speculated that disruption of this early bond produces a gender-specific vulnerability resulting from a "traumatic abrogation of the early holding environment" (p. 41) in little boys' development. This abrogation creates a dynamic foundation that has a profound impact on the boy's later experience of relationships with both other boys and girls. One hypothesized outcome of this developmental process is a defensive firming of interpersonal boundaries, a tendency toward distancing and self-protectiveness in the face of what is ultimately experienced as a pull toward intimacy and connection with others.

A second experience of normative loss in little boys, especially those born prior to and including the post–World War II "baby boomers," is the relative absence of the father, both physically and psychologically (Strauss & Howe, 1991). In our Western culture, in which there is value and honor in a man's providing for his family, such provisioning often takes the father from the home and away from those he loves most (Gilmore, 1990). A number of authors address this key relationship, often focusing on the positive aspects of the father in facilitating the little boy's separation and identity development (e.g., Abelin, 1980). However, with a father away at work, how can a little boy experience the full benefit of this relationship? Osherson (1986) has proposed that for many men, facing the grief and pain over the absence of their father is a critical dimension of men's psychological development. The absence of a stable and enduring relational bond with the father, as well as the grief and pain that is experienced by many men in relation to this absence, further compounds the experience of grief and loss to which boys are subjected in their push from maternal connection.

While, in many cases, the father can be a positive role model for the young boy's separation and identity development, he often is a poor role model in the realm of interpersonal relating. Many boys are left to fend for themselves, superficially imitating their father's independent style but having little substantive guidance on how to manage feelings of hurt, sadness, or grief (Pollack, 1998b). Unlike girls, who are more relationally oriented, boys have little experience managing the grief of making attachments and then separating from them. Instead, many boys learn to avoid the emotional signals that might point toward their grief or confusion and instead develop a more extroverted, activity-oriented lifestyle.

A recapitulation of these earlier interpersonal loss experiences often occurs at adolescence for boys. After a period of years in which they may be growing physically and on the sports field, boys are faced with the demands of interpersonal relationships with the advent of adolescence. These relational challenges often resonate with the confusion and defensiveness that was experienced in conjunction with the dislocation from the emotional holding environment of earlier years. With the onset of adolescence, sex differences in the prevalence of depression become manifest, with girls beginning to lead boys in both symptoms and diagnosis of depression. Before adolescence, little boys are generally diagnosed at least as frequently with depression as little girls (Anderson, Williams, McGee, & Silva, 1987; Kashani, Beck, Hoeper, Fallahi, Corcoran, McAllister, Rosenberg, & Reid, 1987). It is at adolescence that the female preponderance of depressive disorders first begins to emerge (Nolen-Hoeksema and Girgus, 1994).

Young men have been found to exhibit externalizing patterns of defenses and behaviors such as projection, anger, and antagonism (Levit, 1991) and are perceived as disagreeable, aggressive, and antagonistic by others (Gjerde, Block, & Block, 1988). Consistent with this externalizing, activity-oriented style, successful male adaptation in our culture is defined by achievement, intellectual capacity, and competence. As

Gjerde (1995) has found, lack of competence and the presence of allocentric behaviors (self-centered, narcissistic behavioral patterns) in boys as adolescents were related to depression in young men. It is not surprising to find young men channeling their emotional intensity into strivings for success via their careers and the pursuit of "the dream" of success (Levinson, Darrow, Klein, Levinson, MeKee, 1978). During this pursuit, many men also seek out a mate who will support them and help them raise a family. Like his father before him, a man is often better equipped to work than to connect in his relationships. A romantic partner may find a man's energy and activity focus attractive from a provider standpoint. It is often not until a man is faced with the demands of work and family that he is confronted with his poor relational skills. Some men repeat the pattern of their fathers, working hard, but distancing themselves from their spouses and children. Others choose to focus on family but pay the price in the competitive work environment for not being fully on task. Some men find the pressures too great and leave the family totally, retreating to a less complicated and less emotionally demanding relationship situation.

Unfortunately, many men are not well prepared to deal with the limitations of their lives. Taught from an early age to achieve, accomplish, and win, there is no real training in how to psychologically accept one's strengths and weaknesses in a healthy and nonshaming way. Believing that they have more control than they actually do, many men find that when life events do not go their way, they are good at compensating behaviorally but poorly equipped emotionally to absorb the blow. This is especially the case at midlife, where many men are faced with the foreclosure of their occupational and social dreams.

Men often pursue identity through achievement in the workplace (Rabinowitz & Cochran, 1994). Attaining achievement in the workplace is one of the primary ways that a man can erect defenses against other types of threats to his ego. When a man is skipped over for a promotion, downsized out of a job, or told that his skills are no longer needed, he is faced with a loss that cuts deeper than the job itself. It is as if he has been devalued as a man, raising questions about his self-definition. While he may outwardly deny the importance of his work to others, he will experience an internal sense of shame that may dominate his consciousness. A man may find that this shame cuts across his life, coaxing him to question his role as a provider, mate, father, or human being (Krugman, 1995). While some psychologists see this as an opportunity to redefine oneself, most men will struggle to recapture that which they have lost in order to avoid the full brunt of the emotional pain. Often, a man feels he has no choice but to fight back in some way and re-prove his masculinity, even if he feels defeated internally.

Another tragic event for a number of men is the loss of a partner or spouse during midlife to divorce. Divorce is quite common and usually involves a couple's miscommunicating, losing interest in each other, or growing in different directions. Data suggests that marriage serves to protect many men against depression and other mood disturbances (e.g., Wu & DeMaris, 1996; Thoits, 1987). While extramarital affairs may contribute to marital discord, it is usually more a symptom of a problem in the relationship. Traditionally, communication in relationships is in the domain of the female partner, who tolerates a man's less emotionally expressive style as long as her needs are being met. Often, when there are problems in the relationship, men tend to try to problem-solve while women try to work out the problem through talking (Philpot, Brooks, Lusterman, & Nutt, 1997). When a couple finds it can no longer function, one of the partners registers the dissatisfaction and often expects the other to change in response. Fortunate couples who go to therapy often can remedy problems through self-awareness, blame sharing, and mutual problem-solving. Many couples, who do not take this route, conclude the other is to blame. Such a blaming stance on the part of either partner results in a high probability of separation and divorce.

For many men, divorce is not only personally shaming but often involves the loss of regular contact with their children. Most men enter marriage with the intention of being a lifelong partner in a relationship. Choosing monogamy is a very large decision for men, considering that it means limiting one's sexual partner to one individual. Whether caused by death or by divorce, the loss of a long-term relationship or marriage is a painful and devastating experience for many men. Attachment theory suggests that one's connection with another is not easily broken, and severing relational bonds typically results in separation anxiety and depression (Bowlby, 1980). The pain of relationship loss for men is often exacerbated by earlier experiences of dislocation from the maternal holding environment compounded by the accrual of painful loss experiences through adolescence and early adulthood (Cochran & Rabinowitz, 1996).

Another loss for men at midlife is that of losing regular contact with children through divorce or when they grow up and leave home. Most men identify in a proud and positive way with being a father. Much time and energy is involved in raising children. While statistics show that mothers are more involved in the daily lives of children, fathers are still considered extremely important to a child's welfare (Brooks & Gilbert, 1995). Fathers act as role models for young boys and are considered extremely important contributors to the self-esteem of girls, especially as they navigate adolescence (Pipher, 1994). The role of father is an important element of the stage of generativity in Erikson's (1980) scheme of psychosocial development. Deprived of the opportunity to fulfill this important role, many men face a crisis of meaning and purpose during the later stages of the life span.

Until midlife, it is unlikely that the average man will show many of the symptoms that define major depression. Rates of depression increase as men grow into middle age, and peak in the 35–45 age group (Kessler, McGonagle, Swartz, Blazer, & Nelson, 1993). Men may erect defenses against depression by betting that achievement in the external world can substitute for experiences of abandonment and loss absorbed since childhood. It is typically when a man has met his goals or has discovered the limits of his expansion in the world that he begins to doubt, question, or redefine his identity. With an awareness of his mortality, he is thrown face to face with the meaning of his life. The impact of losses experienced in midlife is magnified. Perhaps he is overwhelmed by an accumulation of avoidant coping choices made beginning in boyhood. Maybe he is tired of partitioning his emotions from the instrumental areas of his life in the spirit of the traditional male gender role. Either way, many men are forced to confront aspects of their emotional selves as they traverse midlife and beyond.

As men grow older, the impact of life's slings and arrows begins to chip away at what some have characterized as a narcissistic armor or character structure (Cochran & Rabinowitz, 1996; Pollack, 1995b; Kernberg, 1985). This accrual of loss experiences and the ensuing narcissistic wounding may help explain the increase in rates of depression as men grow older. It may also help to understand the alarming rates of suicide in men, especially elderly men. The eventual breakdown of culturally sanctioned defenses against pain and grief leaves middle-aged and elderly men vulnerable to a breakthrough of depressive mood states. Although these states may not rise to the level of a full-blown depressive episode at any given point in time, this underlying shading of mood is common in many men who eventually make their way to a therapist's office for assistance at these later stages in their lives.

In midlife and beyond, men navigate the final two stages of life that Erikson (1963) termed generativity versus stagnation and ego integrity versus despair. A process of reflection on life and a review of accomplishments and failures often serves as an impetus for emotional engagement for many men. For those men fortunate enough to have successfully navigated the earlier developmental milestones of their life journey, this reflection can be a richly rewarding and gratifying process. For other men who have been less successful in their journeys, late adulthood can be a time of crushing despair and depression. In light of our culture's emphasis on achievement and competence, it is not surprising that those men who are faced with looking back on a life path strewn with failures in relationships and work endeavors may be catapulted into depression. The dramatic increase in suicide rates as men grow older may be partly function of such an impact.

Clinician's Query—"I feel really uncomfortable.
Like I'm some sort of freak"

Jason, an overweight 27-year-old married man, had been referred for psychotherapy by his family physician, who had been treating him for depression and anxiety. Jason, who had been taking buproprion for the past six months, complained to his physician that he was still having trouble sleeping and that he often had intrusive thoughts that were interfering with his relationship with his wife as well as with his coworkers at the manufacturing company where he was employed as a shipping clerk.

"I feel spacey. Sometimes, I miss periods of time, like I have been somewhere else," he described some of his discomfort to his therapist.

While initially hesitant about contacting a therapist, Jason made an appointment at the insistence of his wife. In the first two sessions, Jason spoke about not really knowing his real father, who left his mother when Jason was a baby. His mother had a series of boyfriends during his childhood, eventually marrying one of them when Jason was in high school. Jason revealed little feeling, speaking mainly in a monotone. When asked about his feelings, Jason often replied "I don't know what I am feeling."

He told the therapist that he and his wife had not been having sex for the past year. "It's my fault. She's been trying to get me interested, but my desire just hasn't been there. I just don't feel like it. I don't know what I'm going to do about it, either."

During the third session, Jason responded tentatively to a question from the therapist about anything that stood out from his childhood that he actually did have feelings about. It was at this point that he revealed that he had been sexually molested by one of his mother's boyfriends when he was 10 years old.

"Do you think that after all these years what happened to me then could make me depressed now?" Jason wondered.

"It's possible. How often did it occur?" his therapist asked.

"It happened several times when my mother was out. The bad thing is that I really liked this guy. He listened to me. He seemed to genuinely take an active interest in who I was. He would be really friendly," Jason replied with some animation. Then looking down, his voice slowed. "He'd find a way to touch my penis, like after a bath or shower. He told me he was making sure it was clean or dried off."

"You perceived this as uncomfortable?" his therapist asked.

"Sure. It was weird. I felt kind of creepy and dirty when he did this. Sometimes, my penis would get hard and it felt good. I didn't know what to think. I think it scared me, really."

"So on one hand, it felt really great to get some attention from a father figure, but there was also something disturbing and scary about it."

"During those times, I just kind of blanked out. I pretended like it hadn't happened so I could still enjoy what this guy had to offer me. I wasn't used to having a receptive older guy around the house."

"Did you ever tell anyone about it?" his therapist inquired.

"No. I didn't want to worry my mom. She had enough to worry about. Like I said, I just erased it from my mind so I didn't have to deal with it. I rationalized that he just was being helpful to me at bath time."

"Jason, do you think that your intrusive thoughts are at all related to these incidents?"

"Maybe. The images come and go and when I become aware of where I am, it's like a dream that I can't remember. This whole memory thing is pretty overwhelming to me right now," Jason stated with a look of fear on his face.

"That's understandable. You look afraid."

"I know it happened. But it seems unreal. I've never told anyone about it before today. I don't really know what to make of it or what to do with it. I can feel myself shaking."

"It's o.k. to let yourself feel here. You've put a lot of energy into trying to fight off those feelings."

"I feel really uncomfortable. Like I'm some sort of freak."

- How are childhood sexual abuse and depression related in men?
- How does the traditional male gender role, with its emphasis on strength, stoicism, and avoidance of vulnerability, interfere with the healing process for men who have had traumatic sexual experiences in childhood?

TRAUMA AND DEPRESSION

Trauma involves a severe disturbance of an individual's mental and emotional life through a painfully inflicted experience or series of experiences from outside of oneself. Psychologists have used the term "trauma" to describe the impact of child abuse, sexual abuse, combat, violence, and physical accidents, among other life events (Herman, 1992). Although a number of scientists believe that early traumatic experiences are likely to contribute to depression in later life, experimental findings are somewhat inconclusive. Severe trauma may result in physiological damage to the brain, especially areas in the hippocampus where memory is processed (Butler, 1996). Biondi and Picardi (1996) speculate that trauma in the form of irreparable loss experiences results in increased adrenocortical activity and suppressed immune function in humans. Stressful life events may activate certain neuroendocrine processes that may result in the development of depression (Checkley, 1992). Such activation, which may contribute to irreversible changes in the neurotransmitter systems of the central nervous system, contributes to the emergence and exacerbation of depressive symptoms.

Real (1997) has made a distinction between active trauma and passive trauma. Active trauma involves obvious and dramatic violations of trust, such as child sexual abuse, witnessing or being the victim of physical violence, or the death of one or both parents. Passive trauma situations involve subtle breaches of trust, such as a parent not meeting a child's need to be loved, seen, or valued. Although not as obvious, passive trauma can have a profound effect, since its source may not be found in conscious memory. A man may be left with an unexplained feeling of loss, pain, or emptiness following an interpersonal slight and not have a rationale for its existence.

Men who have experienced active trauma, including childhood sexual abuse, often keep this information to themselves in conformity with the traditional male gender role (Gordon, 1990; Harrison & Morris, 1996; Hunter, 1990). To admit weakness or share emotional vulnerability is to place oneself in a precarious position, especially among other men, who are often perceived as competitors, ready to take advantage of each other. Masculinity is defined partially by one's ability to overcome tragic circumstances without complaining or assuming a victim stance. It is no wonder that, until recently, there has been little information gathered about boys' childhood sexual abuse. Only after investigators were willing to sit down for extended confidential interview sessions and ask questions in non-shame-inducing ways were men who had been abused able to speak honestly about traumatic experiences and their impact (Lisak, 1994).

Active trauma impacts an individual in a number of psychological and emotional ways. The traumatic experience itself is often recalled with vividness, producing feelings of anxiety and shame. For most men, these feelings alone are shameful and lead to conscious and unconscious coping methods. Many men swear, at some point, that they will do everything in their power not to be affected by the memories of trauma. The traditional male gender role, with its emphasis on overcoming pain and achieving success, provides many men with an outlet for their energy and focus. It is extremely manly to be tough, competitive, and not to let anyone interfere with one's goals.

The severity of the abuse and the number of abuse situations endured will have an influence on how an individual is psychologically impacted (Finkelhor, Hotaling, Lewis, & Smith, 1990). In autobiographical interviews of male survivors of sexual abuse, researchers found that several themes emerged in these men's lives. These included feelings of anger, betrayal, fear, helplessness, isolation, loss, shame, humiliation, self-blame, and guilt. They also included themes related to questioning one's masculinity, concerns about sexuality and homosexuality, questions about the legitimacy of one's abuse experience, negative childhood peer relations, and negative schemas about oneself and others (Briere, Evans, Runtz, & Wall, 1988; Dimock, 1988; Dhaliwal, Gauzas, Antonowicz, & Ross, 1996; Lisak, 1994). Many of these feelings and concerns lie at the core of the depression for men who suffered through sexual abuse episodes.

While active traumas like parental abandonment and sexual abuse have obvious impact, passive traumas often go unnoticed in many men's lives. Something as small as an unfulfilled need to be noticed or recognized can have damaging implications on male personality structure. Winnicott (1960/1965) and Kohut (1977) describe the subtly wounded self. Kohut suggests that the developing child has three major needs to be fulfilled. These include the need to be mirrored, the need to idealize, and the need to be like others. The need to be mirrored is best understood as the way that a child develops self-acceptance by having a significant adult validate (mirror) his or her best qualities. Parents often, through subtle gestures and verbalizations, make a child feel as if he is special, important, and desired. When parental mirroring fails, a child who has had significant parental support learns to create his own mirror. This process, called transmuting internalization, allows an individual to gradually create a self-structure, based on the accrual of mirroring experiences, that is stable and relatively positive (Kohut, 1977). If a child does not get enough positive mirroring, he will have difficulty sustaining stable self-esteem. This failure of an internalized sense of positive mirroring results in feelings of low self worth and is defended against by grandiosity. In the normal child, grandiose needs are eventually fulfilled from resources drawn from within. In the child lacking adequate self structure, the need to be seen and validated becomes so strong that it may completely overwhelm the ego structure. This leads to inappropriate exhibitionism to gain attention and only minimal gratification from external sources. Even for men who have not been physically or sexually abused, a lack of mirroring can be a subtle but significant passive trauma that results in an inner hollowness and an overcompensated persona (Pollack, 1998a). For a man who has lacked adequate mirroring, a narcissistic setback such as a job loss or relationship breakup can precipitate strong feelings of emptiness and depression, since these setbacks often activate the pain of prior wounding of an already embattled self (Cochran & Rabinowitz, 1996).

The frustration of the need to idealize a parent can also be damaging to the male self structure. A boy's idealization of his mother and father provide him with hope for the future. By looking up to his parents, a boy can identify and one day imagine himself as a competent and successful adult. If a parent betrays his trust and frustrates his idealization, the growing boy is left with little in which to believe. In child abuse, the violation is obvious and overt. The damage sustained from the trauma makes it difficult for the boy to believe that his own future will be positive. Even subtle betrayals by parents can inflict passive trauma that, if not repaired, can lead to a sense of pessimism or negativity, the source of which is not consciously recalled. Pessimism, negativity, and loss of hope are some of the hallmarks of depression.

Kohut's (1977) final aspect of self is based on the concept of twinship. This is the need to have a double or a playmate who is one's equal to validate each other's feelings, thoughts, and interests. This often occurs in childhood and can lead to a strong sense of belonging. If there has been active trauma, such as child abuse, shame, doubt, and secrecy may replace the openness needed for peer intimacy. For boys, the traditional male code suggests that shameful events not be shared for fear of appearing weak (Pollack, 1998b). For many boys, trauma leads to social isolation or exaggerated nonintimate ways of acting, such as bullying, fighting, or exhibitionism. Passive trauma can also lead to internalized negative feelings about the self, which may keep a boy from sharing personal information with friends or interacting in a spontaneous and uninhibited manner.

Lack of twinship is often reinforced by the male role that pits men against each other in adulthood, in competition for jobs and sexual partners. These restrictive and oppressive norms are transmitted in our child-rearing practices and socialization processes to little boys, who find it difficult to overcome these restrictive aspects of the "boy code" (Pollack, 1998b). As a result, many boys emerge into adolescence and young adulthood isolated and disconnected from these important peer relationships that are viewed as so important to the development of a healthy sense of self. Isolation from other men is a common complaint of men who experience depressive symptoms.

Few men seem to reach adulthood without suffering subtle trauma. Rejection, betrayal, competitive antagonism, and avoidance are part and parcel of life for most boys and men. The male gender-role code makes displays of the painful consequence of these experiences taboo by forbidding crying, emotional displays other than anger, and physical comforting by other males (Pleck, 1995). This leaves men few outlets to express or emotionally soothe themselves in an authentic way. A real man will overcome his traumatic losses through stoicism, strength, and will power. Efforts to distract from or externalize depressed and sad affect may provide relief in the short run, but are ultimately self-defeating strategies. The ineffectiveness of such attempts is reflected in high rates of drug abuse, alcoholism, and other addictions, as well as in higher suicide and accident rates and a shorter life span (Brooks & Silverstein, 1995; Harrison, Chin, & Ficcarrotto, 1989). While effective in the short run to hide weakness and pain, the traditional male way of handling trauma is deadly in the long term.

Throughout the life span, boys and men are subjected to active and passive trauma that is, in part, a consequence of restrictive and dysfunctional gender-role socialization. Gender-role training forces boys and men to utilize maladaptive coping strategies, interferes with effective management of trauma-related depression, and prolongs or derails natural healing processes that repair the impact of traumatic events. Many boys and men experience strong conflict between experiencing and coping with trauma and the externally imposed gender-role norms of our culture. Such conflict often, sadly, results in boys and men erecting defenses against an ever increasing reservoir of unspeakable pain, grief, and sadness, that leaves many men vulnerable to depressive states at various stress-points throughout the life span.

> *Clinician Query*—"It just doesn't get any worse than this."
>
> Paul was an unemployed 38-year-old man who had been laid off from his job as a mechanic at a local automobile repair shop. He contacted a psychotherapist at the insistence of his spouse, who had become concerned about how he was behaving after the layoff. Paul had not had any previous psychological or psychiatric treatment when the first met with his therapist. At this first meeting, he was dressed casually in jeans and a popular sport shirt. He was of medium height and athletic in build. He had short hair and a ruddy, deep complexion. He used a strong grip as he shook hands and introduced himself to the therapist. They entered the consulting room and the therapist asked Paul to just start wherever he would like, and review what had happened that had brought him in to the office that day.
>
> "Well, you know that commercial, `it doesn't get any better than this?' Well, as far as I'm concerned, it doesn't get any worse that this," was Paul's response to this opening question. He continued, "Ever since Jamie died, two years ago now, things have just gone downhill. Ugh. It's just too hard to think about."
>
> Paul glanced out the window.

"You mentioned that on the phone when you made the appointment. What happened?" Paul's therapist inquired, inviting more details about the background and circumstances that had brought Paul to therapy.

"Well, he was diagnosed with leukemia when he was 8 years old. The doctors thought they could beat it, but..." He gazed out the window again. "I remember that day in the hospital when he died. It's so clear to me. I just play it over and over in my head about every day. We were just sitting there, just me and him. He was pretty much out of it, with drugs and all. But I think he was aware enough to open his eyes and hear me talk." Paul paused and struggled to continue. "It was unreal. Here I was, sitting there with my son, my only son, dying, right in front of me. Only 10 years old." Paul paused and was clearly trying to restrain himself from being overcome with grief. His lip quivered as he took a deep breath and continued.

"Well, after he died, I just tried to forget about it. But I guess that's easier said than done. It wasn't too bad, with all the activity around putting on a wake and with relatives visiting, a guy keeps pretty busy. Then, a couple of months after the funeral and everything, my boss comes in and says he's going to have to let me go. Just temporary, he says, until there is more work. We were having the usual winter slowdown, but I just can't help but think he noticed I just wasn't up to par. Well, that was just what I needed. A double whammy!" Paul paused again. "I just haven't been able to pull myself out of it since then. That was over a year ago now. I've been depressed, but what can a guy do? I'm still alive, still eating and sleeping. I guess. Julie thought I should come in and talk. She thought it would help me feel better. Maybe it will, I don't know."

"I'm glad you came in, Paul. I'm just overwhelmed by what you have just said. That's a really sad story about your son, and I'm so sorry it ended the way it did. And to top it off, to lose your job, too. You know, it's not too surprising you would be feeling some depression. I think anyone would after what you've been through. You said you haven't been able to pull yourself out of it? What do you mean?" the therapist continued.

"Well, I just can't get going. I just don't have any get-up-and-go. I'm just stuck. It's like I weigh 600 pounds and can't move myself," Paul described his physical heaviness and inertia. "And I just want to hide. A guy loses his son, and then his job. What's next?"

- How does the traditional male gender role inhibit the expression of grief in men?
- What relationship is there between grief and depression in men?

GRIEF AND DEPRESSION

Grief is defined as the physical and emotional state and the behaviors that accompany the permanent loss of a significant other (Lindemann, 1944). Much of the research literature on men and grief has focused on men who have recently become widowed (Fitzpatrick, 1998) or friends and partners of men who have died from the AIDS epidemic (Martin & Dean, 1993). For men raised in American culture, there is little sanction to outwardly grieve losses with tears or overt emotional expression of sadness. American heroes such as the characters that John Wayne, Clint Eastwood, and Steven Segal portray in film are more likely to show a stiff upper lip and a stoic expression following the deaths of companions. The deaths will likely be avenged in a violent manner, reinforcing a stereotype of men who channel emotional pain into anger.

Freud (1917/1957), in his paper "Mourning and Melancholia," suggested that depression is an affective state related to object loss through death or separation. Through the process of introjection, the lost object or person is retained as an emotionally charged intrapsychic representation incorporated into the self. Identification occurs when the individual modifies his self-image in accordance with certain characteristics of the lost object. This process serves to internally recapture the lost person. Subsequent ego psychologists speculated that the experience of depression is actually an identification with the depressive affect of the lost object (Blanck & Blanck, 1974). Abraham (1911/1948) and Freud (1917/1957) both believed that the lost object is often ambivalently loved. While the individual introjects the good and bad characteristics of the person into his own ego, he is also extremely angry at the lost love object for abandoning him. Anger aimed at the object of loss is directed inward in a punitive manner, resulting in self-condemnation, a wish to die, and in dramatic situations, an active suicide attempt. Klein (1959/1975) suggested that all children go through a phase of extreme rage toward their parents for not meeting their needs, resulting in what she called the "depressive position." The depressive position is a mood state resulting from feelings of guilt following the child's angry outbursts. The child fears that these outbursts have damaged his real relationships resulting in abandonment and a vulnerable state.

For men at midlife, the death of a parent typically precedes a period of personal turmoil, transition, and a deeply felt sense of one's mortality (Douglas, 1990). For aging men, the loss of one's lifetime partner is perhaps the most stressful life event. This loss has been found to result in a significant decline in a man's psychological and physical health (Stroebe & Stroebe, 1987). Changes in life routines, decision-making processes, and social support add stress to a man already shocked by the death of his companion (Fitzpatrick, 1998). The death may also complicate adjustment to the occupational role change of retirement (Berado, 1970). Deaths other than that of a spouse or partner have also been found to be as devastating to an aging man's health. Although the research literature is limited, the death of a parent, child, sibling, or close friend also has a severely destabilizing impact on the psychological health of the older man. The main factor found to mediate the impact of grief for an older man is social support. Those men who have more friends and social networks are less likely to be as psychologically and physically impaired (Fitzpatrick, 1998). For gay men whose partners and friends died during the AIDS epidemic, research suggests that the number of losses, as well as one's HIV status, are predictors of psychological distress (Martin & Dean, 1993), depression, anxiety, and substance abuse (Gluhoski, Fishman, & Perry, 1997).

For many men who have adopted the traditional male gender role, grief is extremely uncomfortable. There is a sense of impotence, frustration, and self-blame that accompanies loss. Women in western culture are more comfortable with the depressive position, perhaps viewing it as a natural consequence of emotional attachment. Men prefer to avoid or suppress the depressive affect that accompanies separation and loss since it exposes vulnerability and perceived weakness (Cochran & Rabinowitz, 1996). A common strategy employed by many men experiencing loss and grief is to split off this affect and focus on external activities that are rational, practical, or goal directed. This masculine way of grieving serves to bolster those socially sanctioned behaviors, values, and norms that comprise traditional masculine coping styles and afford men a sense of control (Carverhill, 1997). While most practitioners encourage men in grief to find social support and safe places to tell their stories and express feelings, most men are uncomfortable seeking help, even in this situation (Stroebe & Stroebe, 1987). Sadly, grief for many men remains an unspoken, hidden experience.

Clinician Query—"A bunch of twisted demons inside."

Lyle, a 51-year-old divorced man, arrived for psychotherapy at the urging of his sister, with whom he lives. Lyle, who is 5 feet 10 inches tall and weighs 325 pounds, has not worked in five years because of physical ailments that have rendered him disabled. Lyle had been a successful attorney for 20 years, specializing in product liability issues for a large law firm. Seven years ago, his wife of 15 years left him for another man. He was involved in a serious car accident approximately two months after she left. This accident left him with chronic back pain and migraine headaches. Lyle had been arrested two times for assault after getting into fights at a local tavern that he frequents. Although he did not serve time in jail, he was put on probation and is still under the jurisdiction of the court.

Lyle was severely beaten by his stepfather as a child, but has tended to diminish the significance of this. "What's done is done. My father was an alcoholic who didn't know what he was doing. It just made me tough," he commented. Both of Lyle's children are adults who live out of state and have no contact with their father.

"I wish he would just lay off me. That probation officer I have to report to is such a weenie. I think he believes I'm just a common criminal. He doesn't seem to believe that at one time I earned five times his puny salary," Lyle complained in an early therapy session.

"You feel like he doesn't really understand you," paraphrased his therapist.

"I find very few, if any, people in this world who do understand me," Lyle replied.

"I wonder if you feel like I understand you."

"You're paid to understand me. You are a bit like a whore, but I forgive you," Lyle joked, laughing to himself.

"Seriously. I sense that you don't trust me with most feelings other than anger," his therapist persisted.

"That's pretty accurate, doc. No one gets inside here, not even me most of the time," he said, pointing at his large belly.

"What do you think I might find if I did get in there?" queried his therapist.

"A bunch of twisted demons, I reckon," Lyle responded.

"Twisted demons?"

"Oh, yeah. They would just torture you with their threats and confuse the hell out of you with their logic," Lyle replied, his eyes going cold, his face rigid.

"Where do the demons come from?" asked his therapist.

"They probably were born some time during one of my father's beatings, I guess. He used to beat the shit out of me for no good reason. Maybe I deserved it, who knows?"

"You really believe that you deserved to get the shit beat out of you?"

"Damn right, partner. If I didn't show him the respect he asked for, I took the blows. Problem was, I didn't always know what kind of respect he was looking for. The bastard, he was drunk most of the time I interacted with him," he replied with an empty laugh.

"You seem like you are proud of yourself for how much pain you could take."

"Right again. There is no way for you to know how much I can take. I outlasted him. He's under ground and I'm still here," Lyle gloated.

"I guess I'm confused. If you're so strong, why are you here with me?" his therapist asked, confronting Lyle's grandiosity.

"I told you before. It's the damn demons. I want to care about people, my kids, my sister. But I get so disheartened. Everyone doesn't want to see how screwed up this culture is. Why can't an intelligent man like me find some use for myself out there? It's enough to make you want to give up. What's the point? You let me know that and we can end this therapy."

"Lyle, you seem strong on the outside, but the demons are eating you up right now. What do you say we take a good, hard look at those demons and see if we can find a way to beat them?"

"Good luck."

- What role does childhood physical abuse have in the manifestation of depression in adult men?
- What clues of depression are present in this case and in other cases in which anger is a prominent affective state?

MANIFESTATIONS OF COVERT DEPRESSION IN MEN

Bio-psycho-social models of depression emphasize a complex interplay of biological and genetic vulnerability, psychological mechanisms, and behavioral tendencies shaped by social and cultural norms. Within this framework, many have speculated that mood disorders are frequently masked by various physical and behavioral phenomena (DiGiuseppe, 1986; Harrington, 1993; Baker, 1996; Charatan, 1985; Weiss, Nagel, & Aronson, 1986). Alexithymia, literally, "without words," is thought to be related to the masking of mood difficulties that are unable to be expressed via language (Lesser, 1985). Such masking, termed "masked depression," "depressive equivalent," or "covert depression," can be defined using an exclusive or inclusive approach. The exclusive approach seeks to discover depression underlying only vegetative, somatic, or physical complaints. The inclusive approach considers a wider spectrum of problems, including alcohol and substance abuse, delinquency, anger and aggressive behavior, accidental injuries, and self-injurious behavior. In comparison to women, men are more likely to be perceived and identified as less verbally expressive, less psychologically oriented, and less willing to acknowledge emotional distress (Levant, 1995). The masking of depressed mood may be a "face-saving" strategy for many men, who are less skilled at emotional expression and more bound to societal expectations of masculinity.

Empirical support for the construct of masked depression is mixed, owing to difficulty operationalizing this construct and to its exclusion from formal diagnostic and research categories. Case reports in the literature have indicated success in treatment of anger associated with depression (Albritton & Borison, 1995) and of alexithymia associated with depression in a Holocaust survivor (Fisch, 1989). In a study of 46 boys manifesting antisocial behavior, 39 were found to report significant depressive symptomatology, lower self-esteem, higher levels of guilt, and greater cognitive problems compared with those who did not manifest an underlying depression (Harper & Kelly, 1985). Stoudemire, Kahn,

Brown, Linfors, and Houpt (1985) found that of 212 patients in a combined medical–psychiatric unit, 17% were diagnosed as depressed on admission, while over 50% received a diagnosis of depression after a thorough psychiatric evaluation. The depression in these patients was manifest at time of admission mainly by somatic complaints that were not expressed directly through verbal means. Other conditions hypothesized to have complex depressive–vegetative components include insomnia (Fleming, 1993), heart disease (Roose, Dalack, & Woodring, 1991; Lesperance, Frasure-Smith, & Talajic, 1996; Frasure-Smith, Lesperance, & Talajic, 1995), and chronic pain (Magni, 1987). Such findings, on the other hand, raise questions concerning the validity of this construct (e.g., Van Houdenhove, Vestraeten, Onghena, & de Cuyper, 1992; Altshuler & Weiner, 1985; Kellner, Abbott, Winslow, & Pathak, 1989; Oxman, Rosenberg, Schnurr, & Tucker, 1985). Nevertheless, cultural conditioning and internal psychological prohibitions that result in men's suppression of painful, sad, or guilt-laden emotional states suggest that depressed mood may be masked by men in many situations and circumstances. The construct of masked depression is, thus, useful in fully understanding the phenomenon of male depression in all its various manifestations.

Overtly avoiding or repressing feelings of loss, guilt, and depression may lead to indirect behavioral or somatic manifestations of the denied emotional states (Lesse, 1983). Cumulative effects of loss, trauma, and grief impact even the healthiest of men. It is still considered taboo in many circles of our society for men to acknowledge their inner pain. Men who follow traditional male gender-role norms have been found to experience higher levels of emotional distress but a decreased likelihood for seeking psychological help, in general (Good, Dell, & Mintz, 1989; Good & Mintz, 1990; Good et al., 1996; Good & Wood, 1995), as well as for depression in particular (Hoyt, Conger, Valde, & Weihs, 1997). While men have a tendency to avoid primary healthcare settings, it is sometimes more acceptable for a man to seek help for physical pain than psychological pain (Sutkin & Good, 1987). Approximately 12–35% of individuals seeking relief in a primary care medical setting for somatic complaints are thought to be significantly depressed (Lombardi, 1990; Katon, 1987). An empirical study utilizing depression questionnaires showed that physicians missed more than 95% of the cases of depression when depression is not self-reported (Katon, Kleinman, & Rosen, 1982). Many men who are depressed may seek help from primary care physicians for physical problems.

One study of two groups of individuals who had equal levels of anxiety, identified either as somatizers or psychologically minded, found that the somatizers were less likely to report feelings of depression than were those with a more psychological orientation (Goldberg & Bridges, 1988). The authors suggest that somatization functions as a defense against personal responsibility for life predicaments. Those who somaticize can project their troubles onto something physical or outside of themselves and avoid internal self-blame. This process functions similarly to the male gender-role socialization pattern, whereby men disavow psychological weakness in order to appear in control and avoid shame. Such a process makes it extremely probable that men will detach, disassociate, and displace emotional distress, resulting in what a number of authors have termed depressive equivalents or masked depression (Lesse, 1983).

Somatization functions as an equivalent outlet for the recognition and expression of emotion (Lombardi, 1990). However, without the mental awareness of what is bothering him, a man will find that his body repeats its outlet of expression, resulting in his noticing a somatic area of anxiety or pain (i.e.. racing heart rate, migraine headaches, lower back pain). Even for men conscious of their bodies, it is not unusual for a man to engage in some sort of physical activity that leads to injury or negative consequences during a period of stress, worry, or loss. Several theorists have suggested that the body and mind could not be separated, that all somatized symptoms, injuries, and diseases were connected to both external and intrapsychic events (Groddeck 1923/1949; Lowen, 1975).

In addition to these speculations on the vicissitudes of repressed emotion, a common theme from the psychoanalytic literature on somatization is the connection between loss and depression. Winnicott (1936/1978) found that many of the children he treated for eating disorders were experiencing anxiety and depression from the earliest days of life. A syndrome identified as anaclitic depression was found to emerge within four to six months after a child separated from his or her mother or caregivers. Symptoms of anaclitic depression included withdrawal, sadness, lack of physical growth, anorexia, weight loss, insomnia, and psychomotor retardation (Bowlby, 1980; Spitz & Wolf, 1946). Spitz (1951) suggested that the psyche and somatic systems are actually merged as one and form an ego structure that allows for psychic discharges through the body.

Winnicott (1960/1965) hypothesized that persons who had to adapt to inconsistent or abusive parenting were forced to split emotional experiences from their bodies and create a false self that complied outwardly with parental wishes and demands. For a man with this experience, the body may speak an emotional truth that is nothing like the reality to which he has adapted (Lowen, 1972). Somatization may be his only way of self-expression, revealed to himself and others as a physical symptom such as overeating, high blood pressure, excessive sleeping, chronic back pain, or difficulty concentrating.

The Kleinian object-relations focus on the depressive position may offer an understanding of why men may have a difficult time tolerating depression. Most men have been able to tolerate depression as children. However, the male gender role reminds boys and men that they are not to show weakness or vulnerability, characterized by the longing and sadness of the depressive position. The forgotten trauma of separation from mother makes boys and men unconsciously sensitive to depressive affect (Pollack, 1995b).

For some men, the acting out of aggression, one of the few acceptable forms of emotional release, may be conceptualized as a cathartic expression of sadness, grief, or depression. While a man may feel some sense of relief following an aggressive action, there are few places where this behavior is acceptable. The exceptions for this emotional outlet are aggressive sports and physically active forms of psychotherapy (e.g., Lowen, 1975). Unfortunately, the recipient of a socially inappropriate aggressive act is typically a person the individual knows or with whom he is intimate. Although there may be immediate relief, the likely overriding emotional response for the sensitive man will be self-blame, self-hatred, and a repetition of the cycle. Thus, for men who grieve through aggression, there is likely to be a further internalization of self-criticism and a propensity toward withholding any type of emotional reactivity until the internal pain is again unbearable. Is it possible that certain types of aggressive actions in men may be disguised loss or grief reactions? Other men who have more fully disconnected from their empathic connection to others may find that aggression is an adaptive way of life that allows them to meet basic needs and externalize their huge reservoir of pain, betrayal, loss, and humiliation (Lisak, 1998).

Another form of masking depressive mood states is mood alteration through alcohol, drugs, or other addictive activities. We know that men suffer from alcohol and drug abuse in significantly greater numbers than women. Could the dramatically higher rates of alcohol and other drug abuse and dependence in men represent this masking on a large scale? In order to calm feelings of impotence, anger, and self-reproach brought on by trauma or loss, biochemically adjusting mood in a predictable manner allows a man to regain an illusion of control and power in his emotional life (Diamond, 1987; Ritter & Cole, 1992). At the first sign of discomfort, a man can change his body's biochemistry in a direction he finds desirable at the time (Cooper, Frone, Russell, & Mudar, 1995). Such activity is consistent with the traditional male gender role that emphasizes strength, power, and control. In the short run, this may relieve his pain and provide a false sense of wholeness. However, most men keep the long-term consequences of this lifestyle out of conscious thought. The man who reaches for a cigarette is not worried about his unconscious self-destruction nor is the man who drinks beer to anesthetize negative feelings aware of how he is avoiding the sources of his frustrations. With more potent narcotics such as heroin or cocaine, men are even more removed from their internal psychological reality, masking impotence with an illusion of power. More socially acceptable addictions, such as work, gambling, or sex, also serve the same function for many men as drugs, altering body chemistry, diverting thoughts and feelings about inner conflict, and minimizing awareness of the effects on others. It is no wonder that some men unconsciously choose various types of addictions to avoid shameful and depressing feelings (Real, 1997). While the addiction may have originated as a means to cope with depression and reduce anxiety, it often tends to exacerbate the condition, leading to more severe cycling of depressive affect when not engaged in the addictive behavior (Khantzian, 1985).

SUMMARY

Our understanding of the way men are socialized informs us that male depression is often a result of the combined effects of biological predisposition, early childhood loss and trauma, gender-role restrictions in behavior, life disappointments, unresolved grief, poor social support, and a growing awareness of mortality. Theory and research suggest that depression is often manifest differently in men and women. With little tolerance for overt emotional expression of trauma, loss, and grief, men may find it more acceptable to act out their feelings through more socially acceptable, although often covert, channels. While depressive symptoms may be hidden to others, subtle behavioral and somatic indicators can be seen through the empathic lens of a male psychology that transcends the blinders of the traditional male gender role (Levant &

Pollack, 1995). From this perspective, men are appreciated for their strengths, while recognition is given to areas of functioning that are limited by gender socialization.

Masking of male depression may occur through somatization or psychophysiological disorders, addictions, and aggressive behavior outbursts. Many of these hypothesized outlets for male depression are categories in which men are proportionally overrepresented compared with women. For example, men are three to five times as likely to suffer from alcohol abuse and dependency as women. Given the documented connection between depression and these various conditions that could serve as covert outlets for depression in men, could this be where men find expression of their psychic pain? Are these outlets not socially sanctioned for men, thus making men more inclined to express depressive affect through such socially acceptable channels as addiction, aggression, and avoidance?

CHAPTER 4

Assessing Depression in Men

He who conceals his disease cannot expect to be cured.

Ethiopian Proverb

Symptom Profiles in Mood Disorders
Interviewing Men for Depression
Instruments to Assess Depression
Masculine–Specific Assessment of Depression
Summary

The title of Whybrow's (1997) popular treatise on mood disorders, "A Mood Apart," anticipates the difficulty clinicians encounter when attempting to accurately assess depressive conditions. What "sets apart" those mood states that we know as depression, which require medical and psychological treatment, from the normal spectrum of human emotions? How are we to know that a deeper sadness or an extended period of elation is truly the beginning of a mood disorder and not just a peak or valley in the human experience? What signs and symptoms might we look for in men, whose moods may be obscured or blunted by cultural conditioning and shame-induced repression? Do men's depressed moods become intertwined in physical or psychosomatic phenomena that further complicate accurate assessment of depression in men? These questions form the basis for our exploration of the assessment of depression in men.

Assessment of depression is accomplished using several different strategies. These include clinical interviewing designed to identify the extent to which a man meets established criteria of depression. The use of self-report depression checklists and assessment questionnaires may also be used to gain information about depressive symptomatology. Objective and projective psychological assessment techniques have a long history of use in the assessment of depression. And finally, the use of clinician ratings to assess an individual's mood state is a popular strategy that is used both in clinical and research settings. Each approach to the assessment of depression views the person's experience and symptoms through a window designed to illuminate the symptomatology from a particular vantage point. Each has advantages and disadvantages, especially with regard to assessing depression in men. For example, men may respond differently than women do to an interviewer of a particular sex (e.g., Pollner, 1998). Men may be less likely to report certain symptoms when questions are couched in terms of assessing specifically for depression, but may be more likely to admit to symptoms when assessment is phrased in terms of "hassles" or difficulties in managing daily life (Page & Bennesch, 1993). Men may respond differently than women do to certain objective or structured measures of depression (Gumbiner & Flowers, 1997), and this response bias may vary with age as well as gender (Wallace & Pfohl, 1995). These findings remind any clinician interviewing men that specific attention must be given to the clinical process of the assessment as well as methods used for the assessment.

Evidence that men may mask or hide depressive moods as a result of the complex interplay of cultural conditioning and internal psychodynamic processes requires clinicians to look carefully not only at the obvious overt symptoms of depression but at ways a man may submerge or "camouflage" his pain and suffering (Warren, 1983). Masking of depression may occur through use of mood-altering substances such as alcohol or other drugs. Other addictive processes men may favor as a consequence of their cultural conditioning include over-involvement in work, sexual conquests, gambling, or other high-risk or self-defeating behaviors. To be sure, these behaviors should never, in isolation, be taken to indicate that a given man is suffering from depression. However, when assessing men's moods, it is important for the clinician to look beyond the presence or absence of symptoms traditionally associated with depression and consider the meaning of all aspects of the man's life, including those aspects that may serve a containment function for dysphoric, depressed mood states.

Clinician Query—"Everybody does it;
what's the problem?"
Bill sought therapy after having been reprimanded at work for irregularities in his expense account records. He

had been adding mileage to his monthly expense account and altering receipts for his meal expenses. After these irregularities were uncovered, he was put on probation and strongly encouraged to seek therapy to help him prevent further recurrences of this problem. He opted to seek help for his difficulties. However, his presentation to his therapist was characterized by excuses and rationalizations for his behavior, as he struggled to avoid taking responsibility for what had happened.

"What's the big deal? Everybody does it. I don't get it," Bill lamented as he told his story to his therapist. Bill was a big, friendly man, and chuckled a lot as he talked. As the interview progressed, his therapist realized that his sense of humor covered up his unhappiness with his employment and his life in general. Interspersed in his protests and excuses, the therapist detected feelings of discontent and frustration with his work and life. Bill had been divorced for five years and lived alone. He had kept the same sales position after his divorce, but was having trouble making ends meet with the alimony and child support payments each month, combined with his own increased living expenses.

"No one will ever notice this extra little bit in the expense account. Besides, they owe it to me for sticking me with this crummy job," he rationalized as he completed his expense account each month.

"I see what you're saying," his therapist commented, "but what I don't understand is why you decided to solve your tight financial situation in this manner. It seems awfully risky to me."

For the first time in the session, Bill paused and reflected on this confrontation. "It is risky," he said with a lowered tone of voice. "I don't know. A lot of the time I just don't think about what I'm doing or why I'm doing it. It's that way with the expense accounts. I just don't think about it. It's automatic. It's what Sarah used to complain about a lot of the time. That I just didn't seem to think about what I did. I guess it keeps my mind off me."

"Keeps your mind off you?" his therapist repeated. "I think we better take a look at that one, Bill. What exactly do you mean by that?"

"I guess I've just never really felt very happy since I got divorced. I miss Sarah and the kids so much." Bill looked down at his shoes and rubbed his hands together. He looked up with a sheepish smile, and said, "It's all I had."

Bill and his therapist sat for several seconds in silence, just looking at each other.

"How do you feel talking about this right now, Bill?"

"Pretty lousy. I just want to get up and get going," Bill replied. "What a mess I've gotten myself into here. I might lose my job. I've already lost my family. What would I do?"

- How does the typical, traditional male role in our culture encourage men to deny or to avoid awareness of depressed mood states?
- What are the main symptoms of depression that men and women experience, and what are some symptoms that men appear to experience more than women?

SYMPTOM PROFILES IN MOOD DISORDERS

A primary consideration in the assessment of depression is a careful review of the individual's symptoms. A diagnosis of depression, as defined in the fourth edition of the *Diagnostic and Statistical Manual of Mental Disorders (DSM-IV)* of the American Psychiatric Association (1994), is built on a foundation of those symptoms that constitute a depressive episode. The length and intensity of such an episode plays an important part in the diagnosis of a depressive disorder. We may all experience a depressed mood from time to time, but what distinguishes a normal deflated mood from a depressive episode? According to the *DSM-IV,* a depressed mood that persists beyond two weeks and that represents a departure from a person's usual mood state warrants attention. In addition to this temporal criterion, there are a number of specific symptoms that an individual must endorse that would confirm the diagnosis of a depressive episode. These symptoms include, in addition to the presence of a depressed mood, loss of interest or pleasure in most activities, weight change, difficulties with sleep, fatigue and loss of energy, restlessness or feeling slowed down, trouble concentrating, feelings of worthlessness or guilt, and thoughts about death.

One aspect of research in the area of sex differences in depression has been the study of symptom profiles of men and women. Might men endorse different symptoms of depression than do women? Could this possibly account for the discrepancy observed between rates of depressions reported for men and women? What are the baseline data when we look at the occurrence of symptoms in depressive episodes in men and women?

The Epidemiological Catchment Area survey (Robins & Reiger, 1991) included in its design a thorough assessment of all subjects' depressive symptoms. The Diagnostic Interview Schedule was designed to assess a number of signs and symptoms of mental disturbance, including depressive episodes experienced in the past 12 months and at any point in the subject's lifetime. Table 4-1 summarizes the data from this study for both men and women with regard to the prevalence of depressive symptoms experienced over the individual's lifetime.

In all categories, fewer men than women reported depressive symptoms at any time during their lives. However, the specific symptoms endorsed most frequently by men and women do not differ. In fact, the most frequently reported symptoms (e.g., dysphoria, death thoughts, changes in appetite and sleep, fatigue, difficulties with concentration) are identical for both men and women. The National Comorbidity Survey (Kessler *et al.*, 1993) similarly found that a greater percentage of women than men endorsed a query involving depressed mood in general, as well as items asking about an increasing number of specific symptoms. However, the percentages of women compared to men who endorsed these criteria and the ratio of women-to-men who would be diagnosed as depressed using such criteria was consistently less than similar ratios from the Epidemiologic Catchment Area survey. One possible reason for this is that men may tend to "forget" symptoms of depression. In order to

TABLE 4-1   Lifetime prevalence of depressive symptoms reported by men and women age 18–65+

Symptom (lasting 2 weeks or longer)	% men reporting (n = 8311)	% women reporting (n = 10,971)
Dysphoria	23.5	35.7
Death thoughts	22.8	33.0
Appetite change	18.8	28.5
Sleep change	18.3	27.0
Fatigue	11.6	19.9
Diminished concentration	10.8	16.7
Guilt	8.6	12.3
Psychomotor change	7.9	10.2
Loss of interest	3.4	6.8

Summarized from Weissman *et al.* (1991).

obtain accurate symptom reports for the determination of lifetime prevalence estimates of the various disorders, a Life Review Section of the assessment process was utilized in the National Comorbidity Survey to assist respondents in focusing on symptoms that may not have been available for immediate recall. The investigators believe that this may have tended to stimulate recollection of depressive episodes or symptoms for the men, thus accounting for the almost fourfold increase in prevalence estimates for men between the Epidemiological Catchment Area study and the National Comorbidity Survey.

In studies involving clinical populations, the identification and reporting of symptoms by men appear to parallel that of women. Young, Scheftner, Fawcett, and Klerman (1990) found that the clinical symptom profiles of men and women with unipolar depression were very similar. Only weight gain and appetite problems were reported more frequently among women than men. Other symptoms, including insomnia, fatigue, somatic concerns, and difficulties with concentration, were reported at similar levels between men and women. Two additional investigations (Frank, Carpenter, & Kupfer, 1988; Kornstein, Schatzberg, Yonkers, Thase, Keitner, Ryan, & Schlaqer, 1996) conclude that there are minimal differences in severity of symptoms among depressed men and women when their symptoms are rated by clinicians. However, self-report measures such as the Beck Depression Inventory tend to reveal that women report more symptoms, different symptoms, and may endorse more severity in the symptoms that are reported. In general, women tended to endorse symptoms related to weight gain, appetite loss, and anxiety. In a related investigation, Williamson (1987) performed factor analyses of the responses of men and women who were seen in a general medical practice clinic to the Beck Depression Inventory. She found sex differences in the factor structure of the responses, indicating that men and women tend to report different patterns of depressive symptoms. Dysphoric mood and performance difficulties were found in both men and women, but a unique component, interpersonal behavior changes, was found in the men in this study. This finding is consistent with other reports of changes in interpersonal behavior, such as an increase in interpersonal conflict and anger for men who are depressed (Heifner, 1997; Melamed, Kushnir, Strauss, & Vigiser, 1997; Barbee, 1996).

Although men and women are generally comparable in their overall symptom profiles in depressive episodes, there are important masculine-specific differences in these profiles that can be used as a guide for the assessment of depression in men (see Table 4-2). Some of these dif-

TABLE 4-2   Clinical Features Associated with Depression in Men

- Strain between gender-role expectations and performance (Heifner, 1997; Good & Wood, 1995)
- Assertions of autonomy and interpersonal distance, increased conflict, and anger in relationships (Frank *et al.*, 1988; Williamson, 1987)
- Withdrawal from and decreases in social contacts (Oliver & Toner, 1990)
- Perceived threats to self-esteem and self-respect (narcissistic wounding), disappointment in self (Ahnlund & Frodi, 1996)
- Alcohol and other drug abuse and dependence (Grant, 1995)
- Inability to cry (Hammen & Padesky, 1977)
- Antisocial, narcissistic, and compulsive personality traits (Black *et al.*, 1995; Frank *et al.*, 1988)
- Decreases in sexual interest but not sexual activity (Nofziger *et al.*, 1993)
- Somatic complaints (Hammen & Padesky, 1977)
- Work-related problems and conflicts (Vredenburg, Krames, & Flett, 1986)
- Difficulties with concentration and motivation (Maffeo, Ford, & Lavin, 1990)

ferences include the findings that men have a greater incidence of comorbid drug and alcohol dependence in depression (Grant, 1995), may present with associated anxiety disorders and antisocial traits (Black, Baumgard, & Bell, 1995) as well as compulsive personality traits (Frank *et al.*, 1988), may be experiencing overt strains in gender-role expectations (Heifner, 1997; Good & Wood, 1995), may be responding with depressed mood to perceived threats to self-esteem or self-respect (Ahnlund & Frodi, 1996), may present with a loss of sexual interest rather than decreased sexual activity per se (Nofziger, Thase, Reynolds, Frank, Jennings, Garamoni, Fasiczka, & Kupfer, 1993), and may present with exaggerated or defensive assertions of autonomy (Pollack, 1998a; Frank, Carpenter, & Kupfer, 1988). Such symptom constellations are consistent with the male tendency to externalize problems, discharge uncomfortable dysphoric affective states through anger and aggression, and self-medicate mood difficulties with mood-altering substances.

In addition to the presence of overt depressed mood, men presenting for evaluation or treatment for depression may exhibit some or all of the features detailed in Table 4-2. Although many men may not express overt symptoms of depressive disorders initially, many men will exhibit tearfulness, guilt, sadness, and concerns about weight and sleep that are characteristic of depressive symptoms in women. However, unlike women, many men may also display anger and overt defensiveness at initial points in the evaluation of depression, which often complicates assessment of classical depressive symptoms.

Clinician Query—"It runs in the family."

James had seen a therapist for four sessions. He met diagnostic criteria for severe recurrent major depression, with primary symptoms including depressed mood, guilt, insomnia and loss of appetite, suicidal thinking, and feelings of persecution with ideas of reference. James was single, 28 years old, and worked as a convenience store manager. He had finished college with a degree in sociology and had continued working at the same store where he had worked part-time to help pay his college bills. He lived alone, did not socialize, and did not have many friends. He was, though, a hard worker and had a lot of energy when he was at work. He had been promoted to his current position as store manager three months prior to the development of his current depressive episode. His first episode occurred when he was 18 years old and a first-year student in college. He had struggled off and on with depression through college and had been helped somewhat with imipramine that was prescribed by a psychiatrist at his campus' health service. He occasionally obtained short-term support through his campus' counseling services.

James' general approach to life was bitter, aggressive, and hostile. He was often argumentative and held himself aloof. As long as "things" were fine, he was "fine." When things weren't fine, he looked for someone to blame. His employees didn't work "hard enough" and this meant that he had to spend extra time at the store. His suppliers didn't make deliveries on time, and thus he couldn't plan the activities of the work day because of their likely interruptions. His supervisor didn't give him "enough backing" in handling a difficult employee he had to reprimand. He had many problems, none of them of his own making. In his fifth session with his therapist, he was describing his deepening depression.

"I just don't give a shit anymore about anything. Who cares?" James moaned dramatically. "What's the point? You get born, you live, you die. There's nothing for me to really look toward. I'm just sick of it. I gotten to the point where I don't really care what happens to me anymore. It's too much."

James' therapist struggled to maintain empathy. "Yeah. You've had a difficult couple of months getting settled into this new job and the new responsibilities. But it sounds like it's more than that, James. You sound today like you're really at the end of your rope."

James tapped his foot and looked impatiently out the window. His eyes moved from the window to the desk to the therapist's face to the floor. "I don't like this job. I'm sick of working so hard. For what? I don't like this town. I don't like anything. I feel like ending it sometimes."

"You feel like ending it sometimes?" his therapist followed.

"Yeah." James paused. "Like my old man. He just offed himself when he couldn't deal with his life. That bastard. That's what I should do."

"I remember you said you father had killed himself when you were a boy. It sounds like you're thinking about him today. What happened?"

"I don't even really know. He was always mad about something. He was a rage-aholic. He would stomp around, pissing and moaning, all the time. Just like me, huh? Then one day when I came home from school, there were police and an ambulance there. Mom just took me aside and said dad had been hurt and would have to go to the hospital. I knew right then what had happened. He used to threaten to kill us all the time. What an asshole."

James paused after describing the day his father had committed suicide and looked out the window. He was quiet. Then he looked at the therapist but did not say anything.

"That sounds terrible, James. What a terrible trauma for a little boy. And now you're feeling like doing the same thing?"

"I just don't feel like dealing with this. I'm tired of working so hard and getting nowhere. I'm tired of not having any friends. I'm tired of being alone." James began sobbing. "I should just kill myself. It runs in the family."

- What assessment issues should James' therapist explore with James in this interview?
- What is the relationship between a man's expression of anger and hostility and underlying feelings of depression?

INTERVIEWING MEN FOR DEPRESSION

In light of the evidence indicating that men underreport specific symptoms of depression, careful clinical interviewing and assessment is necessary. The foundation of any careful clinical assessment of depression is the clinical interview. Practice guidelines and formats for the clinical interview designed to assess the symptoms and severity of depression are described by a number of authors (American Psychiatric Association, 1994; Beck, Rush, Shaw, & Emery, 1979; Gotlib & Hammen, 1992; Shaw, Vallis, & McCabe, 1985; Sholomskas, 1990). In addition to a review and assessment of symptoms present and the severity of these symptoms, the assessment of suicidal and homicidal ideation and plans is of crucial importance when assessing depression in men. A complete chapter is devoted to this important topic.

In parallel with the epidemiological surveys and diagnostic nomenclature schemes developed over the last 20 years, structured interview formats and interview schedules have been developed to increase reliability of assessment and diagnosis of depression. These include the Diagnostic Interview Schedule (Robins, Helzer, Croughan, & Ratcliff, 1981), the Composite International Diagnostic Interview (Robins, Helzer, Babor, Burke, Fariner, Jablenski, Pickens, Reiger, Sartorius, & Towle, 1988); the Schedule for Affective Disorders and Schizophrenia (Endicott & Spitzer, 1978) and its revised cousin the Structured Clinical Interview for *DSM-III-R* (Spitzer, Williams, Gibbon, & First, 1990); and the Hamilton Rating Scale for Depression (Hamilton, 1960). These structured, clinician–directed interview protocols provide a guide for the specific assessment of depression, in the case of the Hamilton Rating Scale, and for depression as well as other *DSM* Axis I conditions, in the case of the Structured Clinical Interview for the *DSM* and the Composite International Diagnostic Interview.

The most frequently used of these clinician–rated instruments is the Hamilton Rating Scale for Depression. This scale was developed to assess severity of depression in patients already diagnosed with depression. It is composed of 21 items. A clinician rates the patient's level of depressive symptomatology after an interview with the patient. The items are used to guide the give–and–take of the assessment interview and the clinician establishes ratings based on patient responses to the items. This instrument has advantages in that it is widely used, mainly by researchers but also by clinicians. It is easy to complete, and can be used in situations in which completion of a self–report instrument would be difficult (e.g., reading level, intoxication, combativeness, etc.).

The next most frequently used instruments are the Diagnostic Interview Schedule, the Schedule for Affective Disorders and Schizophrenia, and the Structured Clinical Interview for *DSM-III-R*. The Diagnostic Interview Schedule was developed for use by lay interviewers gathering information for the Epidemiological Catchment

Area study. The Schedule for Affective Disorders was an early effort to standardize interviewer assessments of psychiatric diagnoses and to increase inter-rater reliabilities when assessing these conditions. Similar to the Diagnostic Interview Schedule, the Schedule for Affective Disorders and Schizophrenia is used to diagnose conditions besides depression. The Structured Clinical Interview for the *DSM-III-R* is a somewhat revised and updated version of the Schedule for Affective Disorders and Schizophrenia, and was specifically designed to be used as an aid to diagnose *DSM-III-R* disorders. It, too, covers conditions in addition to depression, including anxiety disorders, psychoses, eating disorders, and substance use disorders.

These instruments have been used extensively in both clinical and research settings, and are the foundation of many empirical investigations of mood disorders. Gotlib and Hammen (1992), Sholomskas (1990), and Shaw *et al.* (1985) summarize the psychometric properties and use of these instruments. All have demonstrated good reliability and validity when used for the assessment of depression, although none has been shown to offer special value when teasing out any possible differences between men's and women's symptom profiles in depression. Seller, Blascovich, and Lenkei (1981) suggest that sex stereotyping, and not objective criteria, may play a more important role in how clinicians diagnose depression in men and women. They found that, despite similar symptom profiles of depression, women were diagnosed more frequently with depression than were men in a study that used a sample of family practice patients. Even though this investigation used family practice residents as the clinicians, other studies have found similar biases in mental health clinicians (e.g., Pollner, 1998).

INSTRUMENTS TO ASSESS DEPRESSION

In addition to structured clinical interview methods for assisting the clinician in assessing depression, there are a number of popular self-report measures that can also be used to supplement the clinical interview. These include the Beck Depression Inventory (Beck, Ward, Mendelsohn, Mock, & Erbaugh, 1961), the Zung Self-Rating Depression Scale (Zung, 1965), the Minnesota Multiphasic Personality Inventory Depression Scale (Hathaway & McKinley, 1942), the revised Minnesota Multiphasic Personality Inventory Depression Scale (Butcher,

Dahlstrom, Graham, Tellegen, & Kaemmer, 1989), and the Center for Epidemologic Studies Depression Scale (Radloff, 1977).

The Beck Depression Inventory is the most widely used self-report instrument for assessing depression. This is most likely due to its short length and ease of administration and scoring. The Beck Depression Inventory consists of 21 items designed to assess the extent to which a patient has experienced or exhibited various aspects of depressive symptomatology over the past week. Results indicate the extent of depressive symptoms and the severity of these symptoms, ranging from normal mood range through mild depression, moderate depression, and severe depression. A similar self-report scale used in assessing depression is the Zung Self-Rating Depression Scale. This scale, like the Beck Depression Inventory, is a self-report scale composed of 20 items. The Zung Self-Rating Depression Scale is self-administered and also requires minimal time for the patient to complete. The items are scored on a scale from 1 to 4, and a depression index is derived as the final estimate of depressive severity by dividing the raw score by 80, the total possible score. This results in a depression index that ranges from 0.25 (minimal) to 1.00 (maximum). The Center for Epidemiologic Studies Depression Scale was developed to measure depressive symptomatology in the general population. This scale, like the Zung Self-Rating Scale for Depression, consists of 20 items. The patient responds to each item by indicating how much each symptom had troubled him or her over the past week, with 0 corresponding to very little or none of the time, and 3 corresponding to most all of the time. The resulting sum of scores indicates the severity of the person's depressive symptoms, with 0 being the lowest score an individual can obtain and 60 being the highest. The Minnesota Multiphasic Personality Inventory (MMPI), and its revised successor, the MMPI-2, was developed to assess a range of psychiatric and psychological syndromes and conditions, including unipolar depression. Scale 2, the depression scale in both the original and the revised MMPI, consists of 57 items designed to reliably differentiate normal control subjects from depressed patients. As part of the complete MMPI, the individual responds "yes" or "no" to a number of items that describe their feelings, thoughts, and behaviors. Scoring is empirically derived, based on the extent to which groups of items consistently differentiate the clinical group (in this case, depressed patients) from the normal control groups. Higher raw scores translate to higher standard scores, with clinical cutoffs established at $t = 70$ for MMPI, and $t = 65$ for the MMPI-2.

Psychometric properties for the Beck Depression Inventory, including Cronbach alpha values ranging from .86 through .90, are summarized by Beck, Steer, and Garbin (1988). Guidelines for the use of the Beck Depression Inventory are detailed by Kendall, Hollon, Beck, Hammen, and Ingram (1987). Since the Beck Depression Inventory is used widely in both research and clinical settings, a number of studies have reported sex-related differences in responses to items on the inventory. A number of these reports are consistent with a model that emphasizes the social conditioning women and men experience around depressive symptom expression, and have consequently yielded findings of differential response patterns for men and women. Hammen and Padesky (1977) found that men and women reported similar severity of depression on the Beck Depression Inventory, but men were more likely to report an inability to cry, a loss of social interest, somatic complaints, and a sense of failure. This finding is consistent with Vredenburg, Krames, and Flett (1986), who found that men tended to endorse symptoms on the Beck Depression Inventory that were consistent with aspects of the male gender role, such as somatic problems and work performance-related difficulties. Oliver and Toner (1990) found that men reported more withdrawal and somatic symptoms on the Beck Depression Inventory than did women, supporting the hypothesis that symptom expression is shaped by cultural norms. In addition to these findings, Nolan and Willson (1994) found that the item concerning tiredness was most discriminating between men and women. Page and Bennesch (1993) found that men were more likely to report more symptoms of depression when items from the Beck Depression Inventory were phrased in terms of "hassles," instead of in terms of symptoms of depression.

In addition to these findings, which may be interpreted as confirming the importance of gender-role conditioning in responses to the Beck Depression Inventory, Wallace and Pfohl (1995) reported that scores for men on the Beck Depression Inventory were negatively correlated with age. In contrast, scores for women did not vary with age. The older the men in the study, the lower their obtained scores on the Beck Depression Inventory. However, in this investigation, the Hamilton Scale did not demonstrate this age-related correlation.

Gumbiner and Flowers (1997) reported sex differences in MMPI-2 profiles from a population of outpatient community mental health clinic patients. They found that men consistently elevated subscales related to antisocial behavior, authority problems, addiction problems, amorality, and Type A behavior patterns. Women, in contrast, elevated clinical scales measuring depression, hypochondriasis, hysteria, and paranoia and subscales related to depression, need for affection, health concerns, and somatic complaints. Maffeo, Ford, and Lavin (1990), using the MMPI as well as other measures of depression, found that depressed men tended to have greater difficulty with concentration and motivation than did depressed women.

Schaefer, Brown, Watson, Plemel, DeMotts, Howard, Petrick, Balleweg, and Anderson (1985) reported a study that compared the validity of the Beck Depression Inventory, the MMPI depression scale, and the Zung Self-Rating Depression Scale. Subject ratings on each of these three scales were correlated with clinician-derived *DSM-III* diagnostic ratings. The Zung Self-Rating Depression Scale produced the best validity coefficients when related to these clinician-based ratings of depression.

Studies that have utilized the Center for Epidemiological Studies–Depression scale have not typically reported sex differences found when using this scale. Clark, Aneshensel, Frerichs, and Morgan (1981), however, did report sex differences in item correlations and factor loadings and concluded that the scale may measure different phenomena in men and women.

Overall, it is incumbent upon any clinician assessing male depression and who is planning to utilize any of the common self-report depression inventories to be familiar with the research on various sex differences in these instruments. Considerable research with the Beck Depression Inventory has suggested that men may respond to this instrument in ways consistent with gender-stereotyped symptom expression. For example, men may endorse items related to crying less, and may endorse items related to concentration difficulties, work difficulty, or somatic concerns more frequently. MMPI-2 subscales and the Center for Epidemiological Studies–Depression scale may similarly be prone to such variations. One investigation found the Zung Self-Rating Depression Scale demonstrated the best external validity compared with the MMPI Depression Scale and the Beck Depression Inventory when used with male inpatient psychiatric ward and chemical dependency ward patients.

Clinician Query—"I didn't mean to hurt her."
Greg was a 27-year-old married man with one child who was referred for therapy by the court after he was charged with assault of his wife following a domestic dispute. Greg was employed by the telephone company. Because this was his first prosecuted offense, he was given the option to receive counseling and be placed on probation rather than serve time in jail. Greg arrived for therapy with a smile on his face. It was

later found out that he uses his charm to make positive impressions in social situations, especially first meetings.

Greg was relatively open about his behavior but spent a good deal of the first session describing how much better he was than his own father, who had beat him, his brother, and his mother mercilessly. Greg also stated that his wife's father was abusive and that she had learned how to set him off. What was apparent was that Greg did not want to take much responsibility for his aggressive behavior. In his fourth session, his therapist confronted Greg about what his aggression meant.

"So you say that you have only hit your wife a few times, and that usually she had provoked you. I wonder what was going on inside of you when you heard her words?"

"You mean what was I thinking?"

"Thinking and feeling," added his therapist.

"The last time this happened, she had just told me that I was stupid for not having stopped for baby formula and diapers on my way home from work."

"How did this feel when she said it?"

"I hate being called stupid. She knows that will piss me off," replied Greg.

"So what was going on in your body? What were you feeling?"

"I could feel myself get hot. I had an impulse to want to grab her neck," Greg responded, squirming somewhat in his chair.

"Can you remember ever being called stupid or made to feel stupid when you were growing up?" his therapist queried.

"My old man used to call me that all the time."

"What did that feel like, when he would call you stupid?"

"It felt lousy. I already felt stupid, and when he said it, it validated how I felt about myself. I never got really mad at him because he would beat the shit out of me if I talked back to him or showed any defiance in my face."

"So you felt helpless or hopeless when he did this?"

"I don't know what I felt," Greg answered, his smile gone from his face.

"Sounds to me like you were feeling pretty sad," replied his therapist, offering some emotional vocabulary.

"I hate to be sad. I'll do anything to get a smile back on my face. What I want to do right now is tell you a joke," Greg responded.

"So you avoid feeling sad as much as possible?"

"Yeah. I don't want to cry or act like I can't take it. My dad would call me a girl or a fag if I showed any tears. He was harsh."

"So instead of feeling sad or hurt, you either crack a joke or get angry."

"Yeah. I'd rather joke around. But sometimes if someone catches me off guard, I get angry."

"Like your wife?"

"Yeah. She can be a bitch."

"So with the big world, you're a joker. But with her you get angry?"

"I guess. I think she should know better," Greg retorted.

"She should know that you are really hurt by her comments?" his therapist asked.

"Yeah."

"So why can't you say `that hurts me' instead of raging at her?" asked his therapist.

"I don't know," Greg replied, his eyes cast downward.

"It looks like we have some work to do, Greg," his therapist suggested.

"You're probably right," Greg finally admitted.

- To what extent do men who batter conceal an underlying mood disorder or depression?
- How might therapy help impulsive or aggressive men by encouraging expressions of sadness, loss, or grief?

MASCULINE-SPECIFIC ASSESSMENT OF DEPRESSION

Pollack (1998a) has proposed a change in the way clinicians assess male depression. This new approach to assessing depression in men emphasizes the important role covert or masked depressive phenomena, as well as the role that comorbid conditions, play in men's mood disorders. This assessment model de-emphasizes the traditional diagnostic criteria that are viewed as biased toward feminine means of expressing emotional distress. By proposing diagnostic criteria for "major depressive disorder–male type" (see Table 4-3) Pollack directs clinicians' attention to a number of often seemingly unrelated symptom, that often signify the presence of a mood disorder in men.

This important recommendation, that clinicians focus on male-specific symptom clusters when assessing men for depression, has implications for clinicians. Interviewing men for depression requires balancing knowledge of the typical symptom profiles seen in depressive episodes with an awareness of the ways in which men might be likely to conceal, obscure, or otherwise hide these symptoms of depression. Table 4-4 outlines areas for assessment when interviewing men. As noted, when asked directly about symptoms of depression, men and women report the same symptoms with remarkable consistency. Men report dysphoria most, as do women. Thoughts of death, problems with sleep, appetite, and fatigue are next in frequency for both men and women. In addition, many men will reveal long suppressed feelings of sadness, guilt, shame, and inadequacy that have built up over the years but have been suppressed in conformity to gender-role restrictions.

TABLE 4-3   Proposed Criteria for Major Depressive Disorder-Male Type (Pollack, 1998a)

---

1. Increased withdrawal from relationships: May be denied by patient
2. Overinvolvement with work activities: May reach a level of obsessional concern, masked by comments about "stress" (burnout)
3. Denial of pain
4. Increasingly rigid demands for autonomy
5. Avoiding the help of others: The "I can do it myself" syndrome
6. Shift in the interest level of sexual encounters: May be either a decrease or an increase (differentiate from mania)
7. Increase in intensity or frequency of angry outbursts
8. New or renewed interest in psychiactive substance self-administration: To create self-numbing tension relief states without classic dissociative mechanisms
9. A denial of any sadness and an inability to cry
10. Harsh self-criticism: Often focusing on failures in the arenas of provider and/or protector
11. Impulsive plans to have loved ones cared for in case of patient's death or disability: "The wife and/or kids only need me for the money."
12. Depleted or impulsive mood
13. Concentration, sleep, weight disorders

From Pollack (1998a) "Mourning, Melancholia, and Masculinity: Recognizing and Treating Depression in Men" in W. Pollack and R. Levant (Eds.), *A New Psychotherapy for Men* (pp. 147-166). New York: Wiley. Copyright 1998 by W. Pollack and R. Levant. Reprinted by permission of John Wiley & Sons, Inc.

TABLE 4-4   Masculine-Specific Assessment of Depression

- Direct symptom assessment
  1. depressed mood
  2. decreased interest in activities
  3. sleep and appetite disturbances
  4. fatigue
  5. guilt
  6. concentration difficulties
  7. suicidal ideation, plans, and intent (see Chapter 7)
- Precipitating factors or events
  1. rejection in significant relationship
  2. loss of employment or other role status
  3. narcissistic wounding
  4. third-party coercion (employer, partner, spouse)
- Related comorbid conditions
  1. alcohol abuse and alcoholism
  2. other substance abuse or dependence
  3. antisocial behaviors
- Somatic and physical complaints
- Recent interpersonal loss or separation
- Paranoia and increased interpersonal sensitivity (assess for risk of stalking)

Since many men may not directly reveal a sad mood to an interviewer, consideration of the context of the man's presenting situation often reveals important information. Examining the circumstances surrounding the initial visit to the therapist is important. Specific questioning of these circumstances often reveals a pattern of emergent depressive symptoms that may have become too intrusive or problematic for a man to manage. Examination of the precipitating circumstances will also yield valuable insights into the psychodynamic meaning and implications of many of the depressive symptoms that may have led to a man's seeking help. An important aspect of the circumstances precipitating a man's visit to a therapist is whether he has experienced a recent narcissistic wound. Rejections in significant relationships, loss of role status in employment or leisure activity pursuits, and other symbolic losses represent failure in many men's eyes and often are associated with significant depressive sequelae. Left to smolder, many such wounds and losses often emerge later as precipitant in acts of homicidal and suicidal violence perpetrated by disgruntled, depressed men. Kahn (1990) emphasizes the importance of narcissistic injury and the activation of envy and rivalry issues in assessing depressed men for suicidal risks.

In addition, it is important to note to what extent a man might have been coerced into seeing a therapist. Such coercion may be in service of forestalling one of the previously mentioned narcissistic injuries, such as an opportunity to preserve a job if he enters treatment. Such coercion may also occur after some aspect of the patient's behavior has exceeded the limits that important persons in his environment, such as a spouse or employer, are willing to tolerate. Whatever the circumstances, it is important in the context of coerced therapy to balance a desire to challenge the implications for motivation such a presentation suggests with a recognition that many men may need a "problem," often imposed externally, to sanction a first visit to a therapist. Conveying empathy to the male client and the recognition of his frustration at having been "given a problem" will often lay a foundation of acceptance that ensures continuation in treatment.

As noted, many men present for help with the typical constellation of depressive symptoms. These include sad mood and guilt feelings, difficulties in eating and sleeping, withdrawal from most activities, physical and health complaints, and thoughts of death and suicide. In addition to these common symptoms, many men will also exhibit anger, irritation, frustration, and increased conflict in interpersonal relationships. Such symptoms are characteristic of a pattern of managing depressed mood that is based on withdrawal, externalization, and distraction. Any time the clinician encounters a pattern of such behaviors and symptoms she or he should look further for an underlying depressive condition.

The clinician must also carefully assess the presence of any comorbid clinical conditions, which frequently complicate the clinical picture. Different patterns of comorbidity are associated with clinical samples of depressed men and women (Fava, Abraham, Alpert, Nierenberg, Pava, & Rosenbaum, 1996; Grant, 1995; Dunne, Galatopoulos, & Schipperheijn, 1993). Men are more likely to exhibit comorbid alcohol abuse and dependence, other substance use and dependence, and antisocial personality traits. Since these comorbid conditions are common in men and because they contribute significantly to increased risk of violence and suicide, especially in younger men, they must be addressed directly and completely in assessment.

Finally, since depressed men are at such increased risk for suicide at all ages, a careful inquiry into the presence of suicidal ideation, suicidal plans, and suicidal intent is crucial any time a clinician establishes the existence of depression in a male patient. Specific recommendations for this assessment are offered elsewhere in this volume, but the importance of such inquiry in the complete assessment of depression in men is impossible to overstate.

SUMMARY

Since men will often suppress overt expression of depressed mood in conformity with cultural norms, a clinician assessing depression in men must carefully balance direct inquiry into traditional symptoms associated with depression with sensitivity to the ways in which men conceal depressive symptoms. Thus, assessing depression in men requires knowledge of the common symptoms of depression, the various comorbid conditions associated with male depression, and the unique ways that men often conceal depressed mood from themselves and others.

The foundation of assessment is based on interviewing that is designed to identify the presence of symptoms enumerated in the *DSM-IV.* The symptom profiles of depressed men typically parallel those profiles found in depressed women. However, since many depressed men may be missed in a quick or superficial questioning about their symptoms, a clinician must often carefully probe not only for the typical symptoms of depression but for other related symptoms and conditions. The clinician must carefully assess for the presence of alcoholism and drug abuse, since these conditions are commonly related to depression in men. In addition to these conditions, many men who are depressed exhibit a constellation of externalizing defenses and symptoms that are typical of antisocial traits. These include increased interpersonal conflict, prominent anger and aggressive outbursts, and other self-destructive or self-defeating behaviors. The presence of any of these common symptom clusters in the absence of a specific complaint of depression should immediately alert the interviewer to the strong possibility that depression may exist.

Clinician rating scales and patient self-report instruments are helpful in assessing male depression. Men may respond differently from women to some scales and instruments. Research has indicated that responses to some items of the Beck Depression Inventory and the Center for Epidemiologic Studies–Depression Scale may be influenced by the sex of the patient. It is important for a clinician to review how men might respond to a chosen instrument and to be prepared to incorporate such findings into her or his assessment regimen.

CHAPTER 5

*Psychopharmacologic Treatment of Depression in Men

I could feel the tears within me, undiscovered and untouched in their inland sea. Those tears had been with me always. I thought that, at birth, American men are allowed just as many tears as American women. But because we are forbidden to shed them, we die long before women do, with our hearts exploding or our blood pressure rising or our livers eaten away by alcohol because that lake of grief inside us has no outlet. We, men, die because our faces were not watered enough.

Pat Conroy

Biological factors have long been known to play a role in depression in both men and women. Spurred primarily by the recent development of antidepressant medications with relatively few side effects, psychopharmacologic treatments for depression have become the norm for men presenting with complaints of depression. This increased use of medica-

*Written by Scott Stuart, M.D., Department of Psychiatry, University of Iowa, Iowa City, Iowa

Beach Music (p. 216)

tion for depression has also been driven by two additional forces. First, insurors believe that providing antidepressant medication is more cost effective than providing psychotherapy, either alone or in combination with medical treatment. Second, the frequent prescribing of antidepressant medication by family physicians and internists, who actually treat the majority of cases of depression, also contributes to the increased use of medications to treat depression.

Psychopharmacologic treatment of men is generally considered less complicated than similar treatment of women for several reasons. First, with males, there are no concerns regarding possible medication effects on pregnancy or breastfeeding. Though it is possible that psychotropic medications may be teratogenic in the sense that they may increase the risk for chromosomal abnormalities in the sperm of men exposed to them, there have been no data supporting this conclusion. At present, there are no antidepressant medications which are considered to be teratogenic when used by males (*Physician's Desk Reference,* 1999).

Second, though there is some controversy about the possibility that men may experience clinically meaningful hormonal cycling, there is as yet no evidence supporting this position. Thus, treatment issues which might parallel those involved in treating women at various phases during their menstrual cycles are not present. There is as yet no validated male equivalent to what the *DSM-IV* has labeled "Premenstrual Dysphoric Disorder" (American Psychiatric Association, 1994) in women. Additionally, though there is some evidence that there are changes in male sexual hormones that may be associated with aging and depression (e.g., Sternbach, 1998), there are no clinical phenomena in males that are similar to the climacteric in women.

Though depression is diagnosed more frequently in women, men are typically overrepresented in drug treatment trials for depression, particularly in the early phases of testing, in large part because there are fewer factors which may complicate treatment response and because of the lack of potential for teratogenicity. Empirical data supporting the efficacy of antidepressant medication in men is, therefore, abundant and compelling.

There are two facts that serve as the foundation upon which the pharmacologic recommendations in this chapter rest. First, there is no evidence that there is any differential treatment response to pharmacologic interventions when men and women are compared. In other words, men and women respond at equal rates across all antidepressant medication treatments. Given the extensive literature regarding antidepressant medications, it is unlikely that any differences will be detected in the future.

Second, despite the claims made by different pharmaceutical companies, there is no evidence that any of the antidepressant medications is superior in treating depression. Head-to-head comparisons of antidepressants and parallel comparisons to placebo treatment across studies have all demonstrated approximately equal response. As a caveat, it is important to realize that there is also a relatively large placebo response rate for patients with major depression.

Clinician Query—"I'm concerned about
my sexual performance."

Jon, a 35-year-old male, presented with a 4-week history of depressive symptoms, which had worsened over time. Prominent among his symptoms were insomnia, decreased appetite, anhedonia, and poor concentration. He denied suicidal ideation. He reported a decrease in libido that had also worsened over the last month. No other sexual dysfunction was reported. He reported no previous psychiatric history, but had been in counseling for ongoing marital problems intermittently in the past.

Family history was significant for alcohol abuse and depression in the patient's father, though the patient denied any substance abuse himself. He reported that his father had been successfully treated with fluoxetine several years ago, though his father had been only sporadically compliant with the medication after recovery. The patient reported no medical problems and he was not taking any other medications. On exam, he appeared depressed in mood and affect, but did not appear to be particularly anxious or have any psychomotor disturbances.

Because of the positive family history of response to fluoxetine, he was started on a dose of 20 mg per day. The patient returned two weeks later stating that he was experiencing some improvement in mood and concentration and noted that, as his mood had improved, he had experienced some increase in his sexual interest. He noted that on one occasion, however, he had experienced some difficulty in achieving orgasm. Both the patient and his clinician agreed to continue with the same dose of fluoxetine.

Two weeks later, the patient reported that his mood had returned to near normal levels. Despite the improvement in sleep, appetite, and mood, however, he noted that his libido had decreased to pretreatment levels, and that he continued to have ejaculatory problems that were worsening. In particular, he noted that, on two occasions, he had been unable to come to climax during intercourse, and appeared to be quite distraught about this. He also reported that his wife was dissatisfied with their sexual relationship.

Several options were discussed, including switching medications and adding another medication on an as-needed basis to counteract the effects of the fluoxetine. Since he had a good response to the fluoxetine, it was agreed that he would attempt a reduction in dose with close monitoring of any sexual side effects. At his next appointment two weeks later, the patient reported that though his sexual functioning appeared to be improving, his depression had worsened, with a decline in sleep and appetite once again.

A decision was made to switch to a different medication at this point. Buproprion was chosen because of the evidence suggesting that it likely has fewer sexual side effects. After a week of continued decline, the patient noted improvement in his depressive symptoms thereafter. His sexual dysfunction also continued to diminish, and four weeks after switching medications, he reported no sexual problems. He continued on buproprion for another six months without sequelae.

- What are some of the common sexual side effects associated with antidepressant treatment for depression in men?
- What considerations should be given to decision-making regarding choice of antidepressant medication for men?

ANTIDEPRESSANTS AND DEPRESSION IN MEN

Though the population-based data demonstrate equal response to antidepressant medication, there are, of course, compelling reasons to choose a particular medication for a given individual. Primary among predictors of depression remission is previous response to a medication—if a patient has done well before with particular medication, then it should obviously be the first choice should a new episode of depression occur.

A family history of response to a specific antidepressant medication is also a response predictor, and a reason to make that agent a first-line choice for the treatment of depression.

In most cases, however, notably those of new onset depression, there is often no history of either personal or familial response. In these instances, considerations such as ease of administration and potential interaction effects with other medications or medical conditions are important in rational prescribing. The next section of this chapter, however, will be devoted to what is probably the most compelling factor in making a prescription decision: the side-effect profile of the medication.

Numerous texts have been written regarding the side effects of antidepressant medications, and much of the advertising of pharmaceutical companies focuses on the lack of side effects of their particular medication. Though side-effect profile in general should obviously be considered when choosing an antidepressant, there are several side effects that are specific to men, which should be considered by both clinicians and their patients. With males, these are related to sexual functioning, and include changes in libido, erectile dysfunction, and anorgasmia or delayed ejaculation. Table 5-1 summarizes the potential antidepressant-induced side effects related to sexual functioning in men.

Antidepressant-Induced Sexual Side Effects: General Considerations

Untreated affective disorders have long been known to be associated with impaired sexual functioning. Successful treatment of the depression has been shown to result frequently in improvement in or a

---

TABLE 5-1   Antidepressant-Induced
Changes in Sexual Functioning in Males

Changes in libido
Changes in erectile functioning
Anorgasmia
Delayed ejaculation
Priapism
Penile anesthesia
Painful orgasm

---

return to normal sexual functioning (Casper, Redmond, & Katz, 1986). Because of this, differentiating sexual impairment due to depression from that which may be caused by medication is often very difficult. The clinician is obligated to take a very careful history. Often, the time course of changes in sexual functioning can help determine whether it is a primary symptom of depression or due to medication. Cases in which sexual functioning is initially impaired, and continues to be so even after medication treatment has brought about resolution of other neurovegetative symptoms, may also make determination of the cause of impairment difficult. In addition to depression, many other factors that may cause sexual problems which must also be considered. Table 5-2 outlines some of the potential causes of sexual dysfunction in depressed men.

Another factor that profoundly affects the diagnosis and treatment of sexual dysfunction during depression is the effect of the source of the report of the symptoms. The incidence of sexual problems spontaneously reported by patients during clinical encounters is dramatically less than that reported when patients are directly questioned about sexual problems. Monteiro, Noshirvani, Marks, and Lelliott (1987), in a study evaluating the sexual side effects of clomipramine, a tricyclic antidepressant used for both depression and obsessive–compulsive disorder, found that while only about one-third of patients with obsessive–compulsive disorder spontaneously reported sexual problems, 96% of patients reported becoming anorgasmic on the medication when directly queried about sexual side effects. Similarly, Montejo, Llorce, and Izquierdo (1996) reported that sexual dysfunction was spontaneously reported by about 2–7% of depressed patients treated with selective serotonin reuptake inhibitors as compared to 55% of patients who reported such symptoms on direct questioning.

It is also extremely important when considering sexual side effects to recognize that patients who are receiving placebos in medication trials

TABLE 5-2   Causes of Sexual Dysfunction
in Depressed Men

Depression
Antidepressant-induced side effects
Primary sexual dysfunction
Medical illness
Marital conflict
Multifactorial causes

typically report significant rates of sexual dysfunction. Though sexual functioning is multidetermined, and is highly correlated with many psychological factors, reports of changes in sexual functioning may be widely reported by patients receiving placebo because of the subjective nature of many of the complaints. Thus, the calculation of rates of sexual dysfunction due to medication should include the rate reported by patients taking the medication less the placebo rate. Most calculations are simply estimates based on small, retrospective series. The bias towards reporting adverse effects of medication also influences the estimates of incidence rates adversely. In sum, the rates of sexual dysfunction induced by antidepressant treatment are unknown.

Antidepressant-Induced Changes in Libido

Almost all of the antidepressant medications have been reported to have an effect on libido in males. These include the monoamine oxidase inhibitors (MAOIs—phenelzine and tranylcypromine), tricyclic antidepressants (TCAs—amitriptyline, imipramine, desipramine, clomipramine, nortriptyline), the selective serotonin reuptake inhibitors (SSRIs—fluoxetine, paroxetine, sertraline), as well as the newer generation antidepressants such as venlafaxine (*Physician's Desk Reference*, 1999; Segraves, 1998, 1993) and citalopram (Michael & Herrod, 1997). Both buproprion (Crenshaw, Goldberg, & Stern, 1987) and trazodone (Assalian & Margolese, 1996) have been reported to increase libido above predepression levels, in some cases. However, the prescribing information for buproprion indicates that libido was reported as decreased in about 3% of patients receiving the medication and in about 1.5% of patients receiving placebo, while the reported rate with trazodone was about 1% with a less than 1% report by patients receiving placebo. It has been the experience of the author that, although rare, depressed males treated with the SSRIs may also report increased libido.

The incidence of sexual side effects in comparison to placebo are typically reported for all phase III medication efficacy trials, along with information about all other side effects which are spontaneously reported. The prescription inserts for most antidepressant medications report decreased libido in approximately 2–5% of patients, and a placebo rate of about 1%. There have been very few placebo controlled studies comparing the sexual side effects of antidepressants. In one study comparing imipramine and phenelzine, Harrison, and Morris (1986) found that decreased libido was reported on direct inquiry in about 30% of patients taking phenelzine and about 20% of patients treated with imipramine, as compared to 10% who were taking a placebo.

With the data that is available at present, the incidence of antidepressant-induced changes in libido is not clear. Based on efficacy trials of antidepressants, the incidence appears to consistently be in the range of 2–5%, with an incidence of about 1% related to treatment with placebo. In contrast, studies in which sexual side effects are specifically evaluated have reported much higher rates. What is clear is that for some patients, decreased libido is a substantial problem that warrants either a change in medication or some other type of intervention.

Management of antidepressant-induced decreased libido requires close clinical consultation with the patient being treated. During the evaluation, close attention must be paid to the time course of the development of the dysfunction—libido problems which develop after the initiation of the medication and which persist for several weeks during treatment can be considered to be due to the medication. It is also crucial to work collaboratively with the patient regarding possible treatment options. Some patients, despite a decrease in libido, will opt to continue the antidepressant medication if it has otherwise been effective rather than risk the return of depressive symptoms with a drug holiday or a switch to another medication. Patients who opt to continue with the same medication should be assured that all data suggests return of sexual functioning to baseline once the medication is stopped.

There are several options for those patients who do not wish to continue the same antidepressant. The most obvious is to switch from the antidepressant suspected of causing the libido problems to one in another class. There is some evidence that buproprion may be associated with a lower incidence of decreased libido, making it a reasonable choice in such cases. Two open-label studies involving a switch from either a variety of antidepressant medications (Gardner & Johnston, 1985) or from fluoxetine (Walker, Cole, & Gardner, 1993) to buproprion noted an increase in libido with buproprion for those patients who had complaints on their initial antidepressants. Another small study of patients switched from sertraline to nefazodone also noted improvement in libido, suggesting that nefazodone may be associated with fewer libido problems (Ferguson, Shrivastava, & Stahl, 1996).

Several other recommendations have been made regarding treatment of the decreased libido. The use of 7.5 to 15 mg of neostigmine prior to coitus has been reported to restore libido in some cases (Kraupl-Taylor, 1972), and yohimbine has also been recommended and has been shown to be of benefit in an open trial (Jacobsen, 1992).

One last option is to plan a drug holiday. However, careful consideration should be given to stopping antidepressant medication given the morbidity associated with depression. In addition, the rather lengthy half-life of many of the newer antidepressants would suggest that a rather long drug holiday would be required before sexual functioning normalized. Moreover, the provision of drug holidays may undermine the physician's message to the patient that daily compliance with medication is needed to treat depression. Given these risks, the weight of evidence at present would suggest that, for those patients who cannot tolerate a change in libido, a switch to another category of antidepressant medication, particularly buproprion or nefazodone, is indicated. Table 5-3 summarizes recommendations for the management of medication-induced sexual side effects.

Antidepressant-Induced Erectile Dysfunction

Historically, the TCAs have been anecdotally associated with reports of erectile dysfunction in depressed males. As with changes in libido, how-

TABLE 5-3   Management of Antidepressant-Induced Sexual Side Effects

Decreased libido
    Continue the same antidepressant medication if otherwise effective
    Switch to different class of antidepressant
    Add Neostigmine before coitus
    Add yohimbine before coitus
Erectile dysfunction
    Dose reduction
    Switch to different class of antidepressant
    Add Bethanechol before coitus
Delayed ejaculation
    Dose reduction
    Switch to different class of antidepressant
    Add Cyproheptadine before coitus
    Add Bethanechol before coitus
    Add yohimbine before coitus

ever, case reports abound for nearly all of the antidepressant medications, including imipramine, desipramine, nortriptyline, amitriptyline, fluoxetine, paroxetine, sertraline, trazodone, doxepin, and venlafaxine *(Physician's Desk Reference, 1999;)* Hsu & Shen, 1995; Barnes & Harvey, 1993). As with impairment of libido, erectile dysfunction can also be a symptom of depression, making it difficult to distinguish drug effects. A careful review of the time course of the problem will usually identify the cause.

The incidence of antidepressant-induced erectile dysfunction is not known. Data from efficacy trials of antidepressant medications suggest that it is fairly infrequent—while case reports are found frequently, erectile dysfunction is rarely reported as a side effect in efficacy trials, meaning that it does not surpass the threshold of 1% incidence during either antidepressant or placebo treatment. Data from the few studies that have specifically examined erectile dysfunction also suggest that the incidence is low. A double-blind, placebo-controlled study of imipramine and phenelzine found minimal evidence that either medication interfered with erectile function (Harrison, Rabkin, Erhardt, Stewart, McGrath, Ross, & Quitkin, 1986). In a double-blind study using nondepressed volunteers, amitriptyline and mianserin (the latter is not currently available in the United States) were found to slightly decrease the magnitude and duration of nocturnal erections as measured by penile tumescence, but there was no reported difference in waking sexual functioning in the exposed subjects (Kowalski, Stanley, Dennerstein, Burrows, & Maguire, 1985).

Treatment options for patients experiencing antidepressant-induced erectile dysfunction are similar to those for decreased libido. There is some evidence that buproprion may be a reasonable alternative antidepressant: a clinical series found that patients who were receiving a variety of antidepressant medications who reported erectile problems reported resolution of the problems with substitution of buproprion (Gardner & Johnston, 1985). Bethanechol taken prior to intercourse has been reported to be of benefit (Assalian & Margolese, 1996), though its use has not been empirically evaluated. The available evidence suggests that switching to a different class of antidepressant medication is the best course, and that buproprion may be associated with a lower incidence of erectile dysfunction than other antidepressants (see Table 5-3).

Antidepressant-Induced Anorgasmia and Delayed Ejaculation

Although anorgasmia can certainly be induced by antidepressant medication, it is probably more accurate to speak of delayed orgasm, or more specifically in men, delayed ejaculation, than of complete absence of orgasm. Much attention has been given to this issue in the medical press—the SSRIs in particular have been associated with this side effect. As with other antidepressant-induced sexual side effects, the true incidence of delayed ejaculation is not known. Rates vary greatly, depending on the method by which reports about side effects are elicited. Anecdotally, however, delayed ejaculation does appear to present a greater clinical problem than either loss of libido or erectile dysfunction.

Case reports have suggested all of the SSRIs are associated with delayed ejaculation (Hsu & Shen, 1995). From these case reports, it has been estimated that up to 30% of patients taking an SSRI will experience problems with ejaculatory delay (Hsu & Shen, 1995). The validity of establishing incidence from retrospective cases, however, makes the estimates of side effect incidence with the SSRI's suspect. In contrast, the *Physician's Desk Reference* (1999), reporting information from efficacy studies in which patient self-report was used to determine the incidence of treatment–emergent side effects, reports an incidence of less than 1% (comparable to placebo) for depressed patients and 7% for obsessive–compulsive patients treated with fluoxetine; 7% for depressed patients and 17% for obsessive–compulsive patients treated with sertraline, and 1.6% for depressed patients and 2.1% for obsessive–compulsive patients receiving paroxetine. Though it is likely that the SSRIs are associated with a much higher incidence of ejaculatory problems than the TCAs, case reports of such side effects have also been published regarding the use of amitriptyline, desipramine, and nortriptyline (Segraves, 1993). Doxepin and trazodone have also been implicated (Segraves, 1993).

Two additional lines of evidence exist, however, which strongly suggest that the SSRIs are associated with delayed ejaculation The TCAs (with the exception of clomipramine) have not been systematically studied in the same fashion. In addition to controlled studies of sertraline, several of the SSRIs have been evaluated as treatments for premature ejaculation, lending credence to their ability to induce delayed orgasm.

Several controlled studies have been conducted in which the sexual side effects of antidepressant medication were evaluated. Harrison and colleagues (Harrison & Morris, 1996; Harrison, Stewart, Ehrhardt, & el Allali, 1985) compared imipramine and phenelzine over six weeks. Questionnaires about sexual functioning were administered prior to treatment and at the end of the treatment trial. Delayed orgasm was reported by 21% of the men taking imipramine, and by 30% of the men taking phenelzine; none of the men taking placebo reported problems.

Sertraline was compared to nefazodone in a controlled double-blinded study of depressed patients (Feiger, Kiev, Shrivastava, Wisselink, & Wilcox, 1996). Sixty-seven percent of the men taking sertraline reported emergence of delayed ejaculation with treatment on direct questioning, while there appeared to be no increase in incidence with nefazodone. There was no difference, however, in the reported incidence of changes in libido or erectile functioning. Another study of men with orgasmic problems while taking sertraline assigned patients in double-blinded fashion to either sertraline or nefazodone for eight weeks (Ferguson, Shrivastava, & Stahh, 1996). Seventy-one percent of patients who continued on sertraline reported continued delayed ejaculation, while only 30% of those who switched to nefazodone reported such problems. Sertraline has also been used to treat premature ejaculation (Mendels, Camera, & Sikes, 1995). No controlled trials examining the sexual side effects of fluoxetine and paroxetine have been conducted; however, both have been reported to be beneficial in the treatment of premature ejaculation (Lee, Song, Kim, & Choi, 1996; Waldinger, Hengeveld, & Zwinderman, 1994).

While the true incidence of ejaculatory delay with antidepressant treatment is unknown, it is clearly a clinically significant side effect of the SSRIs and may occur, though likely less frequently, with other antidepressant medications as well. In the author's experience, it is a significant, though not highly prevalent, problem which is spontaneously reported by male patients much more frequently than either decreased libido or erectile dysfunction.

In addition to switching antidepressants, several other treatment strategies have been reported in the literature. There have been some reports of tolerance developing with some of the antidepressants (Reimherr, Chouinard, Cohn, Cole, Itil, LaPierre, Masco, & Mendels, 1990; Nurnberg & Levine, 1987) and the effect on ejaculatory dysfunction may be dose related. Several reports have noted that decreasing the dose of medication may be effective in relieving anorgasmia (Patterson, 1993; Barton, 1979).

There have been several medications that have been used to counteract the delayed ejaculation associated with antidepressant medications. Cyproheptadine at 4–8 mg prior to coitus has been reported to be of benefit for patients taking clomipraine (Riley & Riley, 1986), nortriptyline (Sovner, 1984), imipramine (Steele & Howell, 1986), tranlcypromine (DeCastro, 1985), fluoxetine (McCormick, Olin, & Brotman, 1990; Cohen, 1992; Hsu & Shen, 1995), fluvoxamine (Arnott & Nutt,

1994), and citalopram (Lauerma, 1996). Yohimbine at 5.4 to 10.8 mg 1–32 hours prior to coitus has also been reported to reverse anorgasmia associated with use of SSRIs (Hollander & McCarley, 1992; Segraves, 1994) and with clomipramine (Price & Grunhaus, 1990). Bethanechol given 1 to 2 hours prior to coitus has been reported to reduce ejaculatory dysfunction when used with impramine (Segraves, 1987). Case reports describing successful treatment of SSRI-induced anorgasmia have also been published regarding amantadine (Balogh, Hendricks, & Kang, 1992; Shrivastava, Shrivastava, & Overweg, 1995), buproprion (Labbate & Pollack, 1994), dextroamphetamine (Bartlik, Kaplan, & Kaplan, 1995), and buspirone (Norden, 1994). A small open trial of buproprion also suggests that it may be effective in the treatment of delayed ejaculation induced by other antidepressants (Labbate, Grimes, Hines, & Pollack, 1997).

Based on the available evidence, it appears that delayed ejaculation and anorgasmia are relatively common side effects of antidepressant treatment, particularly with the SSRIs and clomipramine. A trial of a decreased dose or a switch to another class of antidepressants is usually indicated. There is some evidence that buproprion is associated with a lower incidence of sexual dysfunction, and switching to buproprion, from SSRIs in particular, may be effective in relieving the dysfunction (see Table 5-3).

Other Sexual Side Effects Induced by Antidepressant Medications

Among other antidepressant-induced side effects, priapism, though apparently quite uncommon, is the most serious. Trazodone has been reported to be associated with priapism (Thompson, Ware, & Blashfield, 1990), though the incidence is unknown. A single case report also describes priapism associated with paroxetine (Bertholon, Krajewski, & el Allali, 1996). Painful ejaculation has been reported with imipramine and clomipramine (Balon, Yeragani, Pohl, & Ramesh, 1993). Penile anesthesia has been reported with fluoxetine (Neill, 1991).

In sum, there are a variety of sexual side effects which may result from use of antidepressant medication in males. The incidence of these dysfunctions is unknown, but it does appear that they may be more common during treatment with the SSRIs and that delayed ejaculation is the most clinically significant of the reported side effects. The incidence is not great enough, however, that it should outweigh other considerations noted above which are associated with a positive response, namely, previous response to a particular antidepressant or a familial response to a particular antidepressant.

In those cases in which intolerable sexual side effects do develop, rational prescribing suggests either a trial of a reduced dose of medication or a switch to a different class of antidepressant. For males, buproprion and nefazodone appear to be associated with a lower incidence of sexual side effects. Other strategies, such as the addition of medications to counteract the sexual dysfunction caused by the antidepressant, may also be tried, but there is a lack of compelling empirical data supporting their use.

TESTOSTERONE AND DEPRESSION IN MEN

Another issue which is unique to the assessment and treatment of depressed men is the potential role played by testosterone in the genesis and maintenance of low mood. There is some evidence that reductions in testosterone levels may be associated with depression, particularly in elderly men, and it has been speculated that testosterone may be useful in the treatment of depression in those cases in which testosterone levels are low. Several hypotheses have been proposed. First, depression that occurs in the setting of hypogonadism may remit or improve with testosterone replacement therapy. Second, some depressive subtypes that occur in males with normal testosterone levels may respond to testosterone. Third, depression which occurs in hypogonadal males, though not responding to testosterone directly, may be more difficult to treat with conventional antidepressants. Finally, testosterone, though not an efficacious primary treatment for depression, may benefit some male patients when used as an adjunct to antidepressant treatment (Seidman & Walsh, 1999).

Association of Depression and Testosterone in Men

Several lines of empirical evidence provide some support for the hypothesis that testosterone is associated with depression. First, several cross-sectional studies have examined the relationship between depressive symptoms and testosterone levels. The gonadotropin levels of depressed and nondepressed cohorts have also been compared cross-sectionally. Second, there are several longitudinal studies examining the testosterone levels of men during an episode of depression and following recovery.

Though several studies have provided data regarding the relationship between testosterone and depression, none of them was designed to examine the prevalence of psychiatric symptoms specifically. Additionally, the instruments used to assess depressive symptoms are variable, as are the criteria (if any) used to determine cases of depression. These methodologic limitations make it difficult to determine if any relationship exists between testosterone levels and major depression.

Two epidemiologic studies assessing the cross-sectional relationship between testosterone and depressive symptoms have been conducted. Both were population based. Due to random sampling, each contained some depressed men, but the vast majority of subjects were nondepressed. The first, the Massachusetts Male Aging Study (Araujo, Durante, Feldman, Goldstein, & McKinlay, 1998), was a cross-sectional population-based survey of about 1700 men, aged 40–70, designed to examine the correlation between depression and erectile dysfunction. Morning levels of testosterone were measured and compared to self-reported levels of depression, which were obtained using the Center for Epidemiologic Studies Depression Scale (CES–D). Though there was a significant correlation between depression and erectile problems, there was no correlation between CES–D scores and testosterone level in these men.

The second study, the Veteran's Experience Study (Mazur, 1995; Dabbs, Hopper, & Jurkovic, 1990), surveyed over 5000 veterans between the ages of 33 and 42. Morning testosterone samples were compared to depressive symptoms obtained by structured interview using the Diagnostic Interview Schedule (DIS) (Robins, Helzer, Cottler, & Goldring, 1989). Testosterone levels were only very weakly associated with depression ($r=.04$), a level which, though significant at $p<.01$, has little clinical relevance. The study did not disaggregate men with low testosterone levels for further analysis, though the weak correlation between testosterone levels and depressive symptoms would suggest that further analysis would have little yield.

There have also been a number of studies examining the cross-sectional testosterone levels of men who are depressed with men from a nondepressed cohort, and studies which compare the testosterone levels of men during an episode of depression and after recovery. Most of the studies that have examined the relationship between depressed and non-depressed men have shown that there are no detectable differences in testosterone (Amsterdam, Winokur, & Caroff, 1981; Levitt & Joffe, 1988; Rubin, Poland & Lesser, 1989; Unden, Ljunggren, Beck-Friis, Kjellman, & Wetterberg, 1988; Rupprecht, Rupprecht, Rupprecht, Noder, & Schwarz, 1988), though one study reported that depressed men have slightly lower levels (Vogel, Klaiber, & Broverman, 1978). Two studies reported a negative correlation between testosterone level and age among depressed men, but not among age-matched controls (Levitt & Joffe, 1988; Rubin, Poland, & Lesser, 1989). The significance of this finding may be that older men with low testosterone levels may be more susceptible to depression than are their younger colleagues. Other studies have demonstrated a negative correlation between testosterone levels and severity of depression (Yesavage, Davidson, Widrow & Berger, 1985; Wexler, Mason, & Giller, 1989; Vogel, Klaiber, & Broverman, 1978) and melancholia (Rubin, Poland, & Lesser 1989). Davies, Harris, Thomas, Cook, Read, & Riad-Fahmy (1992) found no significant difference between a cohort of men with melancholic depression and age-matched controls, but did find that, in the depressed group alone, the testosterone level was negatively correlated with depression severity.

Studies that have examined testosterone levels during and after depression have also reported inconsistent results. Of the five longitudinal studies, testosterone levels were lower during depression in three studies (Rupprecht, Rupprecht, Rupprecht, Noder, & Schwarz, 1988; Unden et al., 1988; Steiger, von Bardleben, Wiedemann & Holsboer, 1991), higher in one (Mason, Giller, & Kosten, 1988), and no different in one (Sachar, Halpern, Rosenfeld, Galligher, & Hellman, 1973).

The role of testosterone in depression is unclear, based on the available data. Most of the studies are limited by small sample sizes or methodologic problems, and the results across studies are contradictory. It is unclear what the significance of subnormal testosterone levels may be, particularly when they occur in the presence of depression. It is also unclear whether hypogonadism has differential effects on mood in older cohorts of men. Consequently, it is difficult to make recommendations to clinicians. However, testosterone levels can be easily measured, and consultation with an endocrinologist may be advised for those depressed men with subnormal levels.

Treatment of Male Depression with Testosterone

There have been several trials of testosterone or testosterone derivatives for depression in men. Itil, Hermann, and Blasucci (1978) conducted several treatment trials with mesterolone. In the first of these, they treated 17 depressed men for 3 weeks in an open trial, finding that 8 were improved after treatment. A second placebo-controlled double-blind study included 38 men who were treated with mesterolone or placebo for 4 weeks. Treatment was reported to be associated with improvement in such symptoms as lack of motivation and anhedonia. In the last of these trials, mesterolone was given over 6 weeks to men with major depression, dysthymia, or bipolar depression, who were randomized to mesterolone or placebo (Itil, Michael, Shapiro, & Itil, 1984). Both the treated group and the placebo group improved significantly, and no difference was found between the two with respect to depressive symptoms. Interestingly, those patients with higher testosterone levels appeared to benefit more from treatment than did those who had lower levels.

Vogel, Klaiber, and Broverman (1978) conducted an open trial in which 13 men with refractory depression and normal testosterone levels were treated with mesterolone for 7 weeks. Eleven of the patients responded to the treatment, with a decrease in mean Hamilton Rating Scale for Depression (HRSD) (Hamilton, 1967) scores, decreasing from 21.1 to 5.6. A second randomized double-blind trial compared mesterolone to amitriptyline in 34 depressed, eugonadal men (Vogel, Klaiber, & Broverman, 1985). They were found to be equal in reducing depressive symptoms. Another study of the effects of testosterone on refractory depression was conducted by Seidman and Rabkin (1998), who treated 5 men with SSRI refractory depression in an open trial over 6 weeks. All five of the patients achieved remission of depression, with mean HRSD scores decreasing from 19.2 to 4.0 over the 8-week trial. Three of the four patients who were withdrawn from testosterone relapsed after discontinuation.

In the only study that focused specifically on the treatment of hypogonadal men, Rabkin, Rabkin, and Wagner (1995) administered testosterone to hypogonadal depressed HIV-positive men. Mean HRSD scores decreased from 13.6 to 4.1 over the 8-week trial, with 64% of patients achieving remission of depression.

Several tentative conclusions can be drawn from these studies. There is some evidence that depression which occurs in some males with normal gonadotropin levels may respond to treatment with testosterone, though one well-controlled study did not find any differences between treated men and those receiving placebo. There is, as yet, no information about which men might benefit from such treatment. Testosterone may also be a beneficial treatment for eugonadal men who have not responded to traditional antidepressants, though further study is clearly needed in this area. The treatment of depression with testosterone in hypogonadal men and the use of testosterone as an adjunctive treatment for depression have not been adequately studied. Particularly given the dearth of information regarding efficacy, clinicians are well advised to consider the risks that are posed by testosterone, including potential adverse effects on cholesterol and the prostate (Seidman & Walsh, 1999). Without further evidence of benefit, the use of testosterone as a treatment for depression should be considered with great caution.

SUMMARY

Studies that examine the efficacy of psychopharmacological treatments for depression indicate that men, as well as women, respond well to all classes of drugs. Recently developed antidepressants, the selective serotonin reuptake inhibitors, have demonstrated efficacy when used to treat depression in men. Clinical reports of possible sexually related side-effects that include decreased libido and erectile dysfunction make careful assessment of sexual functioning important. Matching of possible side-effects with desired symptoms targets is often useful in deciding on a medication to prescribe for treating depression in men.

In addition to the use of the common antidepressant medications, the use of testosterone to treat depression in men has been studied and shows some potential. However, clear indications for the use of this and other hormones in the treatment of depression are not clearly defined. Therefore, the use of testosterone or other sex hormones for the treatment of mood disorders in men must be considered very carefully in light of the fact that other efficacious psychopharmacological treatments are available.

CHAPTER 6

Psychotherapeutic Treatment of Depression in Men

(You) can feel the wrath of God kindled against your soul, and anguish of conscience most intolerable, and (you) can find, notwithstanding continual prayer and incessant supplication made unto the Lord, no relief.

T. Bright

Individual Psychotherapy for Depression in Men
  Empirically Validated Treatments
  Innovative Psychotherapies
Couples Therapy
Group Therapy
Summary

Psychotherapy has always been underutilized by men. The reasons for this are not well understood, although traditional male gender roles may be strong forces operating against men's willingness to use an interpersonal, intimate, face-to-face encounter in which to solve problems (e.g., Scher, 1990). Men initiate fewer contacts with therapists than do women (Vessey & Howard, 1993). However, when men do meet with therapists, there is ample evidence that they do continue in treatment and benefit in much the same way as women benefit when treated using well-known empirically verified treatment approaches.

The New Psychology of Men has yielded many perspectives on how to work with men in psychotherapy in individual (Brooks, 1998; Cochran & Rabinowitz, 1996; Osherson & Krugman, 1990; Pollack,

A Treatise of Melancholy (p. 101)

1995a, 1995b, 1990; Pollack & Levant, 1998), group (Andronico, 1995; Rabinowitz & Cochran, 1987; Stein, 1982), couples (Slipp, 1996), and family modalities (Brooks & Gilbert, 1995). One feature that all these approaches have in common is the emphasis on gender-sensitive insights into the struggles that often bring men in to the therapy consulting room. Many of the suggestions offered have been employed by therapists in efforts to reach a greater number of men and involve them in psychotherapeutic treatment. In spite of the obvious merit of such efforts, none of these innovative approaches has been subjected to empirical testing.

Probably the optimal approach for working with men is an approach that combines the gender-sensitive perspective of the New Psychology of Men with the proven efficacy of those psychotherapies that have been well researched and documented in the psychotherapy process and outcome research literature. Cognitive behavioral and interpersonal psychotherapies have been proven useful for treating depression in men in numerous rigorously controlled outcome studies. In addition, both approaches, as well as supportive psychotherapy, have proven effective in treating depression in men in group settings. Behavioral couples therapy is useful in treating men with substance and alcohol abuse difficulties, resulting in both decreases in substance and alcohol abuse and increases in relationship satisfaction. As we can see, these and a number of other approaches have proven useful in treating depression in men. In addition to these empirically verified approaches, innovative, male-sensitive perspectives on psychotherapy have been forumlated as a specific means of engaging and holding men in treatment.

> *Clinician Query*—"The color just faded from everything."
> John entered psychotherapy after dropping out of his second year of medical school. He had been succeeding at his academic work, but had not been enjoying the classes and was becoming increasingly unhappy with his choice of a career in medicine. He explained that he had become gradually more and more withdrawn from his classmates, and finally had stopped attending classes altogether. A phone conversation with his parents had convinced him to take a leave of absence from his studies and spend some time clarifying his purpose and direction in life. He described his situation in an early interview with his therapist.
> "Everything just gradually became empty this year. The classes. My friendships. It was as if the color just faded from

everything. Nothing gave me pleasure or interested me much. Nothing was any fun. Oh, I could still make the grades. But there has to be more to life than making good grades and getting a good Dean's letter."

"That's a really vivid way to put it, John. The color faded from everything. Have you ever had this kind of experience before?" his therapist probed.

John sat in reflection for several seconds and his therapist let the silence ripen. "Well, my junior year in college things were pretty gray. I had broken up with my girlfriend. Or I should say she had broken up with me. I didn't really have any direction or plan or anything at that point. I decided then to take the MCATs and go to medical school. It gave me some purpose. A direction, I suppose. But things were pretty gray during that time. Like now. I felt really alone and hurt by getting dumped by her."

"So the decision to go to medical school was made on the heels of being dumped by your girlfriend?" his therapist clarified.

"Well, now that we're talking about it, I guess it was. I never really thought about it that way before. I just figured it was something to do, go to medical school. I always got good grades, and I thought helping people would be a good way to use my talents. But I remember thinking 'I have to have something to do. I have to have somewhere to go.'"

"Well, I would agree with you on the helping people with your talents part. But, then we have to figure out why medical school lost so much of its appeal all of a sudden. I wonder if the original motivation for going was to take your mind off the ending of your relationship. What do you think?"

"This is really interesting. I remember now that when I was in high school, I got dumped by my very first serious girlfriend when I was a senior. I was devastated and just didn't know what to do. This was right after a disastrous spring break for us. Then, all the college acceptance letters started coming. It was a great way to keep my mind off my relationship with Michelle. The same thing. Somewhere to go. Something to do. But thinking back on it now, I was pretty miserable during that spring."

"Yeah, that really is interesting. I wonder what is worse for you. Making a major decision about your future or being jilted in a relationship."

John sat quietly in reflection. "I've never really thought about it this way before. Making these decisions about my future this way just keeps me away from the pain. I'm focused on the future, something to do, and don't have to feel what I'm feeling at the time. But I can't run forever. I think what all this means is that I need to look at this rejection and pain and see what is so difficult about it for me." He paused again and was quiet. "This fits for me. I can feel sadness just sitting here thinking about this stuff."

- What approaches to psychotherapy are well suited for treating depression in men?
- What psychotherapies incorporate gender-role analysis in the treatment of male depression?

INDIVIDUAL PSYCHOTHERAPY FOR DEPRESSION IN MEN

Empirically Validated Treatments

The quantity and quantity of research reporting empirical tests of the efficacy of individual approaches to psychotherapy have grown dramatically in the past 20 years. The research literature on psychotherapy of depression has yielded consistent results demonstrating a positive response by men (as well as women) to cognitive–behavioral, interpersonal, and brief psychodynamic psychotherapy interventions (e.g., Dobson, 1989; Hollon, Shelton, & Davis, 1993; Luborsky & Crits-Christoph, 1990; Robinson, Berman, & Neimeyer, 1990; Weissman & Markowitz, 1994).

Findings from the National Instutute of Mental Health Treatment of Depression Collaborative Research Program (Elkin, Shea, Watkins, Imber, Sotsky, Collins, Glass, Pilkonis, Leber, Docherty, Fiester, & Parloff, 1989) provided evidence of the efficacy of both cognitive behavioral and interpersonal psychotherapy in the treatment of unipolar depression when these approaches were compared with standard pharmacological treatment (imipramine). This empirical investigation of the effectiveness of two psychosocial treatments for depression examined the responses of

239 patients randomly assigned to four different 16-week treatment conditions (cognitive–behavioral psychotherapy, interpersonal psychotherapy, imipramine with clinical management, and placebo with clinical management). Psychotherapy treatment conditions were carefully controlled through the use of manuals that directed the treatment. Although the psychotherapy treatment conditions were not found to be superior to the pharmacotherapy treatment, they were as effective as the pharmacotherapy treatment in relieving depression for most of the subjects in the study. A generally accepted conclusion based on the results of this investigation is that both psychotherapy treatments are effective for treating mild to moderate unipolar depression.

In an analysis of patient predictors of the responses to these therapies, Sotsky, Glass, Shea, Pilkonis, Collins, Elkin, Watkins, Imber, Leber, Moyer, & Oliveri (1991) found that patient sex was not a predictor of response in any of the treatment conditions. In a follow-up using subjects from this study, Zlotnick, Shea, Pilkonis, Elkin, & Ryan found no differences in depressive symptom severity assessed at 6-, 12-, and 18-month follow-up intervals. This study examined outcomes that were based on either sex alone or in combination with type of treatment received, dysfunctional attitudes, stressful life events, or social support, indicating that men responded as well as women to the treatments received. The conclusion reached was that both psychosocial treatments for depression were effective but that neither showed superior effectiveness with either sex.

The use of cognitive–behavioral therapy (Beck, 1976; Beck, Rush, Shaw, & Emery, 1979; Newman & Beck, 1990) as an efficacious treatment for depression has been well demonstrated, not only in the NIMH Treatment of Depression Collaborative Research Program but in other outcome studies. In a controlled study examining the effectiveness of cognitive–behavioral treatment for depression, Thase, Reynolds, Frank, Simons, Garamoni, McGeary, Harden, Fasiczka, & Gahalane (1994b) found that depressed men responded as well as depressed women to a course of short-term cognitive–behavioral individual psychotherapy. Interestingly, in this study the men required fewer sessions to achieve remission compared with the women. One possible explanation for this was that on average the women's pretreatment level of depression was somewhat higher than the men's pretreatment levels, thus requiring somewhat lengthier treatment for remission. Similarly, Jarrett, Eaves, Grannemann, and Rush (1991) found that sex was not a predictor of outcome in cognitive therapy, but that marital status and initial severity of depression did predict positive response.

A meta-analysis of the efficacy of cognitive therapy for depression found no differences in effect sizes when the proportion of women in the experimental groups was used as a predictor variable (Dobson, 1989). The implication in this analysis was that if women responded more positively than men, then those studies with higher proportions of women would yield greater effect sizes.

Clearly, both experimental as well as meta-analytic inquiry has demonstrated the effectiveness of cognitive–behavioral psychotherapy in the treatment of depression in men. Thase, Reynolds, Frank, Simons, McGeary, Fasiczka, Garamoni, Jennings, & Kupfer (1994a) specifically studied this approach based on the idea that men might respond to a more cognitive, or problem-solving oriented, approach. Although this study did find a positive effect for the men, women included in the study also responded positively. This comparable effect is a consistent finding in studies using cognitive therapy, leading to the conclusion that cognitive–behavioral psychotherapy is an effective treatment for depression, but is not any more effective for men or women as a group. In addition, matching of patient and therapist gender and patient preference for therapist gender did not predict superior outcome in the Treatment of Depression Collaborative Research Program (Zlotnick, Elkin, & Shea, 1998).

Interpersonal psychotherapy (Klerman, Weissman, Rounsaville, & Chevron, 1984) has also been found to be effective in treating depression. The findings of the NIMH Treatment of Depression Collaborative Research Program reported by Elkin *et al.* (1989) confirmed interpersonal psychotherapy as an effective treatment for unipolar depression. In addition, Frank, Carpenter, & Kupfer (1988) reported that men responded positively to interpersonal psychotherapy when this was used in conjunction with imipramine for the treatment of recurrent depression. The men in this study were more likely to be categorized as normal responders than were the women and obtained improvement at a somewhat more rapid rate than did the women in the study. Similar findings have been replicated by a number of researchers at a number of different sites, including five outcome research projects reported by Thase, Greenhouse, Frank, Reynolds, Pilkonis, Hurley, Grochochinski, & Kupfer (1997). Rounsaville, Klerman, Weissman, and Chevron (1985) summarize findings on the effectiveness of interpersonal psychotherapy in the treatment of unipolar depression and find this approach yields consistent and positive responses in the treatment of depression. In addition, Weissman and Markowitz (1994) summarize research that supports the use of interpersonal psychotherapy in the treatment not only of unipolar depression but also of depressed mood that is secondary to other conditions, such as Human Immunodeficiency Virus (HIV) infection (see also Swartz & Markowitz, 1998).

Another psychosocial approach to the treatment of depression that has fared well in empirical efforts to validate its efficacy is the behavioral therapy approach (Hoberman, 1990; Hoberman & Lewinsohn, 1985; Lewinsohn & Gotlib, 1995). This perspective has also enjoyed empirical support in the psychotherapy process and outcome literature (e.g., Bellack, Hersen, & Himmelhoch, 1981; Hersen, Bellack, Himmelhoch, & Thase, 1984). This approach to treating depression is based on a model of depression that relates social and instrumental skill deficits to the extinction of behaviors that result in reinforcing contingencies. Behavioral therapy emphasizes the acquisition of social skills and the increase of behaviors that are experienced as pleasurable and thus result in an uplift of mood. In fact, Addis and Jacobson (1996) showed that the behavioral component of cognitive–behavioral psychotherapy was most beneficial to patients who reported the treatment to be successful. Patients who gave what the investigators described as "existential" reasons for their depression did not fare as well with the behavioral therapy.

As is the case with both cognitive–behavioral and interpersonal psychotherapy, behavioral psychotherapy has not demonstrated a superior effectiveness with either sex, yet appears to be a viable and empirically supported psychosocial treatment for depression (Craighead, Craighead, & Ilardi, 1998).

Persons (1998) reviewed the issues involved in evaluating randomized controlled trials of psychotherapy outcome studies, as well as questions related to combining psychotherapy and pharmacotherapy in the treatment of depression, and supports the use of those treatments that have proven efficacy as a first line of psychosocial treatment. She also gives suggestions on monitoring effectiveness of treatments and recommends the use of psychotherapy as a first choice of treatment for most depressed patients.

Innovative Psychotherapies

In addition to these treatments reported in the psychotherapy process and outcome literature and found to be effective with men who suffer from depression, there are other individual psychotherapies that have been proposed for use with depressed men. Pollack (1998a) has specified a treatment for depressed men based on a psychoanalytic perspective that emphasizes empathic attunement to and repair of childhood relational trauma (abandonment depression) resulting from the socialization process most little boys are subjected to as they are pushed into premature separation from early caretakers. This approach may have particular utility when working with men suffering from a mood disturbance that is in reaction to the loss or disruption of an important interpersonal relationship. Since many men are thought to come to therapy only at the behest of a significant other, and particularly when a relationship is in turmoil and jeopardy, this empathic perspective, based largely on the work of Kohut (1977), would be especially useful.

Cochran and Rabinowitz (1996) proposed a similar approach, focused on issues of grief and loss, which is easily applied to working with men experiencing depression. Their perspective follows men's developmental journeys through childhood, adolescence, and adulthood and demonstrates how experiences of loss at various developmental nodal points may become a focus of psychotherapeutic activity. An integration of the psychodynamic features of Pollack's model (Pollack, 1998a, 1995b) and the gender-role strain features of Pleck (1995, 1981) and O'Neil (1981), this model underscores the central role of loss in men's lives and the relation of loss experiences to mood disorders. The combination of psychological losses experienced in relational discontinuities through the lifespan with social losses experienced in failing to live up to the masculine ideals of our culture are frequent triggers for depressive episodes in men. The psychotherapeutic work in this model focuses on the identification and working through of the various losses a man has experienced. The optimal outcome of working with men from this perspective is a blend of sadness as the affective state that accompanies the recognition and integration of loss with acceptance of the man's life, life choices, strengths, and limitations.

A third perspective on psychotherapy with men that emphasizes psychodynamic aspects of male development and focuses on the experience of shame in men is outlined by Osherson and Krugman (1990) and Krugman (1995). Shame is a "first cousin" of male depression. It is evoked from the crucible containing the developmental struggles and cultural expectations of boys and men that is described by Cochran and Rabinowitz (1996). Shame is a complex physiological and psychological state that arises from a failure to live up to a notion of the "ideal" self, a conception of self that is heavily shaped by cultural expectations of men and the cultural construction of manhood. The emerging recognition of the inability or the unwillingness to meet these expectations is a common breeding ground for shame in men.

The experience of shame is very similar to the experience of depression in many men. Shame has components that closely parallel depression in men. Men experiencing shame may feel a sense of inadequacy, wounded self-esteem, a feeling of danger, and fear of exposure of inadequacies (Osherson & Krugman, 1990). They may hide their "real self" in order to protect it from the crushing impact of shame.

Efforts to conceal the threatened real self are common as men attempt to manage shame. Common shame management strategies parallel depressive syndromes or depressive equivalents in men. These strategies include outbursts of anger, aggression and violence, alcoholism, substance abuse, and isolation and disconnection from others. Paradoxically, such strategies serve only to compound a man's suffering and sense of inadequacy, thus deepening his sense of isolation and alienation. Psychotherapy that is sensitive to shame-based defenses and dynamics in men will counter the sense, felt by many men, that treatment for emotional troubles in "unmanly," threatening, and inappropriate.

All three of these perspectives emphasize the developmental nature of men's psychological growth and the potential for vulnerability to depressive states that is a result of the early "traumatic abrogation" (cf. Pollack, 1995b) of the boy's holding environment in the nuclear family structure. This relational discontinuity is hypothesized to produce an intrapsychic structure in little boys that makes them uniquely vulnerable, as men, to later relational disruptions which often result in mood disturbances.

Clinician Query—"I'd just rather be by myself
most of the time."

Tom and his spouse, Martha, sought couples therapy at Martha's suggestion after she had consulted with her family physician about feelings of depression and frustration with her marriage. Tom and Martha had been married for 15 years, and had 2 children, a son 13 years old and a daughter 10 years old. They had married and set up house in the town where they attended college, and shortly after getting married, their first child was born. They had struggled financially, but Martha's income as a speech pathologist had always been sufficient to keep the bills paid. Tom had taken a series of entry-level positions at various industries around town, but had not persisted in any of these positions beyond one or two years.

Martha had recently become increasingly concerned with Tom's withdrawal, lack of ambition, and increase in drinking over the past couple of years. Tom's father had died two years ago, and he was now the only member of his own family still living. He had an older brother who had been killed in an automobile accident when Tom was a senior in high school. Shortly after this, his mother had died of breast cancer. Tom felt that his father just withdrew and became depressed himself, and had started drinking heavily at the time of his wife's death.

In this interview with their therapist, Martha is raising some of her concerns about what she observes in Tom's behavior at home.

"I just don't know what to do anymore, Tom. It's so frustrating. You just pull back and don't talk. You just want to get a glass of wine and disappear to the back porch. Why don't you talk to me anymore?" Martha pleaded.

Tom sat and stared at Martha, not saying a word. Several seconds passed.

"Tom, do you want to respond to anything that Martha has just said?" their therapist inquired.

"There's nothing to say, really. I don't really have much to say," Tom replied as he looked down at the carpet.

Martha let out a sigh of exasperation. "See? Come on, Tom. We've got to talk. You just seem unhappy all the time. Is it me? What's wrong? You're so negative with everything. Nothing is ever good enough. Kate does the least little thing and you're all over her case. And the same with Bill."

"What do you want from me?" Tom responded, his voice raising in anger. "I'm doing the best I can. I just don't feel like talking sometimes. Can't you just drop it?"

"Tom, you don't sound to me like you heard what Martha was asking. I heard her say that all she wants is to talk. What did you hear?"

"She wants to talk. Great. Whenever we do, I just wind up the bad guy. She is so critical all the time. All she does is complain about me. It's just better for me to mind my own business, so I do." Tom replied.

"Martha, how do you feel when you hear Tom say this?" the therapist inquired in hopes of illustrating to Tom the impact of his negativity and withdrawal.

"I just feel like he doesn't care. Like we're not important to him. He just wants to be alone, by himself. It's sad. It's like I don't have a husband and the kids don't have a father."

"Tom, is that what you intend to communicate?"

"I don't know. Maybe so. I never feel like she really cares, either. She's always so critical of me when I try to say something. She always finds something wrong. I just prefer to be by myself."

"You've come to find that more comfortable, just being by yourself?" their therapist followed, trying to connect with some of Tom's loneliness and isolation.

"Yeah. I feel like I would just rather be by myself a lot of the time."

"What's that about, Tom?"

"I don't know how to open up. I've been shut off for a long time, really. It's just easier to be by myself. I won't get hurt."

"You won't get hurt? What do you mean by that?" their therapist wondered, hoping to start connecting some of Tom's current withdrawal to his feelings of loss and abandonment by his brother, mother, and father.

"It's just easier that way. I don't like to connect to people. It's too painful."

"You're saying it's painful to connect with people, and that you'll get hurt. I don't think I'm really following you here. I wonder where these fears came from, Tom?"

There was a silence in the room. Tom looked down at the carpet again and let out a deep sigh. Martha sat and looked at him, tears filling her eyes.

- Under what circumstances is couples therapy indicated, as either a primary or adjunctive treatment for depression in men?
- Are there any situations in which couples therapy would be contraindicated in treating depression in men?

COUPLES THERAPY

A number of approaches to working with couples have been offered in the past (e.g., Jacobson & Gurman, 1986; Paolino & McCrady, 1978).

One of these which has proven effective in a variety of controlled studies is the behavioral couples therapy approach (Beach, Sandeen, & O'Leary, 1990; Beach, Whisman, & O'Leary, 1994; Christensen, Jacobson, & Babcock, 1995; Jacobson & Addis, 1993). This approach has proven useful for the amelioration of couples conflicts, as well as for reductions in depressive symptoms in either or both partners, decreases in drug and alcohol abuse in male partners, and decreases in couples' violence instigated by male partners (Beach, Sandeen, & O'Leary, 1990; Beach, Arias, & O'Leary. 1987; Fals-Stewart, Birchler, & O'Farrell, 1996; O'Farrell & Murphy, 1995).

In their overview and manual for treating depression with couples therapy, Beach, Sandeen, and O'Leary (1990) provide the context for conceptualizing depression in a relational perspective. They note that clinicians as well as researchers began to notice the convergence of depressive symptoms and marital or couples' discord. As treatment interventions improved the quality of the relationship, depressive symptoms began to abate. These observations led to an explicit model of the relationship between depression and relational discord. Haas, Clarkin, and Glick (1985) offer empirical support for a couples-based treatment for depressive disorders that emphasizes psychosocial dysfunction as an important variable in both precipitating and maintaining depression in couples.

Although any approach that works with heterosexual couples must explicitly address the political and cultural values embedded in its ideology and interventions (cf. Gurman & Klein, 1980), behavioral couples therapy offers interventions for distressed couples that follows the guidelines of gender-aware therapy outlined by Good, Gilbert, and Scher (1990). Regardless of the political persuasion of the therapist, when working with men, it is important to assess the man's relationship status and to consider offering couples therapy as an adjunct to individual treatment if the man is reporting alcohol or substance abuse in addition to depression.

Although couples-based interventions have been successful in reducing relational violence, the use of a conjoint structure in which to address one partner's violence is controversial. The danger in such an arrangement is that violence directed from one partner to the other will be viewed as an interactive, relational phenomenon, thus blurring responsibility for the containment and cessation of the violent behavior. In consideration of this important aspect of the structure of couples' treatment, it is crucial for the clinician to be very clear about her or his perspective on addressing violence in couples therapy. Some clinicians recommend that couples therapy should only be offered in conjunction with specific plans targeted at eliminating violence, such as a referral to individual therapy or a batterers' group focused on personal responsibility for violent behaviors (e.g., Rosenbaum & O'Leary, 1986).

Clinician Query—"It feels good to know someone else knows what it's like."

Tim, a physically fit, 41-year-old man, was having a difficult time deciding whether to stay in his relationship with his wife. He had been with his wife since they were teenagers. They had two daughters who were in high school. Tim was a partner in a modestly successful construction company. He had complained of exhaustion and of being "burnt out" when he saw his family physician. His physician had prescribed sertraline for him and, although he had an increase in energy, Tim still had negative thoughts about himself and his life. He was referred for psychotherapy, where he discussed his ambivalence about his primary relationship. His therapist referred Tim to an all-male psychotherapy group as an adjunct to his individual treatment. His therapist thought that Tim would benefit from contact with other men who were in transition in their lives.

The group met weekly for two hours, and included a variety of experiential exercises and activities to encourage the men in the group to communicate in a more emotionally expressive manner. Although the group had been going for several years, Tim joined after summer break and was one of the "new guys." At first, Tim was quiet and observant of the others' interactions. By the fourth session, he began to participate in the verbal interaction of the group. In the seventh session, after doing an exercise that encouraged him to look at how he suppressed aspects of himself in order to fit in socially with the traditional male role, Tim revealed that he was really depressed about the way his life had turned out.

"I'm totally on the fence with my wife. I find her very immature, and I feel like we haven't grown together much since we were teenagers," he stated, keeping his eyes down in an effort to avoid the attention he was receiving from eight of the group members and the two therapists.

"Why don't you just leave?" queried a group member in a direct fashion.

"I have two daughters who I don't want to let down. My wife is like a child, too. She would freak if I left. She was abandoned by her parents," he replied.

"You seem stuck. What do you feel as you say what you just did?" asked one of the therapists.

"I don't know. I feel a lot of tension right here, in my gut. It feels like it is all knotted up in here," he said, putting a hand on his stomach.

"You seem like you are doing a lot of caretaking," proposed Don, another group member.

"I take care of everyone. My wife. My kids. The other guys at work. That seems like all I do," Tim responded.

"And it puts you into knots. How do you take care of yourself?" asked one of the therapists.

"Are you kidding? About the only thing I do purely for myself is go rock climbing one weekend a month. I love it. It is the most freeing thing to be alone in the mountains. Life seems very simple at those moments," said Tim, his face reflecting a lightness which hadn't been apparent since he joined the group.

"My parents fought and stayed together for the kids, and I hated it. I wished they would have just gotten divorced. The fighting and the negative energy was lethal," blurted out another group member, Lee, who was responding emotionally to Tim's ambivalence about his marriage.

"Well, my parents did get divorced, and it sucked," Tim countered with some strong feeling in his voice.

"So part of your ambivalence has to do with not repeating what happened in your own family?" one of the therapists suggested.

"I hardly ever saw my father when I was younger. He was either working or out getting drunk with his friends. He didn't come home just to be with me and my brothers. We sort of dreaded his appearance since we created a life without him with my mom." After Tim said this, he started to look very sad. He put his hand on his forehead and looked down, seemingly holding back tears. The men were quiet for a few minutes as the impact of Tim's sadness about his father filled the room.

The silence was broken by one of the group's quieter members, Len. He, too, had had very little time with his father during childhood and could relate to Tim's pain and sadness.

"I wish that my Dad had been around more. I'm sorry you had to go through that, Tim. If it helps any, I can really relate to what you are feeling," Len offered.

Tim lifted his head. A single tear had trickled down his cheek. "Thanks, Len. It feels good to know someone else knows what it's like."

- When is group treatment indicated for a man who is depressed?
- How do the dynamics of an all-male group benefit treatment for men struggling with feelings of depression?

GROUP THERAPY

Shortly after the rise of feminist consciousness-raising groups in the late 1960s and early 1970s, men began gathering in groups to discuss the impact of sexism on their lives. A number of approaches to working with men in all-male therapy and consciousness-raising groups have been presented (e.g., Andronico, 1995; Cochran & Rabinowitz, 1983; Heppner, 1981; Rabinowitz & Cochran, 1987; Stein, 1982; Wong, 1978). In addition to these groups that emphasize exploration of the gender-role strains men experience and the impact of these strains on men's relationships, a number of other approaches to working with men in groups have recently been found to be effective in treating depressed men.

Consistent with individual psychotherapy outcome studies, group-based cognitive–behavioral therapy interventions have proven effective in the treatment of depression (Briston & Bright, 1995; Peterson & Halstead, 1998; Oei & Shuttlewood, 1997). A study that examined the effectiveness of cognitive–behavioral therapy when compared to medication found the use of group-based cognitive–behavioral therapy to be as effective as imiprimine in the treatment of major depression (Stravynski, Verreault, Gaudette, & Langlois, 1994). Although gender was not a specific independent variable in these outcome studies, the positive effect of the psychological treatment as well as the proven efficacy of individual cognitive–behavioral therapy with men implicates this modality as a very useful approach to consider when working with depressed men in groups.

Cognitive–behavioral and support-based interventions have also been found to be useful to men who are infected with the human immunodeficiency virus (HIV). Both modalities of group treatment produced decreases in depressive symptoms, hostility, and somatization. The support group intervention additionally yielded reductions in interpersonal sensitivity, anxiety, and the frequency of unprotected sex (Kelly, Murphy, Bahr, Kalichman, Morgan, Stevenson, Koob, Brasfield, & Bernstein, 1993). In contrast to this finding, Zisook, Peterkin, Goggin, Sledge, Atkinson, and Grant (1998) failed to find an enhancement of outcome when supportive group psychotherapy was added to fluoxetine in the treatment of HIV-positive men who met criteria for major depression. Group-based interventions with depressed men with comorbid medical or other psychiatric conditions may be more complicated. The complexity of the subjects' medical conditions in these studies may ultimately attenuate the impact of the psychosocial interventions used, thus making definitive conclusions difficult.

In addition to these findings supporting the use of group therapy in the treatment of depression, other group interventions have proven useful in addressing problems related to depression. One such intervention is a 12-week structured intervention for men who experienced distress after their partners had an abortion. This group intervention resulted in reductions of anxiety, anger, and grief for those men who participated (Coyle & Enright, 1997).

Although group treatment appears to be an efficacious and cost-effective alternative to individual treatment in general (McRoberts, Burlingame, & Hoad, 1998), the efficacy of group treatment for various categories of depressed men awaits empirical validation. In addition, an examination of effective treatments for other variants of depression in men (e.g., bereavement and grief, adjustment disorders, depression comorbid with alcoholism or other substance abuse) is warranted. There is good data recommending the extension of group treatment to men in these categories, but many of the studies have been done primarily with samples that yield limited generalization.

SUMMARY

Cognitive–Behavioral, interpersonal, and behavioral approaches for treating depression all have demonstrated efficacy. Depressed men benefit from treatments utilizing these therapies in much the same way that women benefit. In addition to these empirically verified treatments, innovative individual psychotherapies have been designed which focus specifically on male-related issues, including relationship disconnection, shame, and loss. These psychotherapies suggest specific linkages to depression, and likely will prove promising as treatments for male depression. This is especially important since most evidence indicates that men do not seek psychotherapy as frequently as do women. Perhaps one reason for this is that psychotherapy, as traditionally practiced, is not perceived by the typical male to be particularly welcoming. If use of the innovative treatments described here results in increases in clinician empathy and sensitivity to depressed men, perhaps greater numbers of depressed men will perceive psychotherapy as a viable alternative to living lives of lonely, quiet desperation.

Couples treatments that emphasize relationship issues have proven effective in treating depression in both partners, as well as in decreasing alcohol and substance abuse and violence in the male partners. Such approaches are important because so many depressed men are also found to be at higher risk for alcohol and substance abuse as well as violence. Psychotherapy interventions which focus not only on depression but also on alcohol and substance abuse and violence have obvious merit for men.

Group therapies for treating depressed men have been effective in specific populations of men. Interventions with men with issues related to HIV-infection status have been studied extensively. In general, cognitive–behavioral approaches have proven to be helpful in reducing depression when delivered in a group setting. In addition to the structured, empirically verified group treatments for depression, a number of male therapy groups address issues related to depression in their approach and may also prove to be effective in treating depression in men.

CHAPTER 7

The Murder of the Self: Men and Suicide

Religious and bureaucratic prejudices, family sensitivity, the vagaries and differences in the proceedings of corner's courts and post-mortem examinations, the shadowy distinctions between suicides and accidents-in short, personal, official, and traditional unwillingness to recognize the act for what it is-all help to pervert and diminish our knowledge of the extent to which suicide pervades society.

A. Alvarez

Although prevalence studies utilizing general population samples indicate that men suffer from depression at only about half the rate that women do, the statistics on suicide, both in the United States and in other industrialized nations throughout the world, tell a dramatically different story. At all ages, for all races, men commit suicide at three to

The Savage God (p. 84)
Copyright 1990 A. Alvarez, reprinted with the permission of Gillon Aitken Associates, Ltd.

Men and Depression: Clinical and Empirical Perspectives

135

five times the rate that women commit suicide (Moscicki, 1997). Almost three out of every four suicides in the United States are committed by white men. Suicide rates for elderly white men, those over 75 years of age, may be as much as eight to fifteen times as great as rates for women the same age (Kennedy, Metz, & Lowinger, 1995). For white men, suicide rate is directly correlated with age—as white men get older, they commit suicide at ever-increasing rates (Osgood & Thielman, 1990).

The number of men who commit suicide is probably strongly influenced by our culture's fascination with violence, our national traditions that support the right to purchase and bear arms, and cultural norms that insist it is better for boys to fight or act aggressively than to express any sad, depressed, or hurt feelings. How might these cultural expectations we place on boys and men, to suppress emotion and to act out in aggression and violence at others or the self when containment of these emotions is threatened, contribute to the epidemic of male suicide?

In addition to the overt loss of life and ensuing disruptions in family and community relationships resulting from completed suicides, the myriad self-destructive behaviors that are often related to suicide have a detrimental influence on health and well-being. Specifically, for men, these include increases in alcohol and substance abuse, poor health maintenance and denial of health problems, compulsive work activity, and reckless activities of many kinds. Socialization of men in our society exacts a toll on those who succumb to the glitzy, sexy allure of a lifestyle devoted to risky, self-destructive behavior.

Many men, as they grow older, encounter numerous experiences that bring them face-to-face with their own mortality. The accrual of deaths of friends and family members and life-partners are only the most obvious examples of experiences that force confrontation with a man's own limited life span. Failing health and loss of valued roles amplify the losses many men are forced to cope with as they grow older. How responsive a man might be to the transforming impact of such encounters depends on a number of known and unknown factors. Existential awareness, focusing on the limitations of mortality and the losses inherent in living a full life, may prove overwhelming for many men. They may ultimately choose death over facing their problems in living—relationship losses, employment difficulties, health problems, and role loss—since such problems may represent essential parts of a self not worth preserving any longer. The choice of suicide in the face of human limitations and frailty may represent a masculine effort to regain control over an out-of-control life (Heifner, 1997).

No matter how we might attempt to understand the paradoxical finding that fewer men than women are depressed but that many, many more men than women commit suicide, there is no denying the fact that many men who are depressed end their lives by committing suicide. Suicide is an extreme response to a man's predicament. It represents the erosion of hope and optimism to the point where no light is seen at the end of the tunnel. The fantasy of peace and freedom from suffering eclipses the actual pain of life. Since so many men commit suicide and since suicide impacts so many other persons, it is essential for clinicians to be aware of the enormity of this risk in depressed men. Clinicians must carefully assess for suicide risk all men who come to them for help with any kind of depressive disorder and must actively intervene to manage suicide risk in those men for whom it is appropriate.

Clinician Query—"I just can't go on."

Allen was a 40-year-old man who had lost his job as an engineer due to a downsizing move by the company that employed him. His visit to a therapist was prompted by his wife. She had become increasingly concerned about his lack of energy and motivation to seek employment. When she called to make the initial appointment, she told the therapist that Allen would sleep late in the morning, often until after their two sons, ages 12 and 16, had left for school. He would then get up and watch television, not bothering to get dressed. Both Allen and his wife, Arlene, came to the initial interview. The therapist had encouraged Arlene to accompany Allen if it would make it easier for him to come to the initial appointment. When they arrived for the first interview, the therapist decided to include both Allen and Arlene in the initial consultation.

"Arlene, since you called for the appointment, why don't you get the ball rolling by presenting your perspective on what has brought us together today. Then, Allen, you can give your side of the story," the therapist opened their first session.

"Well, I'm very worried about Allen. He was laid off from his job about six months ago, and he has just gone downhill since then. It was quite a shock, but we were also halfway expecting it. His company has been on some hard times recently, and there was word around that there might be some layoffs. You never really know how you will react to something like that until it actually happens, though. He's been home ever since. Mostly, he just sleeps late, watches television, and sits and reads or stares out the window. I keep telling him he should just get on with trying to find another job. He would feel better, I'm sure. But he just says he doesn't feel like it, and doesn't say much else. I think the boys are beginning to get worried about him. Last week, Ken asked if he was alright. I just don't know what more to do."

"Just leave me alone, that's what you could do!" Allen interjected with an angry tone to his voice.

"Okay, Allen, let me finish up with Arlene, and then you can have the floor to give your side of the story," the therapist responded to Allen. Then, turning to Arlene, "So basically you're very concerned about Allen, in the aftermath of his being laid off from his job, and how he seems to be coping with this, right?"

"Yes. I'm just glad he agreed to come in today. He said he wouldn't ever get help, but I insisted. I called our family doctor and he gave us your name and said we should get ahold of you right away. He said you have dealt with these kinds of things before."

"Yes, I have. I'm glad you decided to come in and talk about the situation. Is there anything else you want to add, Arlene?" the therapist offered one more invitation to Arlene to continue.

"No, not really. I'm just worried about Allen."

"Okay. So you're concerned about your husband. Thanks for getting the ball rolling here." The therapist turned toward Allen. "Now, Allen, why don't you take some time and tell me your perspective on what has brought us all together today."

Allen shrugged, and looked down at his feet. "Well, it's basically like she says. I got laid off from my job about six months ago. I had been working at Mason's Engineering for about 15 years, and, boom, they just let a bunch of us go. It was coming, with new management and company priorities. So I've been in a tailspin ever since. I never dreamed this kind of thing would happen to me. You go to college and get your degree and get a job, and you never expect this to happen. I just don't know what to do."

"What have you been doing, to deal with this?" the therapist asked.

"Well, not much. Just trying to regroup, basically."

"Oh, Allen, it's more that just trying to regroup. I figured a little time would be okay, but this has gone on way too long. And I just feel like you're depressed and don't seem to be getting out of it," Arlene interjected, her voice tinged with obvious frustration at Allen's apparent denial and minimization.

"O.K., Arlene, thanks. Allen, I want to hear it "straight from the horse's mouth," so to speak." The therapist directed the focus back to Allen.

"Well, I guess she's right. I just haven't been myself. I don't feel like doing anything except sleeping and watching TV. I've thought about trying to get out and look for work, but I just never make it through the door."

"What keeps you from getting through the door?" the therapist inquired.

"I just don't feel like it. I'm tired. I don't feel like there's anything I can do with myself now. I just don't have the energy to do anything."

"And you've been sleeping a lot and watching TV?"

"Yeah. I guess I probably sleep 10, 12 hours a night. The TV is a distraction. I can just space off while I watch it. Sometimes, I just don't know where to start."

"So you're sleeping a lot, escaping into TV, and not feeling like doing much about getting another job?"

"That's about it," Allen replied as he glanced at Arlene.

The therapist continued to focus on Allen by inquiring about the position he had lost, how he had liked his work, and if he had had any thoughts about what kind of work he might like to pursue. This was interspersed with questions designed to detect other depressive symptoms and their severity. Allen seemed to prefer to respond mainly to questions from the therapist.

"Have you been drinking more than usual, or taking other kinds of mood-altering drugs?"

"Some. It helps to have a drink. It takes my mind off of my problems."

"Oh, it's more than that, Allen. You drink a six-pack or two a day. Sometimes that's all you do, sit on the couch and drink," Arlene interjected with obvious frustration.

"Thanks, Arlene. We'll get back to that in a moment. Allen, have you had any thoughts of killing yourself, or someone else?"

Allen lowered his eyes. "Yeah, I guess so. They come and go. I've thought of going down to Mason and taking out that bastard that laid me off. But what good would that do? Then I think of just getting rid of myself. I feel like such a loser, such a burden to Arlene and the kids now. And the kids are getting worried. I can tell." Tears welled up in Allen's eyes as he described his dejection and shame.

"What would you do?" asked the therapist.

"Well, I've got some guns. I've been collecting for a while. I think about which one would be neatest, which one would make the most noise, which one would take care of things. I've also thought of just sitting in the car and gassing myself. That would be less messy." Allen chuckled at the thought.

"Yeah, I guess it might. What keeps you from doing it?" the therapist asked.

"That's a good question. I don't really know. I just can't go on," Allen replied.

- What historical factors and current life circumstances influence suicide risk for men?
- How should Allen's therapist proceed with assessment from this point in the interview?

SUICIDE IN MEN: THE FACTS

When data on suicide are examined closely, the grim reality of the impact of depression on men is obvious. Studies of suicide have consistently found that men of all ages are at higher risk for suicide than are women (see Moscicki, 1997; Pritchard, 1996; Tsuang, Simpson, & Fleming, 1992). This finding holds true for men of all races (Buda & Tsuang, 1990). Suicide is the ninth leading cause of death in men, accounting for 25,950 deaths in 1995 (Anderson, Kochanek, & Murphy, 1997). At this rate, 20 out of 100,000 men will commit suicide in any given year, regardless of age or race. Table 7-1 summarizes estimates of suicide rates in men and women for varying age groups.

As demonstrated by the statistics presented in Table 7-1, suicide rates in men vary considerably with age. Suicide rates have increased signifi-

TABLE 7-1   Estimated Annual Suicide Rates per 100,000 by Age and Gender (1992–1997)

Age range	Men	Women	Male : Female
5–14	1.3	0.4	3.25
15–19	18.5	3.7	6.08
20–24	27.2	4.0	7.35
25–29	26.9	4.1	4.29
30–34	25.5	5.3	4.81
35–39	25.2	5.9	4.27
40–44	26.0	7.0	3.71
45–49	24.3	7.1	3.42
50–54	25.1	7.3	3.43
55–59	25.9	6.3	4.11
60–64	26.5	6.0	4.42
65–69	28.5	5.5	5.18
70–74	35.5	5.0	7.10
75–79	46.0	5.0	9.20
80–84	62.0	5.0	12.40
85+	75.0	5.0	15.00

Summarized from Anderson, Kochanek, & Murphy, 1997; Murphy, 1998.

cantly for both young men and older men in the past 25 years. Suicide is now the third leading cause of death for white males between the ages of 15 and 24 (Berman & Jobes, 1991). Suicide rates in men increase with advancing age as older men, perhaps suffering from physical ailments and unable to perceive any further meaning to their existence, take their lives in numbers approximately 8 to 10 times greater than women in similar age groups. Osgood and Thielman (1990) reported rates of suicide for elderly white men (men age 65 and over) to be 46.1 per 100,000 in 1987. The suicide rate was 57.1 per 100,000 for men from 75 to 84 years of age, and an astronomical 66.9 per 100,000 for men over 85 years of age.

In addition to the possible impact of declining health in older men, the effect of widowhood on elderly men has been identified as a prominent risk factor. The recent death of a spouse increases the risk of suicide in widowers to three to four times that of married men (Li, 1995). Marriage provides a protection against suicide for many men in our culture by decreasing the perceived acceptability of suicide for married men compared with married women (Stack, 1998).

Male suicide rates, presented in Table 7-1, document an alarming picture of the reality of suicide in depressed men. Not only do men outnumber women in these statistics, but the ratio of men to women that commit suicide is much higher than two-to-one, exceeding six-to-one in the adolescent–young adult age group, and increasing to an astonishing twelve-to-one to fifteen-to-one ratio for elderly men. How might we understand this dramatic and consistent trend? Do men simply choose more lethal means to commit suicide than women? Do other variables including cultural norms and social-role conditioning provide protection for women but exacerbate the risk of completing suicide in men (Murphy, 1998)? Whatever the reasons, the data compel us to look carefully at this issue for two reasons. First, we must increase our efforts to understand these disturbing findings so that we might begin to mount educational and prevention efforts aimed at decreasing suicide rates in men. Second, as clinicians we must be prepared to actively assess suicide risk and to intervene to prevent suicide when treating depressed men, since simply being a man dramatically increases risk for suicide.

Clinician Query—"I couldn't face not seeing
those kids again."

Tony, a 42-year-old, slightly overweight man, arrived at the inpatient unit of a psychiatric hospital with his friend, Brad. Tony had bags under his eyes, and looked as if he hadn't slept in several days. A few days earlier, Tony's wife had told him that their marriage was definitely over. The couple had been separated for nine months, but, according to Tony, had talked of reconciliation. He suspected that she had been having an affair with another man, but he had no definite proof. Tony had called Brad, a long-time friend, earlier in the evening and told him that he was going to end his life. Brad had rushed over to his house and found Tony sitting in a rocking chair in his living room with a loaded 9 millimeter handgun in his lap. He was staring at a picture of his wife, himself, and his two children. Next to his chair was fifth of tequila, half empty. Brad asked for the gun, and then spent two hours listening to Tony rant and rave about his wife and her unwillingness to give the marriage another chance.

The therapist at the acute psychiatric facility spent the next several hours interviewing Tony, his friend by his side.

"If Brad hadn't been home, what do you think would have happened?" queried the intake therapist.

"I hate to think about it. I was so ready to end it all. But some small part of me didn't want to do it," Tony replied, sipping on black coffee from a styrofoam cup.

"Have you had these suicidal feelings before?"

"Oh, yeah. But they would pass. I know that if Rachel and I were back together, I would be in a totally different state of mind. I miss my kids and that feeling of being a whole family."

"So tonight, you just lost hope that this was ever going to happen?"

"Yeah. I guess you could put it that way. I felt this way when I had to move out of the house several months ago. It was eerie to sit in that bare-walled rental place. It was cold and it reminded me of how bad I had screwed up," Tony recalled.

"You feel like you screwed up your marriage?"

"Definitely. If I wasn't such a prick to Rachel, she would-n't have gotten fed up with me. I took her for granted. All I want to show her now is that I'm willing to work on the relationship. I wish she'd give me one more chance."

"What pushed you to put the gun to your head tonight?"

"Well, I was drinking for one thing. I lost touch with reality there. I thought I'd make her pay for the rest of her life for rejecting me," he said, shaking his head while looking at the floor.

"What stopped you from following through?"

"That picture on the wall with my kids. My son is 9, and my daughter is 7. I couldn't face not seeing those kids again. I thought about how they might remember me. A father who was so selfish he blew his head off." Tony shook his head and glanced down at the floor again.

"Is your father alive?" the therapist questioned, trying to connect to the empathy Tony had for his kids in the moment.

"He's alive somewhere. I haven't seen him in years. What a bastard. I don't want to be a father like he was."

"You have strong feelings. Sounds like he wasn't much there for you"

"Damn straight. The bastard took off when I was a kid. He ran off with some other woman, leaving me and my brother alone with my mom. I don't know how many times I wished I could have killed the asshole. He doesn't have any clue as to how much pain he has caused us," Tony said, his voice escalating in volume as his pupils widened and his face sneered.

"You have a lot of anger at him."

"At times, I am as big an asshole as he was. That's when I get angry at myself. I don't want my kids to have to live through their childhood fearing or hating me," Tony replied with resignation.

"Maybe this time you can get some help in learning how to deal with your anger. You could give your kids a dad who can be there for them."

"I sure hope so," Tony concluded.

- In addition to alcoholism and access to firearms, what are other factors that increase risk of suicide in men?
- What are protective factors that might help decrease the likelihood of a man's committing suicide?

COMORBIDITY AND SUICIDE IN MEN

Men and women who make suicide attempts and who commit suicide have been found to suffer from a number of psychiatric and psychological disturbances. In addition to the obvious contribution of major depression and related mood disorders, two major conditions that dramatically increase risk of suicide for men are alcoholism or other substance abuse and severe personality disorders. Even though mood disorders, typically major depression, are present in completed suicides in as many as 90% of all cases, these two additional complicating conditions (alcoholism/substance abuse and personality disorder) are present in large numbers of suicides, particularly in men. These conditions, when combined with mood disorders, increase suicide risk by estimates that vary from fivefold to as much as twentyfold in instances in which more than one of these comorbid conditions are present.

Alcoholism, Substance abuse, and Suicide

Alcohol and other types of psychoactive substance abuse are associated with suicide in up to as many as 20 to 60% of completed suicides (Conwell, Duberstein, Cox, Hermann, Forbes, & Caine, 1996; Flavin, Franklin, & Frances, 1990; Fowler, Rich, & Young, 1986; Isometsa, Henriksson, Aro, Heikkinen, Kuoppasalmi, & Lonnquist, 1994). A large proportion of these completed suicides are men found to be suffering from both a mood disorder and a comorbid alcohol or substance abuse disorder. Isometsa, Heikkinen, Henriksson, Aro, Mantunnen, Kuoppasalmi, and Lonnquist (1996) found that suicide in men with nonmajor depression occurred primarily in men suffering from alcoholism (59%), personality disorders (53%), severe physical illness (47%), and other recent adverse life events. Young, Fogg, Scheftner, and Fawcett (1994) found that higher suicide rates in men are due to the fact that more men meet the criteria for alcoholism and drug abuse. Roy and Linnoila (1986) summarized findings from a number of studies of the sex distribution in alcoholic suicides and found that almost 90% of alcoholic suicides are committed by men. Alcoholism and alcohol abuse, as well as other drug abuse, clearly increase the likelihood of suicide in depressed men.

In these and a number of other studies, the consistent finding of an association between suicide and alcoholism and drug abuse in men warrants attention. Alcohol and drug intoxication most likely disinhibit the expression of violence. In the context of depression, such violent acting out of anger and aggression can frequently occur against the self (Plutchik, 1995). Since men are diagnosed more frequently with alcoholism and drug abuse, careful examination of the interactions of these conditions with depression and suicidal behavior is essential when working with depressed men.

Personality Disorder and Suicide in Men

The complicating influence of personality disorders in suicide attempts and completed suicides is well documented (Goldsmith, Fyer, & Frances, 1990). In addition to the contributions of alcohol and substance abuse, personality disturbances in the form of antisocial personality and conduct disorder are also implicated in a large percentage of male suicides. This is especially true for suicides in men under age 30. Beautrais, Joyce, Mulder, Fergusson, Deavoll, and Nightingale (1996) found that young men suffering from antisocial personality disorder are at greater risk for making a serious suicide attempt than are young women. In depressed men under the age of 30, the combination of two or more psychiatric disorders, including antisocial personality disorder, increased the likelihood of suicide attempt to high levels, with odds ratios as high as 56-to-1, compared with a comparable control group. Langhinrichsen-Rohling, Sanders, Crane, and Monson (1998) found that in a sample of college students, men reported engaging in more antisocial and potentially suicidal behavior than did women, even though the men and women in the sample reported similar symptoms of depression.

Additional Factors Associated with Increased Suicide Risk in Men

In addition to these obvious complications from comorbid psychiatric and psychological conditions, a number of other factors associated with suicide, suicidal thinking, and suicidal behavior have been identified. A family history of suicide greatly increases the risk of suicide in persons with mood disorders (Moscicki, 1997). Isolation from others has a high correlation with completed suicides, especially for men (Canetto, 1994). Poor health status and the perception of one's physical health as "not good" was associated with suicidal outcome in men in a sample of 2756 suicidal inpatients who were followed for 4 years after discharge from inpatient treatment (Motto & Bostrom, 1997). Disruptions in the family environment, including violence, incest, alcoholism and other substance abuse, and negative parenting, all contribute to increasing the odds of a completed suicide (Brown & Anderson, 1991; Maris, 1997; Moscicki, 1997). Dhaliwal, Gauzas, Antonowicz, and Ross (1996) reviewed studies that examined the effects of childhood sexual abuse on men and found that almost 90% of men in one study reported suicidal ideation or behavior. In another study, as many as 30% of the men who experienced childhood sexual abuse reported having made suicide attempts, while another 45% reported recurrent suicidal ideation. Clearly, the effects of chaotic and dysfunctional family environments in childhood, especially those characterized by violence, sexual abuse, and incest, have a negative and exacerbating effect on the risk of suicide in adult men.

Suicide (violence against the self) and domestic violence (violence against others) are often related. The relationship between depression in men and domestic violence is strong (Hamberger & Hastings, 1991; Pan, Neidig, & O'Leary, 1994). Men are mostly the perpetrators of combined homicide–suicide acts in both the United States and Great Britain. Felthouse and Hempel (1995) found that over 90% of the perpetrators of combined homicide–suicide acts were men, and fully 75 to 90% of the victims were women. Several additional studies have found that men who are at risk of suicide are also at increased risk for violence (e.g., Greenwald, Reznikoff, & Plutchik, 1994; Plutchik, 1995), and that a family history of violence increases these risks significantly (Gortner, Gollan, & Jacobson, 1997). In addition, combinations of alcoholism, substance abuse, and antisocial personality disorder are also associated with increased risk of violence and homicidal behaviors, especially in the context of a mood disorder (Asnis, Kaplan, Hundorfean, & Saeed, 1997). When assessing depressed men for suicide risk, the close connections between depression, suicide, domestic violence, and homicide must be taken into consideration by the clinician.

As men grow older, the influence of antisocial behaviors and alcohol and drug abuse frequently begins to abate. Concerns with health, in conjunction with depression, begin to be more salient for men as they approach the end of their life span. Studies with older men have found that the presence of depression, usually by itself or in conjunction with failing health, is more often associated with suicide (Rich, Young, & Fowler, 1986). Other psychiatric disorders that further exacerbate the likelihood of suicide in depressed men include primary affective disorder and schizophrenia (Black & Winokur, 1990).

Several consistent findings are apparent when the factors that are associated with completed suicides and suicide attempts in men are examined. The influence of alcoholism and other drug abuse is of paramount importance, and makes assessment of these conditions in the context of assessing male depression essential. In addition to these conditions, the association of antisocial personality disorder with completed suicides and suicide attempts has been frequently noted. Additional factors associated with suicide attempts and completed suicide are summarized in Table 7-2.

TABLE 7-2   Factors Increasing Risk for Suicide Attempts and Suicide in Depressed Men

---

- Alcohol abuse and alcoholism
- Drug abuse, especially in young men
- Antisocial personality disorder, especially in young men
- History of conduct disorder
- History of sexual abuse
- History of suicide in family of origin
- History of violence in family of origin
- Co-occurring psychiatric disorder (e.g., schizophrenia, affective disorder)
- Physical illness, especially in older men

METHODS OF COMMITTING SUICIDE

Methods used for committing suicide vary somewhat between men and women. Table 7-3 summarizes the methods chosen by men and women to commit suicide in a selected year (1987) in the United States. As these data indicate, use of firearms is the suicide method chosen most frequently by both men and women. This includes handguns as well as shotguns and other firearms. Hanging is the second most frequently chosen method for men, whereas overdoses of medications are second for women. Asphyxiation by gases or other vapors is next in rank for men, followed by other means such as jumping from building or other self-inflicted violent behaviors intended to kill oneself. Ingestion of drugs or other medicaments is the least chosen suicide method for men (Buda & Tsuang, 1990; National Center for Health Statistics, 1987).

In light of the fact that most men (as well as women) commit suicide by using a firearm, access and availability to firearms is an essential element of assessment of depression and suicide risk in men. Adamek and Kaplan (1996) found that for men over age 65, firearms account for over 80% of suicides, highlighting the importance of this variable in risk assessment for elderly men who are depressed or suicidal.

Although it is tempting to speculate that men's increased suicide rates are simply an artifact of the method chosen, and that men might choose more definitively lethal means, both men and women choose firearms for committing suicide. Perhaps the choice of medications by some women to commit suicide is, in fact, less frequently lethal. However, when the percentages of men using firearms and medications are combined, the resulting numbers are very similar to those for women. Sixty-nine percent of suicides completed by men are accomplished using

TABLE 7-3   Methods of Committing Suicide by Sex (1987)

Method chosen	Men (% suicides)	Women (% suicides)
Firearms (not handguns)	52%	31%
Handguns	11%	9%
Total firearms	63%	40%
Hanging, strangulation	14%	12%
Gases and vapors	10%	13%
Drugs, medications	6%	26%
All other means	6%	9%

Summarized from Buda & Tsuang (1990).

firearms and medications. Sixty-six percent of suicides completed by women are accomplished using firearms and medications. These two methods account for the same proportions of suicides in both sexes.

INCREASED RISK OF SUICIDE IN MEN

Data on suicide attempts and completions clearly paint a grim picture for depressed men: depressed men complete suicide in very high numbers. Even if it is true that there are fewer men who suffer from a diagnosable clinical depression, there are many men who take their own and others' lives and who must be in the throes of some kind of depressive disorder. This is especially troubling since men visit therapists' offices less frequently than do women, and often will mask their depression through alcohol and substance abuse and other dangerous or distracting behaviors. This indirect or masked expression of depressive symptoms, including suicidal thinking and behavior, obscures the issue of suicide in a host of apparently unrelated concerns and complications.

Most persons with major depression who are at risk for suicidal behavior are undertreated (Oquendo, Malone, Ellis, Sackeim, & Mann, 1999). This is especially of concern when taken together with findings from one investigation that found that men who committed suicide had received less treatment than had women (Isometsa, Henriksson, Aro, *et al.,* 1994). Clearly, in addition to depression's being undetected and untreated in men, suicide risk is underestimated and undertreated in men. Such a situation results in large numbers of depressed men being at greatly increased risk for suicide.

Data from suicide attempts and completions enables us to identify a number of risk factors, both historical and immediate, that increase the likelihood that a given man at a given time will commit suicide. This information, combined with the knowledge that depressed men are, by virtue of their sex, at increased risk for suicide, can assist in careful assessment of suicide risk in men.

Clinician Query—"I wish I had known."
The therapist mulled it over again and again. "What could I have done? Why didn't I see this coming? Why didn't I get him into a hospital? Why didn't he tell me he was going to do this? I wonder if I should be practicing therapy?" All of these questions go through the mind of anyone who has been treating a patient who has successfully committed sui-

cide. Even if it was known that a person had made previous attempts, that the problems were longstanding, and that one could not sit watch 24 hours a day with a patient, it is difficult not to find fault with yourself when it happens to you.

Drew was a ruggedly handsome 33-year-old married man who had struggled most of his life with identity difficulties. He had recently gotten married for the third time. Drew had dropped out of college in his sophomore year and never returned, though he often repeated that he wished he had. He had grown up in an affluent area but now lived in a lower middle-class neighborhood. In the past three months, he had lost another job and had again been bailed out by his father, a successful chief financial officer at a large corporation. His father had given him a large sum of money to pay his bills and "hold him over" until he was back on his feet again. This had been a typical pattern since he had dropped out of college. Drew described his wife during sessions as "really nagging" him about finding a good job so they could "get out of this dump" they were living in. His younger brother had recently become an executive with an established company, buying a house in the same affluent area in which his family had lived. Drew often commented that his life felt like a lot of pressures.

The following interchange occurred in the last session before he committed suicide by asphyxiation in the garage of his house.

"I wish I could finish something. I never seem to be able to hang onto jobs or relationships. It's really discouraging."

"This sounds like a broken record. You really want to do life differently, but somehow it's hard for you to see yourself as other than a failure," his therapist commented, having known Drew for four years in their therapy relationship.

"I know you've told me many times that life begins today and that I seem to sabotage myself with the negative self-talk. But it seems like I'm running in place. Dad bails me out as I look for another job. My wife is already getting on my case and we've only been married for six months."

Drew paused and let out a deep sigh.

"You seem overwhelmed. Be honest with me. Are you having any of those suicidal thoughts or feelings?" his therapist inquired, knowing that Drew had a history of suicidal ideation and two attempts, one as a teenager and another in his midtwenties.

"I'm definitely feeling low. I don't know if I'd call it suicidal. I do imagine that it would be easier for my family and my wife to live without me. I'm really tired of my own excuses for my lame life."

"That sounds pretty desperate to me. Have you thought about how you might kill yourself?"

"Wow! I can't believe you are asking me this. I haven't given it much thought. I don't think I have the guts to follow through with it. I can't finish anything else, so I'm not likely to finish my own life in that way."

"I'm still uncomfortable with the fact that you are feeling so low right now. Would you be willing to spend some time at the hospital for a few days voluntarily until some of these feelings pass?"

"I don't think so. I'm not suicidal, just a bit depressed. Nothing worse than it has ever been," Drew said, trying to convince his therapist that he could take care of himself.

"Okay. Would you promise me that you will call me if you feel like you want to take your life so we can talk? I'll be here for you."

"Don't worry. I can take care of myself."

As Drew left the office after his session, his therapist recalled that he felt uneasy but that Drew had sounded this way before and had always faithfully returned for his weekly therapy session. When Drew missed his next session, his therapist became alarmed and called his home. His wife told him that she had found Drew dead in their car in the garage. His therapist tried to keep his composure and strained to help her process her own feelings, but he was internally devastated. He resumed his own psychotherapy to sort out his competency issues that had been stirred up by his patient's suicide.

- What are the most serious risk factors for men who commit suicide?
- How can a therapist minimize the probability that a patient will successfully commit suicide?

ASSESSMENT OF SUICIDE RISK IN MEN

In light of men's higher risk for suicide, careful assessment of suicide risk is essential when treating men for depression. This assessment of risk in men focuses on specifying the level of risk and identifying the contribution of any comorbid conditions that increase suicide risk in the context of male depression. These comorbid conditions include alcohol and other drug abuse, personality disturbances, and other serious psychiatric disorders, such as schizophrenia or bipolar disorder. After assessment of suicide risk is completed, appropriate interventions to minimize the likelihood that a man will commit suicide can be planned and implemented.

The foundation of accurate suicide risk assessment is the clinical interview. A number of authors (e.g., Berman & Jobes, 1991; Bongar, 1991; Chiles & Strosahl, 1995; Hendren, 1990; Sommers–Flanagan & Sommers–Flanagan, 1995) have outlined various approaches to the assessment of suicide risk with adolescents and adults. Hendren (1990) offers specific interviewing and assessment strategies that are geared to the patient's developmental level. Chiles and Strosahl (1995) recommend contextualizing the assessment process, depending upon whether the clinician is working within an assessment of risk context or within a treatment context in which suicidal risk arises. Within each of these contexts, Sommers–Flanagan and Sommers–Flanagan (1995) recommend five foci for assessment: severity of depression, suicidal ideation, suicide plans, capacity for self-control, and suicidal intent.

In addition to these considerations, assessment of both distal and proximal risk factors (Moscicki, 1997) contributes to refinement in understanding the context of a given suicide risk assessment. Distal risk factors decrease the threshold for containment of suicidal action. These include depression, alcoholism, personal vulnerability to abandonment or loss, history of family violence, and an impulsive response tendency. Proximal risk factors act as precipitants for a suicidal act. These can include stressful life events, isolation, medical disorders, accessibility to firearms or medications, and alcohol or drug intoxication. Hall, Platt, and Hall (1999) found that severe anxiety, acute depression, recent relationship loss, alcohol or substance intoxication, hopelessness, insomnia, and medical illness, in descending order, were recent stresses or events most predictive of suicide attempts. The contribution of these and other proximal risk factors must be carefully assessed in any discussion of suicide with depressed men.

Table 7-4 outlines the essential elements of assessment of suicide risk in depressed men. A prerequisite for effective assessment is the rapid establishment of rapport with the patient. This is accomplished by a calm approach to the task at hand, an attitude of respect toward the patient, and an acknowledgement of the psychological pain and suffering of the patient. Establishing rapport with depressed, potentially violent, men may prove challenging for many therapists. Therefore, a thorough grasp of countertransference dynamics that might be activated when working in this context is important for any therapist to have.

The assessment of depression follows the basic points covered in chapter 6. The *DSM-IV* specifies symptoms for assessing and diagnosing

TABLE 7-4   Assessment of Suicide Risk in Men

- Severity or level of depression
  1. based on diagnostic criteria
  2. patient-rated severity and level of distress
- Proximal risk factors
  1. acute intoxication
  2. isolation
  3. psychosis, delusional thinking
  4. relationship or job loss, failure experiences
  5. acute anxiety, restlessness, agitation
  6. medical illness
- Presence and intensity of suicidal ideation
- Presence and specificity of suicide plan
- Access to means to commit suicide
  1. firearms
  2. ropes for hanging
  3. combustion engine and enclosed garage
  4. prescription medications
- Capacity for self-control and containment of depression
  1. previous suicide attempt
  2. willingness to work with therapist to manage depression
- Specific suicidal intent
  1. patient-rated level of intent to follow through
  2. indirect evidence ("put affairs in order," giving away valued possessions, notes)
- Exacerbating conditions or circumstances
  1. anger as predominant affect
  2. hopelessness
- Protective factors available or accessible
  1. social support—family, work, school, neighbors
  2. cooperation with therapist in planning for safety
  3. psychiatric consultation

---

depression. These symptoms include depressed mood; diminished interest or pleasure in daily activities; changes in weight and sleep patterns; psychomotor retardation or agitation; fatigue; feelings of worthlessness or excessive guilt; decreased concentration; and finally, thoughts of death and suicide. Coverage of each of these nine symptoms is best woven into an interview that ebbs and flows as the clinician inquires into the current life circumstances of the patient and the implications of thoughts of death and suicide.

Brief self-report inventories, such as the Beck Depression Inventory or the Beck Hopelessness Inventory, may be utilized for the purpose of obtaining a simple evaluation of the severity of the patient's current mood disturbance. A patient-generated rating scale may also be utilized by asking the patient to rate, on a scale of 1 to 10, or even 1 to 100, the severity of his depressed mood. A rating of 1 would indicate minimal depression, while a rating of 10, or 100, would represent the most extreme feelings of depression that might cause the person to commit suicide. The self-rating gives both a quantitative and a personally meaningful self-assessment of how close the patient may be to a psychological state in which suicide would be not only thinkable but preferred.

The ninth criterion for assessing a depressive episode, thoughts of death and suicide, provides a convenient link to more direct and explicit exploration of these thoughts with the patient. It is common for persons suffering from depression to think of death and suicide. The clinician can evaluate the specificity of these thoughts. This will lead to an exploration of the patient's contemplation of the method for committing suicide as well as the availability of the means to carry out the plan. In evaluating suicide risk, greater specificity of the method and availability of the means greatly increase the extant risk of the patient committing suicide. For men, as well as women, the use of a firearm is a significant risk factor. For men, the use of rope for hanging, the use of a car for asphyxiation, or the use of other means by which to poison or gas oneself are significant risk factors.

The assessment of the patient's capacity for self-control examines current and past efforts to inhibit impulsive acting out as well as previous suicide attempts. The ability to inhibit self-destructive impulses and tolerate painful affective states is of paramount importance in the patient's ultimate decision to choose to stay alive. Past suicide attempts, whether designed to end life or simply to call attention to the patient's suffering, indicate an inability to inhibit the self-destructive impulse and are a significant risk factor. This is especially true if the patient reports that he was disappointed that his attempt to end his life had failed.

In addition to specific suicide attempts, the utilization of other acting out behavior to ward off painful affective states signifies difficulty in managing painful affect and may also signify increased risk. Examples of such behavior include going on a drinking binge after being rejected by a romantic partner, driving recklessly after being informed of a demotion at work, or getting into a fight at a bar after losing a sports event. These behaviors, while not directly intended to end one's life, signify a weakness in the patient's ability to contain and manage disturbing and painful affective states—a key capacity in weathering suicidal feelings.

Finally, within the context of suicidal feelings and thoughts, it is important to assess suicidal intent. Suicidal intent refers to the specific intent to act on a suicidal plan with the expected outcome that the patient would end his life. After questions regarding suicidal thinking and feeling have been explored, and as the interviewer is formulating a specific assessment of suicidal risk, a direct inquiry into the patient's intention to follow through on the plan is recommended. This may take the form of a question such as, "Since we have been discussing the thoughts you have about ending your life, and the way in which you would do this, how likely do you think it is that you will actually act on these thoughts?" Such a question invites the patients to clarify for himself and for the interviewer the extent of his self-control and the degree to which the interviewer must be concerned about the patient's safety. It is not unusual, in the context of evaluating suicidal intent, for a patient to exclaim, "Oh, I would never actually do it; it would be simply devastating to my wife and kids." Such statements must be evaluated carefully and considered in the context of the interview and the patient's involvement in his therapy. A statement such as this may actually refer to the inner capacity to resist such impulses and may lead the clinician to conclude that, at least for now, the patient is relatively safe. Such a statement may also be designed to deflect further inquiry into the area due to the patient's serious and unresolved ambivalence about these feelings.

Clinician Query—"I feel like I've never been wanted
in my life."

Jerry was a large, 53-year-old divorced man with long hair, a beard, and prominent tattoos covering most of his body. He had been admitted to the Veteran's Hospital because of a suicide attempt. Police had arrested Jerry for assault following an altercation at a rock concert in which Jerry had punched a security guard. While in jail, he had cut his wrist on a scrap of metal he had twisted from a spring of the bunk, and he had announced to the jailers that he was going to kill himself. Jerry was transferred to the Veteran's Hospital after the jailer had discovered that he had been an ongoing patient in the outpatient psychiatry clinic and had been frequently admitted to the inpatient unit over the past 20 years.

Jerry had served in a combat unit in the Vietnam War, and had been the lone survivor of a platoon that had been ambushed. He came from an abusive family in which he and his two siblings were moved into group homes during adolescence. Jerry was married for a brief time, and has remained isolated since he was divorced. He was interviewed by a new therapist at the Veteran's Hospital who had not had previous contact with him.

"What happened the other night, Jerry?" he asked.

"I just flipped out. I felt like a caged animal, and didn't have any way to get out of there."

"At the concert or the jail?"

"First, it was at the concert. I was just enjoying myself, smoking a doobie, when this security dude shined his flashlight at me. I smiled at him but he seemed really determined to get me so I tried to take off out of my seat. He must have called some other guys, because before I knew it there were two or three of them on me. I fought them but I got tried and the next thing I know I'm down at the city jail."

"What were you thinking and feeling when you got to the jail?" his therapist inquired.

"I really thought I was going to die. I hate lockup. It's so degrading. I just wanted to get it over with."

"So you tried to kill yourself?"

"Yeah. I began cutting myself with this piece of metal I found sticking out of the bunk. I started bleeding, and the other guys in the cell started calling for the guards."

"How does it feel to be here? Do you still feel like killing yourself."

"It's okay. to be here. I feel pretty safe. I always feel like there is a part of me that wants to die. Do you know what I mean?"

"No, tell me about it," requested his therapist.

"Well, it's a long story. It's like I never felt like I have ever really been wanted, so I've had to pretend my whole life that there was some meaning to things," Jerry started.

"Never felt wanted by who?" his therapist followed.

"My parents. My teachers. My friends. Nobody. I thought that joining the army during the war would give me some purpose. I felt like I had nothing to lose. Man, was I wrong. Those frigging gooks killed all the guys I knew. It was like I finally had some friends. You had to trust these guys with your life, and then in a split moment, they were chopped liver." Jerry stopped abruptly, stared straight past the therapist, and became mute for several minutes.

"What just happened?" his therapist asked when Jerry's gaze returned.

"Oh. I can remember that day like it was yesterday. I still don't know how I live through it. I really wished I hadn't," Jerry responded.

"Like you don't deserve to be alive?"

"Yeah. I just wished God or somebody would get this over with already. Life is too much for me. Just put me out of my misery."

- What effect does early trauma and repetitive trauma have on the development of depression and suicidality in men?
- What is the role of suicidal ideation in the psychodynamics of male trauma survivors?

MANAGEMENT OF SUICIDE RISK

Assessment of suicide risk invariably directs clinician attention to the management of suicide risk. Goals and strategies for management of suicide risk may vary, depending upon the context in which the clinician is functioning. Chiles and Strosahl (1995) outline two contexts in which management of suicide risk occurs: an assessment context and a treatment context. In an assessment context, specification of the level of suicide risk and the implementation of more immediate, shorter-term strategies to contain emergent suicide danger are emphasized. In a treatment context, analysis of the level of suicide risk is balanced with the strength of the therapeutic alliance and active decision-making regard-

TABLE 7-5   Management of Suicide Risk in Men

- Increase tolerance of depressive affect
  1. explicit empathy
  2. cognitive restructuring
  3. behavioral tasks to reduce depressive affect (sporting activities, work out)
  4. reality testing and education regarding pain tolerance
- Decrease access to lethal means of committing suicide
  1. hold weapon
  2. destroy medications
  3. transfer custody of other lethal means to other persons
- Decrease potential impact of other proximal risk factors
  1. decrease isolation
  2. decrease alcohol or other drug use or abuse
  3. psychiatric referral for evaluation of delusional or psychotic symptoms
- Strengthen environmental supports
  1. enlist family and friends as appropriate
  2. work and school release
- Strengthen therapeutic alliance
  1. increase session frequency
  2. allow between-session access (sit in waiting room)
  3. check in between sessions by phone, electronic mail
  4. no-suicide contract
- Consider hospitalization to insure safety
  1. high immediate risk, intent
  2. inability of patient to cooperate in reducing risk
  3. acute intoxication (alcohol or other drugs)
  4. psychosis
  5. absence of family or social support for protection

ing whether treatment would be best served in an outpatient or inpatient setting.

Management of suicide risk will require the clinician to balance an ongoing assessment of the degree of immediate suicide risk with planning and implementing interventions designed to decrease immediate risk. A number of authors offer guidelines and recommendations for decreasing immediate suicide risk in the context of both assessment and treatment (e.g., Berman & Jobes, 1991; Bongar, 1991; Chiles & Strosahl, 1995; Blumenthal & Kupfer, 1990; Maltsberger, 1986).

Several common factors are important as the clinician engages in managing suicidal risk (see Table 7-5). First, therapeutic interventions to increase tolerance of depressive and painful affect are helpful in decreasing the intrusive and burdensome nature of severe depression. Second, strategies designed to limit access to means of committing suicide may interrupt the patient's plans for committing suicide. Third, clinician activities that address other aspects of danger related to proximal risk factors, such as acute intoxication or active psychosis, minimize the negative impact of these risk factors. Fourth, the clinician can make efforts to increase environmental support systems where appropriate. And finally, bolstering the therapeutic alliance by increasing session frequency, offering between-session access, and the use of no-suicide contracts or agreements may increase the level of support felt by the patient.

In working with men, a number of therapeutic interventions may be geared toward increasing tolerance of painful depressive affect. Direct empathy and explicit affirmation of the therapeutic alliance may decrease feelings of isolation and palliate depressed mood. Cognitive therapy interventions that might be used include monitoring and rating level of depression, graded task assignments designed to alleviate depressed mood or increase positive mood states, and analysis and reframing of cognitions related to depression.

At times, direct reality-testing or education-oriented interventions may be helpful. Such strategies are designed to undo the negative effect of male gender-role socialization and to assist in helping the man develop perspective on his emotional life. Male gender-role socialization views sadness and any display of depressive affect as unmasculine and undesirable. Direct statements that support the depressed man in his specific situation while "normalizing" his experience of depression may be helpful in increasing his capacity to tolerate depressed mood. The significance of simply responding directly to the man's affective state can never by minimized when working with men in therapy. Existential approaches to treatment (Cochran & Rabinowitz, 1996; Yalom, 1980) often will help engage the man in a frank and open discussion about his current predicament. This perspective also provides a linkage to direct assessment and discussion of the meaning of life and the option of suicide as a solution to the patients's problems.

Another crucial aspect of therapeutic activity when managing suicide risk is effort designed to decrease access to means of committing suicide. Direct questioning has already helped the therapist gain information about the specificity of the patient's plan and his access to the means of carrying out the plan. Empirical studies show that access to firearms is one of the most dangerous proximal risk factors that significantly increases the immediate probability that a man will commit suicide. Offering to hold a weapon or identifying other persons who might be enlisted to assist in such an intervention would be one appropriate therapeutic strategy to decrease or eliminate access to lethal means. It is generally not useful for the therapist to engage in a debate or power struggle with the man over who will assume custody of a weapon or how such risk will be managed. At times, the impossibility of resolving such debates signifies a level of danger that cannot be managed in the context of a typical outpatient treatment regimen. Such power struggles are often a means by which the patient externalizes his own ambivalence about staying alive. By engaging in such a struggle the patient is expressing his preference for the therapist to take action and help resolve his indecision.

While these strategies are helpful in the context of an established therapeutic relationship with the depressed man, additional therapeutic activity may be directed toward decreasing or diffusing the potential impact of proximal risk factors. In addition to decreasing access to lethal means by which to commit suicide, these activities include efforts to decrease social isolation, efforts to eliminate alcohol or drug use, interventions to manage emergent symptoms that might signify decompensation or psychosis, and continuing focus on treatment of the underlying mood disorder.

Additional clinician activity that might be directed to strengthening environmental supports includes enlisting family or friends to assist in the treatment plan as appropriate. Although often family relationships, or disrupted intimate relationships, may be a root cause of the man's distress, identification of persons the man perceives as supportive will often decrease the intensity of immediate suicidal ideation or intent. Arranging for reduced work or school schedule until the suicidal phase has passed may also be an appropriate support for the clinician to offer.

Within the context of a therapeutic relationship in which suicide risk management emerges, a number of strategies may be enlisted by the clinician to strengthen and bolster the therapeutic bond with the patient. First, the therapist can increase the frequency of session contact. Moving session frequency from one time per week to twice or thrice weekly will often assist in containment of suicidal impulses between sessions. In extreme cases, daily sessions may be required until an immediate crisis has passed. In addition, the therapist can invite extra-session phone contact, or "check-in" calls if extra sessions are not possible. Electronic mail could also be considered as a short-term means of checking in with the therapist. Finally, simply allowing the patient to come to the office and sit in the waiting room if this would result in a greater sense of connection to the therapist would be warranted. Of course, the extent to which such strategies might provide untoward disruptions in the therapeutic framework must be considered. However, it is always important to balance a rigid adherence to the "ground rules" of therapy with those compassionate efforts designed to help a patient "over a hump," so that he can continue and benefit from the ongoing therapy relationship. After all, a dead patient is a treatment disaster in any orientation to therapy.

If a man is unable to cooperate in creating conditions that will assure his own safety, hospital treatment may be warranted. This is always a difficult decision for a clinician to make, since it creates disruptions in the man's life and is often extremely costly financially. However, there are often situations in which the safety of a controlled hospital environment is required to assure the patient's safety. Several factors must be taken into consideration when assessing a depressed man for hospital versus outpatient treatment. First, and foremost, is the level of suicide risk. Obviously, the risk must be high and immediate. Often, this involves strong suicidal ideation, the presence of a plan, the means to carry out the plan, and the intent to take action.

Other factors that increase the immediate risk of suicide and that should be taken into consideration when making decisions about hospital treatment include absence of social support networks, acute intoxication with alcohol or other mood-altering substances, active psychosis, and inability or unwillingness to cooperate with a treatment plan. Each of these factors, taken in isolation, may not trigger the decision to utilize a hospital environment. However, more than one in conjunction with a high level of suicide risk should alert the clinician to the possibility that hospital management might be more appropriate than outpatient management.

CODA: COUNTERTRANSFERENCE AND THE MANAGEMENT OF SUICIDE RISK IN MEN

Maltsberger (1986) and Kahn (1990) both emphasize the importance of therapist countertransference that is frequently activated by working with suicidal patients. In working with men who may be at risk for suicide, there are three sources of potential countertransference interference. These three sources of potential countertransference difficulty arise from therapist internalized gender-role values, threats to the therapeutic alliance, and temptations to debate philosophical issues around suicide. It is important for therapists to examine the potential contribution that each of these areas might make in her or his own countertransference reactions to working with suicidal men.

Therapists are subject to the same cultural conditioning and socialization processes as men. As such, therapists also have been exposed to various dysfunctional and detrimental values and norms relating to masculinity, the same as their male patients. These values and attitudes impact therapists' perceptions of male patients, as well as the responses that therapists make to their male patients' struggles and difficulties. How a given therapist might respond to a male patient's feelings of hopelessness and resignation in the face of seemingly insurmountable personal difficulties is, to a significant degree, shaped by the therapist's own beliefs about appropriate masculine behavior. Is the therapist empathic in responding to a situation such as this, or does he or she respond from a therapeutic stance based on unhealthy or dysfunctional values about male behavior? Therapist values and norms around issues of male anger, hostility, and violence will surely be tested when working with male patients who are suicidal. How does the therapist feel about a male who behaves in a helpless, clinging manner or whose hostility is so frightening to the therapist that it threatens to overwhelm the therapeutic alliance?

Interference from internalized dysfunctional attitudes around masculinity is particularly damaging to the therapist's ability to maintain empathic connection in the therapeutic relationship with the suicidal male client. In the face of hostility, helplessness, and potential violence, it is important for the therapist to maintain connection with the male patient. Yet often it is easier, in the face of such common distancing and controlling tactics of a male patient, for a therapist to disengage and withdraw himself or herself. Such disengagement may only recapitulate relational trauma for the male patient, thus feeding feelings of hopelessness and abandonment. A masculine-sensitive lens through which the therapist can clearly see the emotional pain and neediness that lies beneath such tactics on the part of the patient is an essential support that assists in maintaining therapist connection. By identifying and addressing issues related to internalized dysfunctional attitudes about masculinity within himself or herself, a therapist will be prepared to act decisively and confidently when faced with such behavior in the therapy relationship.

In addition to these obvious countertransference issues that will be activated by the patient's behavior, the therapist should also have a clear position on philosophical questions such as free-will versus involuntary commitment and physician-assisted suicide in the face of protracted suffering and terminal illness. A cognitive "let's debate this issue" stance is commonly encountered when working with men in therapy. Such a stance may be particularly appealing for the suicidal male patient, who would prefer to avoid looking at his own feelings of helplessness and hopelessness rather than engage with the therapist in an effort to manage them. Debating issues related to suicide will serve no useful purpose when working with a suicidal male patient, and may only exacerbate a feeling of disconnection and isolation, since the therapist is communicating that he is uncomfortable confronting these typically unacceptable emotional states in men. Confidence that is gained from clearly thought-out positions on such philosophical issues will assist the therapist in disengaging from debate around such issues when it arises.

SUMMARY

Men commit suicide in alarming numbers. Paradoxically, the men who appear to be most privileged and comfortable in our culture, white American men, are most at risk for committing suicide. Therapists working with depressed men must be prepared to assess and manage suicide risk.

A number of conditions greatly increase the risk of suicide in men. Two particularly dangerous conditions are comorbid alcoholism or substance abuse and antisocial personality. Alcohol and other substance abuse most likely disinhibits the containment and expression of aggressive, suicidal, or homicidal impulses in men. Thus, in men who are also suffering from major depression, a potentially lethal combination is created. The impulsive and dangerous behavior patterns associated with antisocial personality often contribute to the potential for injury or violence. Taken together with an underlying mood disorder that might cause suicidal feelings, factors such as these create a dangerous, although common, situation for depressed men.

Since men commit suicide at such great rates, a clinician working with depressed men must be prepared to assess and manage suicide risk. Guidelines for assessment of suicide risk assist the clinician in navigating this challenging aspect of treatment of depressed men. Recommendations for managing suicide risk lend support and offer guidance for the clinician, who must collaborate with the suicidal patient to insure his safety and survival. In addition to increasing knowledge about guidelines for assessing and managing suicidal risk in men, the clinician must be aware of his or her own countertransference reactions. Working with depressed and suicidal men is difficult, challenging, yet frequently quite rewarding for the therapist who is willing to take on such a task and "hang in there" with her or his male patient.

CHAPTER 8

Reflections on Theorizing, Diagnosing, and Treating Male Depression

In a journey of compassion what we have ultimately as our guide is whatever understanding we may have gained along the way about ourselves and others; chiefly those close to us, so close to us that we have lived daily in their sufferings. From here on, then, in the blinding smoke, it is no longer a "seeing world" but a "feeling world"—the pain of others and our compassion for them.

Norman Maclean

How Do Men Figure in the Research on Depression?
A Research Agenda to Illuminate Male Depression
    Within-Group Differences
    Gender-Role Strain
    Masked Depression
    Depressive Spectrum Disease
    Qualitative Inquiry
Optimizing Assessment and Treatment of Depression in Men
    Psychotherapy and Pharmacotherapy for Depressed Men
    Assessment of Depression Must Identify Depressed Men
    How Can We Reduce the Risk of Suicide in Men?
    Training Programs Must Educate Their Students about Depression in Men

In the numerous articles, monographs, book chapters, and books that have been written on depression, very little specifically addresses male depression. Even less material is available in the research literature that illuminates a clear perspective through which to view the phenomenon

Young Men and Fire (p. 296)

of male depression. Yet, so many men could be helped with the knowledge currently available. As we welcome increasing numbers of men to
our consulting rooms, we will undoubtedly encounter the diverse manifestations of male depression. As we recognize and respond to male
depression, we will find that these men benefit a great deal from treatment interventions offered in an empathic and gender-sensitive context.
Recognition of the scarcity of research findings combined with the
clinical reality of the suffering of depressed men and their loved ones
motivated us to write this book about this neglected, but important,
topic. Having now reviewed the research literature on male depression,
the outcome studies pertaining to the treatment of depression, and the
various theories proffered to account for depression, we come full-circle
to ask what understanding we have gained. Where has our "journey of
compassion" led? Where might it continue to lead into the future?

HOW DO MEN FIGURE IN THE RESEARCH ON DEPRESSION?

As we have studied the research literature on depression, we have asked
what we can learn from it about men and male depression. Much of this
research is characterized by attempts to account for the overrepresentation of women in our diagnostic categories and treatment settings. We
conclude that much of this research is not so clear-cut, but is mixed and
open to various interpretations. In large-scale studies utilizing heterogeneous population samples, the incidence and prevalence statistics on
depression are well known to most professionals. The data from these
studies indicate that men suffer from depression at about half the rate
that women suffer. Fewer men endorse fewer symptoms, and thus we
find fewer men in the final tabulations in all categories of mood disorders. Often, many of us stop here in our attempts to understand male
depression. We may be tempted to conclude that depression is simply
not a serious or widespread disorder in men.

However, there are an increasing number of research findings that
diverge from these well-known results. Chinese-American men, elderly
men, Orthodox Jews in London, men in Canadian Atlantic communities,
all appear to suffer from depression in numbers equal to the women in
comparable populations. In some instances, the men are actually found to
outnumber the women in the mood disorder categories. How are we to
make sense of these results? Something about the men and women in

these studies causes their responses to questions about depressed mood to differ from those men and women in most of the familiar studies.

In spite of the rigorous designs of the Epidemiological Catchment Area study and the National Comorbidity Survey, these two studies have been widely interpreted to support an oversimplistic conclusion that women generally are more depressed than men and that more women than men suffer from depression in all its forms. In the increasing number of studies that find men to be at least as depressed as women, the interplay of cultural forces with psychopathology is clearly implicated. In many cultural groups, perhaps those whose cultural value systems diverge substantially from late twentieth-century American culture, men and women are more alike in terms of identifying and acknowledging psychological distress, including depression.

Then, when we look at the ways in which men and women suffer with depressive disorders, we find that men and women are remarkably alike. The actual course of depression—the type and severity of symptoms experienced, the length of an episode of depression, the time it takes to recover from an episode of depression, as well as the impact of psychotherapy or pharmacotherapy on depression—is, for all practical purposes, identical for men and women. This is borne out in our consulting rooms, too, as both men and women relate to us their suffering associated with depression in much the same way. Empathic listening reveals the same underlying sadness, anxiety, and frustrations in both men and women.

These findings on the clinical nature of depression, taken together with the increasing number of studies that challenge the typical two-to-one ratio of women to men in depressive disorders, cause us to conclude that the characteristics of unipolar depression manifestated by men and women are mainly socially derived. Cultural prohibitions on male depression, including prohibitions on expressing sadness or tears, contribute to a more externalized, idiosyncratic expression of depression in men. This male depression, contorted by the restrictive and silencing impact of contemporary cultural norms about masculinity such as "Big boys don't cry," "Keep a stiff upper lip," and "Be strong and in control," is channeled into socially sanctioned outlets.

These outlets for male depression frequently include anger, aggression, addictions, and violence. Many more men are found to be suffering from alcoholism, drug addictions, and violence-related syndromes in the large epidemiological studies we have reviewed. When the numbers of men in the addiction and aggression-related categories are added to the numbers of men in the depression categories, we find totals very comparable to the numbers of women in the depression categories. Do cultural forces shaping the expression of depressed mood disperse men who suffer from depression into these various categories? We think they do.

To be sure, depression is a very real and very deadly disorder for both men and women. Depression is, in fact, deadlier for men, since suicide rates are dramatically higher for men. But as the research tells us over and over, the actual experience of depression on a number of levels, including the somatic and symptomatic levels, is quite similar for both men and women. Human suffering knows no sex-delineated or gendered boundaries. The underlying physical, somatic, and emotional phenomena that correspond to depression are probably very much the same for men and women. A complex overlay of culturally shaped norms and expectations related to expression of distress, labeling of somatic body states, and the meaning of such experiences will more likely be found to account for the sex differences in depression. Such an overlay of culturally shaped phenomena shade the experiences of depression for men and women much more strongly than essentialist or biologically derived explanations that have been offered to account for the observed sex-differences in rates of depression.

A RESEARCH AGENDA TO ILLUMINATE MALE DEPRESSION

Our assessment, then, is that the research that is available does not go far enough in capturing the reality of male depression. There are significant gaps in our understanding of the causes and manifestations of male depression. We feel the time has come for workers in this area to take up the challenge and to turn their attention to the reality of male depression and to begin to design studies that will help further our understanding of this disorder in men. After reading this research, we offer some possible directions for future research inquiry in this area.

Within-Group Differences

One important finding gleaned from the epidemiological studies on the incidence and prevalence of depression is that not all men are at comparable risk for suffering a depressive episode. What men are at increased or decreased risk, and how do we define the characteristics that correspond with their levels of risk? Does alcoholism, drug abuse, or sociopathy, so prevalent in the general population of American men, serve to mask male depression? Do cultural subgroups of men, in which such behavior is less prevalent, turn out to be at greater risk for developing depression? What factors within these specific sub-groups might increase or decrease risk further? These and related questions that focus on delineating differences between men will help in understanding what contributes to increased or decreased risk of developing depression. Such inquiry will offer a complement to the many studies that have focused solely on identifying between-sex differences in depression.

Gender-Role Strain

Recent research has suggested a strong gender-role strain component to depression in men. Specific aspects of gender-role strain have been related to increased levels of depression in men as well as to decreased interest or willingness to seek help. Are men who subscribe to traditional or nontraditional gender roles afforded any protection from depression? What kinds of personal value systems might enhance protection from depression for men? Are men with strong networks of friends protected from depression? Do strong family relationships or a solid primary relationship protect men from depression? Do men with traditional masculine value systems suffer from depression at levels comparable to women's but merely manifest this depression differently? Such questions will help us understand the important role that culturally mediated aspects of masculinity and masculine value systems play in the development of depression in men.

Masked Depression

Masked depression as a construct has a mixed status in most of the research literature we reviewed. It has considerable intuitive appeal as a model for understanding male depression since so many men appear to express depressed mood through behaviors considered "depressive equivalents." Studies devoted to confirming the usefulness of this construct as one component of a comprehensive model for depression in men should be considered. Is it true that certain men manifest depression through anger, hostility, aggression, or other more socially accept-able outlets? What might cause one man to become depressed and sui-cidal, another man to become depressed and homicidal, and yet another to merely become depressed? Do the high rates of fatal accidents or vio-lence in men suggest a depressive component? Do alcoholism, drug abuse, and personality difficulties, identified as more prevalent in men, also contain a depressive component? There are certainly connections between these various potential depressive equivalents and depression in men suggested in the research literature. Perhaps more attention devoted to these patterns would help us more fully characterize the reality of depression in men.

Depressive Spectrum Disease

The depressive spectrum disease conceptualization of major depression appears to be a model that would link depression to a number of related conditions more commonly diagnosed in men. This model would also suggest reasons for the underrepresentation of men in the diagnostic categories of depression and related disorders such as dysthymia. In this model, men who are alcoholic, antisocial, or addicted to other mood-altering substances are suspected of suffering from an underlying depres-sive disease. These men would therefore not be counted in the tradi-tional mood disorder categories. They would, though, be represented in other diagnostic groupings. Genetic and family studies have been promising in confirming some of the predictions this model generates. A number of other findings that document comorbidity patterns of cer-tain disorders with depression and suicide in men point toward a poten-tial role this model has in furthering our understanding of depression in men. We would like to see more studies that are based on the depressive spectrum disease conceptualization of depression.

Qualitative Inquiry

Finally, well-designed qualitative studies on the male experience of depression might point us in further, as yet unspecified, directions in our efforts to understand depression in men. Simply asking men to discuss their experiences of depression may be the simplest and most direct route to increasing our empathy for and understanding of this disorder.

Such inquiry helps us look beyond the superficial aspects of the traditional male gender role and increases our understanding of what lies beneath this role for most men.

These are five important areas of research that, if pursued, will contribute substantially to our understanding of depression in men. There are a number of important findings that have grown from the important work on depression in women. Now it is time to complete the task as it relates to men and include inquiry specifically geared toward illuminating the phenomenon of male depression. Only by integrating what we have previously learned about depression with our current knowledge of the psychology of men will we achieve a complete understanding of depression in men.

OPTIMIZING ASSESSMENT AND TREATMENT OF DEPRESSION IN MEN

A number of encouraging and hopeful conclusions are warranted after sifting through the research literature, clinical case reports, and descriptions of innovative psychotherapies for men. In spite of the fact that fewer men than women seek psychotherapy, those men that do seek treatment are helped a great deal. As clinicians with a great deal of experience working with men, this does not surprise us. However, it does cause us to wonder how we might disseminate such findings so that greater numbers of men will seek care for depression. Efforts to reach colleagues with the good news that men can be treated effectively for depression will increase awareness of the treatment options that are available. By increasing our knowledge of the diagnosis and treatment of depression in men perhaps we will also enhance our empathy and sensitivity for our male patients. Our belief is that the men who don't come to therapy are telling us something—that we have not been sensitive enough to their concerns and their frustrations.

Psychotherapy and Pharmacotherapy for Depressed Men

Research and clinical literature on treating depression in men bears good news. Empirically validated treatments, studied thoroughly for their efficacy in the treatment of unipolar depression in the National Institute of Mental Health's Collaborative Treatment of Depression

Research Project, are effective in helping men. Both psychosocial treatments, cognitive–behavioral and interpersonal psychotherapy, and pharmacological treatments have been proven effective in relieving depression in men. In some instances, men may actually respond more quickly than women to psychotherapy. Recent developments in psychopharmacological therapies have provided increased options for physicians. New antidepressants with proven efficacy offer a number of prescribing choices in the treatment of male depression.

In addition to these empirically validated treatments, there are a number of promising, gender-sensitive, innovative treatments for depressed men that we are confident will also prove beneficial. Drawn from the extensive experiences of clinicians who regularly treat depression in men, these innovative psychotherapies combine the best of the empirically validated treatments with a gender-sensitive perspective that welcomes and supports men in their efforts to overcome the burden of depression.

One aspect of optimizing clinical care for depressed men must address creative means to "get the word out." Since treatments are effective in relieving depression in men, why do not more men avail themselves of help? We believe the answer lies in our failure to characterize psychotherapy in ways that welcome men. Popular media, as well as clinical writing, often create an impression that entering therapy is, for men, an admission of weakness, or only for "sensitive" men, or those seeking "self-exploration." All of these manners of characterizing psychotherapy will assure that men will stay away in great numbers. Of course, in reality, nothing could be further from the truth. New, innovative psychotherapies have shown that they are, indeed, welcoming to men and sensitive to men's pain and suffering. Many men have benefited from these new psychotherapies. Now, we must educate our patients, their families, our colleagues, and the public at large about the reality that psychotherapy is good for men. Men should not stay away from the help that is available.

Assessment of Depression Must Identify Depressed Men

This statement is self-evident. After examining the literature on clinical assessment of depression and then placing these findings side-by-side with studies of the prevalence of depression, we conclude that many men are simply not identified by clinicians as depressed. Traditional models of assessment of depression are not geared toward identifying the various ways in which men experience and express depressed mood. Most men don't cry or proclaim their sadness. Many men may simply be unaware of feelings of depression. They may, instead, engage in increased conflict with loved ones, increase their consumption of mood-altering substances, or act out their depression in ways designed to take their mind off their mood state. Assessment of male depression must begin to take these realities into account as we strive to increase our accuracy in diagnosing depression in men.

We must always look carefully for depression when working with a man with a substance abuse or alcohol problem. We must suspect depression when a man has been coerced into seeking help as a result of trouble that his behavior has created. We must inquire about possible depression when relationship difficulties are a presenting focus. Of course, we are not suggesting that all problems that men bring to therapy are somehow rooted in a depressive disorder. We are suggesting, though, that a great number of men who are suffering from depressive disorders enter and leave our offices and "slip through the cracks." These men are never asked to reflect on or describe their moods to us and, therefore, never have the opportunity to address their mood disorders with us.

In addition to educating our clinical colleagues about the importance of identifying depression in men, we must recognize the benefit of educating our colleagues in primary care medical settings, employment settings, and educational settings. In these environments, there are many men who could be identified and referred for treatment for depression. Awareness of the problem of depression in men must extend beyond the walls of our consulting rooms and offices. The greater the number of professionals who are made aware of the problems of depression in men, the more likely they will be to identify and refer men for appropriate treatment.

How Can We Reduce the Risk of Suicide in Men?

In the research literature on suicide, the numbers of men who succumb to suicide are simply overwhelming. This is particularly true, and especially sad, as men grow older. The rates of suicide among older men in the United States are a national crisis. How we as a society conscience the unnecessary loss of such wisdom, talent, and insight that our society's elders carry is beyond comprehension. We have come a long way in our understanding of the risk factors for increased suicide risk in men. We now must educate not only ourselves, but our patients, their families, and loved ones about these risk factors, warning signs, and symptoms of depression and suicide risk in men.

Suicide prevention programs designed to reduce suicide in certain age groups have demonstrated only modest success. However, the possibility of saving one man's life through efforts aimed at educating the general public as well as professionals about this dramatic problem would justify the expenditure of energy and funds. This is particularly compelling since we know beyond a doubt that depression in men can be effectively treated with psychotherapy, pharmacotherapy, or combinations of the two and that there are many well-trained professionals equipped to provide this care. There is simply no reason for the numbers of men who commit suicide to continue to be ignored. Were this any other health problem, it would be decried as a major public health crisis in our country.

Training Programs Must Educate Their Students about Depression in Men

Finally, since our culture values education to such a great extent, we must begin to educate our students about the psychology of men in general and about the problem of undiagnosed and untreated depression in men in particular. So many problems we encounter in our consulting rooms, as well as in our neighborhoods and on our streets, are related to violence that is perpetrated by men. Men have difficulties with alcoholism, substance abuse, and other conditions related to depression. If we are to begin to make progress in eliminating these problems, we must begin to recognize the contribution untreated depression in men makes to these phenomena. One of the best ways to accomplish this is to begin teaching our students about how to apply gender-sensitive insights into the assessment and treatment of the men with whom they work. They must be taught to create a welcoming and affirming relationship with the men they will encounter in their practices. They must be exposed to the new and innovative approaches to psychotherapy with men which have been developed in the last decade. They must be taught to apply these effective treatments with men. By emphasizing the positive value in working with men, perhaps more men will begin to see that help is available and that psychotherapy or pharmacotherapy are not instruments designed to induce shame and guilt but rather are the means by which we can eliminate suffering and loss of life. We owe this to the men in our lives and in our communities.

So, having now come full circle in our journey, we are encouraged and optimistic. There are clear research directions that will lead to increasing our understanding of depression in men. Findings to date suggest a number of unanswered questions that will enhance and deepen our appreciation of the quality and quantity of depression in men. Similarly, the findings from treatment studies teach us that men can be effectively treated for depression, and that new psychotherapies will add even more value to these approaches for working with men. As we enter a new century, we look forward to working toward further enhancing the care all men receive for their psychological suffering.

References

Abelin, E. L. (1980). Triangulation, the role of the father and the origins of core gender identity during the rapprochement sub-phase. In R. Lax, S. Bach, & J. A. Burland (Eds.), *Rapprochement: Essays in honor of Margaret Mahler.* New York: Jason Aronson.

Abraham, K. (1911/1948). Notes on the psychoanalytical investigation and treatment of manic–depressive insanity and allied conditions. In *Selected papers of Karl Abraham,* (pp. 137–156). London, UK: Hogarth Press.

Adamek, M., & Kaplan, M. (1996). Firearm suicide among older men. *Psychiatric Services, 47,* 304–306.

Addis, M., & Jacobson, N. (1996). Reasons for depression and the process and outcome of cognitive–behavioral psychotherapies. *Journal of Consulting and Clinical Psychology, 64,* 1417–1424.

Ahnlund, K., & Frodi, A. (1996). Gender differences in the development of depression. *Scandinavian Journal of Psychology, 37,* 229–237.

Albritton, J., & Borison, R. (1995). Paroxetine treatment of anger associated with depression. *Journal of Nervous and Mental Disease, 183,* 666–667.

Ali, A., & Toner, B. (1996). Gender differences in depressive response: The role of social support. *Sex Roles, 35,* 281–293.

Altshuler, K., & Weiner, M. (1985). Anorexia nervosa and depression: A dissenting view. *American Journal of Psychiatry, 142,* 328–332.

American Psychiatric Association. (1994). *Diagnostic and statistical manual of mental disorders* (4th ed.). Washington, DC: American Psychiatric Association.

American Psychiatric Association. (1994). Practice guidelines for major depressive disorder in adults. In *American Psychiatric Association practice guidelines* (pp. 78–134). Washington, DC: American Psychiatric Association.

Amsterdam, J., Winokur, A., & Caroff, S. (1981). Gonadotropin release after administration of GnRH in depressed patients and healthy volunteers. *Journal of Affective Disorders, 3,* 367–380.

Anderson, J., Williams, S., McGee, R., & Silva, P. (1987). DSM-III disorders in preadolescent children. *Archives of General Psychiatry, 44,* 69–76.

Anderson, R., Kochanek, K., & Murphy, S. (1997). Report of final mortality statistics. *Monthly Vital Statistics Report, 45*(11). Hyattsville, MD: National Center for Health Statistics.

Andronico, M. (Ed.). (1995). *Men in groups: Insights, interventions, and psychoeducational work.* Washington, DC: American Psychological Association.

Araujo, A., Durante, R., Feldman, H., Goldstein, I., & McKinlay, J. (1998). The relationship between depressive symptoms and male erectile dysfunction: Cross-sectional results from the Massachusetts Male Aging Study. *Psychosomatic Medicine, 60,* 450–465.

Arnott, S., & Nutt, D. (1994). Successful treatment of fluvoxamine-induced anorgasmia by cyproheptadine (letter). *Journal of Clinical Psychiatry, 53,* 174.

Asnis, G., Kaplan, M., Hundorfean, G., & Saeed, W. (1997). Violence and homicidal behaviors in psychiatric disorders. *Psychiatric Clinics of North America, 20,* 405–425.

Assalian, P., & Margolese, H. (1996). Treatment of antidepressant-induced sexual side effects. *Journal of Sex and Marital Therapy, 22,* 218–224.

Baker, F. (1996). An overview of depression in the elderly: A U.S. perspective. *Journal of the National Medical Association, 88,* 178–184.

Balogh, S., Hendricks, S., & Kang, J. (1992) Treatment of fluoxetine-induced anorgasmia with amantadine. *Journal of Clinical Psychiatry, 53,* 212–213.

Balon, R., Yeragani, V., Pohl, R., & Ramesh, C. (1993). Sexual dysfunction during antidepressant treatment. *Journal of Clinical Psychiatry, 54,* 209–212.

Barnes, T., & Harvey, C. (1993). Psychiatric drugs and sexuality. In A. Riley, M. Peet, & C. Wilson (Eds.), *Sexual pharmacology* (pp. 176–196). Oxford: Clarenden Press.

Barash, D. (1982). *Sociobiology and behavior* (2nd ed.). New York: Elsevier.

Barbee, M. (1996). Men's roles and their experience of depression. *Art Therapy, 13,* 31–36.

Bartlik, B., Kaplan, P., & Kaplan, H. (1995). Psychostimulants apparently reverse sexual dysfunction secondary to selective serotonin re-uptake inhibitors. *Journal of Sex and Marital Therapy, 21,* 264–271.

Barton, J. (1979). Orgasmic inhibition by phenelzine. *American Journal of Psychiatry, 144,* 805–807.

Beach, S., Arias, I., & O'Leary, K. (1987). The relationship of marital satisfaction and social support to depressive symptomatology. *Journal of Psychopathology and Behavioral Assessment, 8,* 305–316.

Beach, S., Jouriles, E., & O'Leary, K. (1985). Extramarital sex: Impact on depression and commitment in couples seeking marital therapy. *Journal of Sex and Marital Therapy, 11,* 99–108.

Beach, S., & O'Leary, K. (1986). The treatment of depression occurring in the context of marital discord. *Behavior Therapy, 17,* 43–49.

Beach, S., Sandeen, E., & O'Leary, K. (1990). *Depression in marriage.* New York: Guilford.

Beach, S., Whisman, M., & O'Leary, K. (1994). Marital therapy for depression: Theoretical foundation, current status, and future directions. *Behavior Therapy, 25,* 345–371.

Beautrais, A., Joyce, P., Mulder, R., Fergusson, D., Deavoll, B., & Nightingale, S. (1996). Prevalence and comorbidity of mental disorders in persons making serious suicide attempts: A case-control study. *American Journal of Psychiatry, 153,* 1009–1014.

Bebbington, P., Dunn, G., Jenkins, R., Lewis, G., Brigha, T., Farrell, M., & Leltzer, H. (1998). The influence of age and sex on the prevalence of depressive conditions: Report from the National Survey of Psychiatric Morbidity. *Psychological Medicine, 28,* 9–19.

Beck, A. (1976). *Cognitive therapy and the emotional disorders.* New York: International Universities Press.

Beck, A., Rush, A., Shaw, B., & Emery, G. (1979). *Cognitive therapy of depression*. New York: Guilford.

Beck, A., Steer, F., & Garbin, M. (1988). Psychometric properties of the Beck Depression Inventory: Twenty-five years of evaluation. *Journal of Clinical Psychology, 40,* 1365–1368.

Beck, A., Ward, C., Mendelsohn, M., Mock, J., & Erbaugh, J. (1961). An inventory for measuring depression. *Archives of General Psychiatry, 4,* 561–571.

Beckham E., & Leber, W. (Eds.). (1995). *Handbook of depression* (2nd ed.). New York: Guilford.

Bellack, A., Hersen, M., & Himmelhoch, J. (1981). Social skills training compared with pharmacotherapy and psychotherapy in the treatment of unipolar depression. *American Journal of Psychiatry, 138,* 1562–1566.

Berado, F. M. (1970). Survivorship and social isolation: The case of the aged widower. *The Family Coordinator,* January, 11–25.

Bergman, S. (1995). Men's psychological development: A relational perspective. In R. Levant & W. Pollack (Eds.). *A new psychology of men* (pp. 68–90). New York: Basic Books.

Berman, A., & Jobes, D. (1991). *Adolescent suicide: Assessment and intervention*. Washington, DC: American Psychological Association.

Bertholon, F., Krajewski, Y., & elAllai, A. (1996). Adverse effects: Priapism caused by paroxetine. *Annales Medico-Psychologiques, 154,* 145–146.

Betcher, R., & Pollack, W. (1993). *In a time of fallen heroes: The recreation of masculinity*. New York: Atheneum.

Bibring, E. (1953). The mechanism of depression. In P. Greenacre (Ed.), *Affective disorders* (pp. 14–47). New York: International Universities Press.

Biondi, M., & Picardi, A. (1996). Clinical and biological aspects of bereavement and loss-induced depression: A reappraisal. *Psychotherapy and Psychosomatics, 65,* 229–243.

Black, D., Baumgard, C., & Bell, S. (1995). A 16- to 45-year follow-up of 71 men with antisocial personality disorder. *Comprehensive Psychiatry, 36,* 130–140.

Black, D., & Winokur, G. (1990). Suicide and psychiatric diagnosis. In S. Blumenthal & D. Kupfer (Eds.), *Suicide over the life cycle: Risk factors, assessment and treatment of suicidal patients* (pp. 135–154). Washington DC: American Psychiatric Press.

Blackburn, L., & Moore, R. (1997). Controlled acute and follow-up trial of cognitive therapy and pharmacotherapy in outpatients with recurrent depression. *British Journal of Psychiatry, 171,* 328–334.

Blanck, G., & Blanck, R. (1974). *Ego psychology: Theory and practice*. New York: Columbia University Press.

Blumenthal, S., & Kupfer, D. (Eds.). (1990). *Suicide over the life cycle: Risk factors, assessment, and treatment of suicidal patients*. Washington, DC: American Psychiatric Press.

Boggiano, A., & Barrett, M. (1991). Gender differences in depression in college students. *Sex Roles, 25,* 595–605.

Bongar, B. (1991). *The suicidal patient: Clinical and legal standards of care*. Washington, DC: American Psychological Association.

Bowlby, J. (1980). *Loss: Sadness and depression*. New York: Basic Books.

Brannon, R. (1976). The male sex role: Our culture's blueprint for manhood and what it's done for us lately. In D. David & R. Brannon (Eds.), *The forty-nine percent majority: The male sex role* (pp. 1–48). Reading, MA: Addison-Wesley.

Briere, J., Evans, D., Runtz, M., & Wall, T. (1988). Symptomatology in men who were molested as children: A comparison study. *American Journal of Orthopsychiatry, 58,* 457–461.

Bright, T. (1586). *A treatise of melancholy.* London, UK: John Windet.

Briston, M., & Bright, J. (1995). Group cognitive therapy in chronic depression: Results from two intervention studies. *Behavioral and Cognitive Psychotherapy, 23,* 373–380.

Brooks, G. (1998). *A new psychotherapy for traditional men.* San Francisco: Jossey-Bass.

Brooks, G., & Gilbert, L. (1995). Men in families: Old constraints, new possibilities. In R. F. Levant & W. S. Pollack (Eds.), *A new psychology of men* (pp. 252–279). New York: Basic Books.

Brooks, G., & Silverstein, L. (1995). Understanding the dark side of masculinity: An interactive systems model. In R. F. Levant & W. S. Pollack (Eds.), *A new psychology of men* (pp. 280–333). New York: Basic Books.

Brown, G., & Anderson, B. (1991). Psychiatric morbidity in adult inpatients with childhood histories of sexual and physical abuse. *American Journal of Psychiatry, 148,* 55–61.

Brown, S., Inaba, R., Gillin, C., Schuckit, M., Stewart, M., & Irwin, B. (1995). Alcoholism and affective disorder: Clinical course of depressive symptoms. *American Journal of Psychiatry, 152,* 45–52.

Bruder-Mattson, S., & Hovanitz, C. (1990). Coping and attributional styles as predictors of depression. *Journal of Clinical Psychology, 46,* 557–565.

Buda, M., & Tsuang, M. (1990). The epidemiology of suicide: Implications for clinical practice. In S. Blumenthal & D. Kupfer (Eds.), *Suicide over the life cycle: Risk factors, assessment, and treatment of suicidal patients* (pp. 17–38). Washington, DC: American Psychiatric Press.

Butcher, J., Dahlstrom, W., Graham, J., Tellegen, A., & Kaemmer, B. (1989). *The Minnesota Multiphasic Personality Inventory-2.* Minneapolis, MN: University of Minnesota.

Butler, K. (1996). The biology of fear. *Family Therapy Networker, 20,* 39–45.

Butler, L., & Nolen-Hoeksema, S. (1994). Gender differences in responses to depressed mood in a college sample. *Sex Roles, 30,* 331–346.

Canetto, S. (1994). Gender issues in the treatment of suicidal individuals. *Death Studies, 18,* 513–527.

Carlson, N. (1987). Woman therapist: Male client. In M. Scher, M. Stevens, G. Good, & G. Eichenfield (Eds.), *Handbook of counseling and psychotherapy with men* (pp. 39–50). Newbury Park, CA: Sage.

Carverhill, P. (1997). Bereaved men: How a therapist can help. *Psychotherapy in Private Practice, 16,* 1–16.

Casper, R., Redmond, E., & Katz, M. (1986). Somatic symptoms in primary affective disorder. *Archives of General Psychiatry, 42,* 1098–1104.

Charatan, F. (1985). Depression in the elderly: Diagnosis and treatment. *Psychiatric Annals, 15,* 313–316.

Checkley, S. (1992). Neuroendocrine mechanisms and the precipitation of depression by life events. *British Journal of Psychiatry, 160* (Supp.), 7–17.

Chevron, E., Quinlan, D., & Blatt, S. (1978). Sex roles and gender differences in the experience of depression. *Journal of Abnormal Psychology, 87,* 680–683.

Chiles, J., & Strosahl, K. (1995). *The suicidal patient: Principles of assessment, treatment, and case management.* Washington, DC: American Psychiatric Press.

Chodorow, N. (1978). *The reproduction of mothering.* Berkeley, CA: University of California Press.

Chodorow, N. (1989). *Feminism and psychoanalytic theory.* New Haven:Yale University Press.

Christensen, A., Jacobson, N., & Babcock, J. (1995). Integrative behavioral couple therapy. In N. Jacobson & A. Gurman (Eds.), *Clinical handbook of couples therapy* (pp. 31–64). NewYork: Guilford.

Clark,V., Aneshensel, C., Frerichs, R., & Morgan,T. (1981). Analysis of effects of sex and age in response to items on the CES-D scale. *Psychiatry Research, 5,* 171–181.

Cochran, S., & Rabinowitz, F. (1983). An experiential men's group for the university community. *Journal of College Student Personnel, 24,* 163–164.

Cochran, S., & Rabinowitz, F. (1996). Men, loss, and psychotherapy. *Psychotherapy, 33,* 593–600.

Cohen, A. (1992). Fluoxetine-induced yawning and anorgasmia reversed by cyproheptadine treatment (letter). *Journal of Clinical Psychiatry, 53,* 174.

Conroy, P. (1996). *Beach music.* NewYork: Ballantine Books.

Conwell,Y., Duberstein, P., Cox, C., Hermann, J., Forbes, N., & Caine, E. (1996). Relationships of age and axis I diagnoses in victims of completed suicide: A psychological autopsy study. *American Journal of Psychiatry, 153,* 1001–1008.

Cooper, A., Finlayson, R.,Velamoor,V., Magnus, R., & Cernovsky, Z. (1989). Effects of ECT on prolactin, LF, FSH, and testosterone in males with major depressive illness. *Canadian Journal of Psychiatry, 34,* 814–817.

Cooper, M., Frone, M., Russell, M., & Mudar, P. (1995). Drinking to regulate positive and negative emotions: A motivational model of alcohol use. *Journal of Personality and Social Psychology, 69,* 990–1005.

Coryell,W., Endicott, J., & Keller, M. (1992). Major depression in a non-clinical sample: Demographic and clinical risk factors for first onset. *Archives of General Psychiatry, 49,* 117–125.

Coyle, C., & Enright, R. (1997). Forgiveness intervention with postabortion men. *Journal of Consulting and Clinical Psychology, 65,* 1042–1046.

Craighead, W., Craighead, L., & Ilardi, S. (1998). Psychosocial treatments for major depressive disorder. In P. Nathan & J. Gorman (Eds.), *A guide to treatments that work* (pp. 226–239). NewYork: Oxford University Press.

Cramer, D. (1993). Living alone, marital status, gender, and health. *Journal of Applied Community Social Psychology, 3,* 1–15.

Crenshaw, T., Goldberg, J., & Stern, W. (1987). Pharmacologic modification of psychosexual dysfunction. *Journal of Sex and Marital Therapy, 13,* 239–252.

Crook, T., & Eliot, J. (1980). Parental death during childhood and adult depression: A critical review of the literature. *Psychological Bulletin, 87,* 252–259.

Culbertson, F. M. (1997). Depression and gender. An international review. *American Psychologist, 52,* 25–31.

Dabbs, J., Hopper, C., & Jurkovic, G. (1990). Testosterone and personality among college students and military veterans. *Personality and Individual Differences, 11,* 1263–1269.

Davies, R., Harris, B.,Thomas, D., Cook, N., Read, G., & Riad-Fahmy, D. (1992). Salivary testosterone levels and major depressive illness in men. *British Journal of Psychiatry, 161,* 629–632.

DeCastro, D. (1985). Reversal of MAOI-induced anorgasmia with cyproheptadine (letter). *American Journal of Psychiatry, 142,* 783.

Dhaliwal, G., Gauzas, L., Antonowicz, D., & Ross, R. (1996). Adult male survivors of childhood sexual abuse: Prevalence, sexual abuse characteristics, and long-term effects. *Clinical Psychology Review, 16,* 619–639.

Diamond, J. (1987). Counseling male substance abusers. In M. Scher, M. Stevens, G. Good, & G. Eichenfield (Eds.), *Handbook of counseling and psychotherapy with men* (pp. 332–342). Newbury Park, CA: Sage.

DiGiuseppe, R. (1986). Cognitive therapy for childhood depression. *Journal of Psychotherapy and the Family, 2,* 153–172.

Dimock, P. (1988). Adult males sexually abused as children: Characteristics and implications for treatment. *Journal of Interpersonal Violence, 3,* 203–221.

Dobson, K. (1989). A meta-analysis of the efficacy of cognitive therapy for depression. *Journal of Consulting and Clinical Psychology, 57,* 414–419.

Dohrenwend, B. P. (1995). The problem of validity in field studies of psychological disorders: Revisited. In M. Tsuang, M. Tohen, & G. Zahner (Eds.), *Textbook in psychiatric epidemiology* (pp. 3–22). New York: Wiley-Liss.

Douglas, J. D. (1990). Patterns of change following parent death in midlife adults. *Omega, 22,* 127–137.

Dunne, F., Galatopoulos, C., & Schipperheijn, J. (1993). Gender differences in psychiatric morbidity among alcohol misusers. *Comprehensive Psychiatry, 34,* 95–101.

Eaton, W., Anthony, J., Gallo, J., Cai, G., Tien, A., Romanoski, A., Lyketsos, C., & Chen, L. (1997). Natural history of diagnostic interview schedule/DSM-IV major depression. *Archives of General Psychiatry, 54,* 993–999.

Egeland, J., & Hostetter, A. (1983). Amish Study I: Affective disorders among the Amish. *American Journal of Psychiatry, 140,* 56–61.

Egeland, J., Hostetter, A., & Eshelman, S. (1983). Amish Study III: the impact of cultural factors on diagnosis of bipolar illness. *American Journal of Psychiatry, 140,* 67–71.

Elkin, I., Shea, M., Watkins, J., Imber, S., Sotsky, S., Collins, J., Glass, D., Pilkonis, P., Leber, W., Docherty, J., Fiester, S., & Parloff, M. (1989). National Institute of Mental Health Treatment of Depression Collaborative Research Program. General effectiveness of treatments. *Archives of General Psychiatry, 46,* 971–982.

Endicott, J., & Spitzer, R. (1978). A diagnostic interview: The Schedule for Affective Disorders and Schizophrenia. *Archives of General Psychiatry, 35,* 837–844.

Erikson, E. E. (1963). *Childhood and society.* New York: W. W. Norton.

Erikson, E. E. (1980). *Identity and the life cycle.* New York: W. W. Norton.

Fals-Stewart, W., Birchler, G., & O'Farrell, T. (1996). Behavioral couples therapy for male substance-abusing patients: Effects on relationship adjustment and drug-using behavior. *Journal of Consulting and Clinical Psychology, 64,* 959–972.

Farrell, W. (1975). *The liberated man.* New York: Random House.

Fasteau, M. (1974). *The male machine.* New York: McGraw-Hill.

Fava, M., Abraham, M., Alpert, J., Nierenberg, A., Pava, J., & Rosenbaum, J. (1996). Gender differences in Axis I comorbidity among depressed outpatients. *Journal of Affective Disorders, 38,* 129–133.

Feiger, A., Kiev, A., Shrivastava, R., Wisselink, P., & Wilcox, C. (1996). Nefazodone versus sertraline in outpatients with major depression: Focus on efficacy, tolerability, and effects on sexual function and satisfaction. *Journal of Clinical Psychiatry, 57* (supplement 2), 53–62.

Felthous, A., & Hempel, A. (1995). Combined homicide–suicides: A review. *Journal of Forensic Sciences, 40,* 846–857.

Ferguson, J., Shrivastava, R., & Stahl, S. (1996). Effects of double-blind treatment with nefazodone or sertraline on re-emergence of sexual dysfunction in depressed patients. *New Research Program and Abstracts of the 149th Annual Meeting of the American Psychiatric Association* (Vol. 358, pp. 164). Washington: American Psychiatric Association.

Ferraro, K. F., Multran, E., & Barresi, C. M. (1984). Widowhood, health, and friendship in later life. *Journal of Health and Social Behavior, 25,* 245–259.

Finkelhor, D., Hotaling, G., Lewis, I., & Smith, C. (1990). Sexual abuse in a national survey of adult men and women: Prevalence, characteristics, and risk factors. *Child Abuse and Neglect, 14,* 19–28.

Fisch, R. (1987). Masked depression: Its interrelations with somatization, hypochondriasis and conversion. *International Journal of Psychiatry in Medicine, 17,* 367–379.

Fisch, R. (1989). Alexithymia, masked depression and loss in a Holocaust survivor. *British Journal of Psychiatry, 154,* 708–710.

Fitzpatrick, T. R. (1998). Bereavement events among elderly men: The effects of stress and health. *The Journal of Applied Gerontology, 17,* 204–228.

Flavin, D., Franklin, J., & Frances, R. (1990). Substance abuse and suicidal behavior. In S. Blumenthal & D. Kupfer (Eds.), *Suicide over the life cycle: Risk factors, assessment and treatment of suicidal patients* (pp. 77–204). Washington DC: American Psychiatric Press.

Fleming, J. (1993). The difficult to treat insomniac patient. *Journal of Psychosomatic Research, 37* (Supp.), 45–54.

Flett, G., Vredenburg, K., & Krames, L. (1997). The continuity of depression in clinical and nonclinical samples. *Psychological Bulletin, 121,* 395–416.

Fortner, E., Gollan, J., & Jacobson, N. (1997). Psychological aspects of perpetrators of domestic violence and their relationships with the victims. *Psychiatric Clinics of North America, 20*(2), 337–352.

Fowler, R., Rich, C., & Young, D. (1986). San Diego Suicide Study: 2. Substance abuse in young cases. *Archives of General Psychiatry, 43,* 962–965.

Frank, E., Carpenter, L., & Kupfer, D. (1988). Sex differences in recurrent depression: Are there any that are significant? *American Journal of Psychiatry, 145,* 41–45.

Frasure-Smith, N., Lesperance, F., & Talajic, M. (1995). The impact of negative emotions on prognosis following myocardial infarction: Is it more than depression? *Health Psychology, 14,* 388–398.

Freud, S. (1917/1957). Mourning and melancholia. In J. Strachey (Ed. and Trans.), *The standard edition of the complete psychological works of Sigmund Freud* (Vol. 14, pp. 243–258). London, UK: Hogarth Press.

Gardner, E., & Johnston, J. (1985) Buproprion: An antidepressant without sexual pathophysiologic action. *Journal of Clinical Psychopharmacology, 5,* 24–29.

Gaylin, W. (1983). The meaning of despair. In W. Gaylin (Ed.), *Psychodynamic understanding of depression* (pp. 3–25). New York: Jason Aronson.

Gilligan, C. (1982). *In a different voice.* Cambridge, MA: Harvard University Press.

Gilmore, D. D. (1990). *Mankind in the making: Cultural concepts of masculinity.* New Haven, CT: Yale University Press.

Girling, D., Barkley, C., Paykel, E., Gehlhaar, E., Brayne, C., Gill, C., Mathewson, D., & Huppert, F. (1995). The prevalence of depression in a cohort of the very elderly. *Journal of Affective Disorders, 34,* 319–329.

Gjerde, P. (1995). Alternative pathways to chronic depressive symptoms in young adults: Gender differences in developmental trajectories. *Child Development, 66,* 1277–1300.

Gjerde, P., Block, J., & Block, J. (1988). Depressive symptoms and personality during late adolescence: Gender differences in the externalization–internalization of symptom expression. *Journal of Abnormal Psychology, 97,* 475–486.

Gluhoski, V., Fishman, B., & Perry, S. (1997). The impact of multiple bereavement in a gay male sample. *AIDS Education and Prevention, 9,* 521–531.

Gold, J. R. (1990). Levels of depression. In B. Wolman & G. Stricker (Eds.), *Depressive disorders: Facts, theories, and treatment methods* (pp. 203–228). New York: Wiley.

Goldberg, D., & Bridges, K. (1988). Somatic presentations of psychiatric illness in primary care settings. *Journal of Psychosomatic Research, 32,* 137–144.

Goldberg, H. (1976). *The hazards of being male.* New York: Nash Publishing.

Goldsmith, S., Fyer, M., & Frances, A. (1990). Personality and suicide. In S. Blumenthal & D. Kupfer (Eds.), *Suicide over the life cycle: Risk factors, assessment, and treatment of suicidal patients* (pp. 155–176). Washington: American Psychiatric Press.

Golomb, M., Fava, M., Abraham, M., & Rosenbaum, J. (1995). Gender differences in personality disorders. *American Journal of Psychiatry, 152,* 579–582.

Good, G., Dell, D., & Mintz, L. (1989). The male role and gender role conflict: Relationships to help-seeking. *Journal of Counseling Psychology, 68,* 295–300.

Good, G., Gilbert, L., & Scher, M. (1990). Gender aware therapy: A synthesis of feminist therapy and knowledge about gender. *Journal of Counseling and Development, 68,* 376–380.

Good, G., & Mintz, L. (1990). Gender role conflict and depression in college men: Evidence for compounded risk. *Journal of Counseling and Development, 69,* 17–21.

Good, G., Robertson, J., Fitzgerald, L., Stevens, M., & Bartels, K. (1996). The relation between masculine role conflict and psychological distress in male university counseling center clients. *Journal of Counseling and Development, 75,* 44–49.

Good, G., & Wood, P. (1995). Male gender role conflict, depression, and help-seeking: Do college men face double jeopardy? *Journal of Counseling and Development, 74,* 70–75.

Gordon, M. (1990). Males and females as victims of childhood sexual abuse: An examination of the gender effect. *Journal of Family Violence, 5,* 321–332.

Gortner, E., Gollan, J., & Jacobson, N. (1997). Psychological aspects of perpetrators of domestic violence and their relationships with the victims. *Psychiatric Clinics of North America, 20,* 337–352.

Gotlib, I., & Hammen, C. (1992). *Psychological aspects of depression.* New York: Wiley.

Grant, B. (1995). Comorbidity between DSM-IV drug use disorders and major depression: Results of a national survey of adults. *Journal of Substance Abuse, 7,* 481–497.

Greenson, R. R. (1968). Dis-identifying from mother. *International Journal of Psychoanalysis, 49,* 370–374.

Greenwald, D., Reznikoff, M., & Plutchik, R. (1994). Suicide risk and violence risk in alcoholics: Predictors of aggressive risk. *Journal of Nervous and Mental Disease, 182,* 3–8.

Groddeck, G. (1923/1949). *The book of the It.* New York: Vintage Books.

Gumbiner, J., & Flowers, J. (1997). Sex differences on the MMPI-1 and MMPI-2. *Psychological Reports, 81,* 479–482.

Gurman, A., & Klein, M. (1980). Marital and family conflicts. In A. Brodsky & R. Hare-Mustin (Eds.), *Women and psychotherapy* (pp. 159–188). New York: Guilford.

Haas, G., Clarkin, J., & Glick, I. (1985). Marital and family treatment of depression. In E. Beckham & W. Leber (Eds.) *Handbook of depression* (pp. 151–183). Homewood, IL: Dorsey Press.

Hall, R., Platt, D., & Hall, R. (1999). Suicide risk assessment: A review of risk factors for suicide in 100 patients who made severe suicide attempts. *Psychosomatics, 40,* 18–27.

Hamberger, K., & Hastings, J. (1991). Personality correlates of men who batter and nonviolent men: Some continuities and discontinuities. *Journal of Family Violence, 6,* 131–147.

Hamilton, M. (1960). A rating scale for depression. *Journal of Neurology, Neurosurgery, and Psychiatry, 12,* 56–62.

Hamilton, M. (1967). Development of a rating scale for primary depressive illness. *British Journal of Social and Clinical Psychology, 6,* 278–296.

Hammen, C., & Padesky, C. (1977). Sex differences in the expression of depressive responses on the Beck Depression Inventory. *Journal of Abnormal Psychology, 86,* 609–614.

Handal, P., Gist, D., & Wiener, R. (1987). The differential relationship between attribution and depression for male and female college students. *Sex Roles, 16,* 83–88.

Hanna, E., & Grant, B. (1997). Gender differences in DSM-IV alcohol use disorders and major depression as distributed in the general population: Clinical implications. *Comprehensive Psychiatry, 38,* 202–212.

Harper, J., & Kelly, E. (1985). Anti-social behavior as a mask for depression in year five and six boys. *Mental Health in Australia, 1,* 14–19.

Harrington, R. (1993). Similarities and dissimilarities between child and adult disorders: The case of depression. In C. Costello *et al.* (Eds.), *Basic issues in psychopathology* (pp. 103–124). New York: Guilford.

Harrison, J., Chin, J., & Ficcarrotto, T. (1989). Warning: Masculinity may be dangerous to your health. In M. Kimmel & M. Messner (Eds.), *Men's lives* (pp. 296–309). New York: Macmillan.

Harrison, J., & Morris, L. (1996). Group therapy for adult male survivors of child sexual abuse. In M. P. Andronico (Ed.), *Men in groups: Insights, interventions, and psychoeducational work* (pp. 339–356). Washington, DC: American Psychological Association.

Harrison, W., Rabkin, J., Ehrhardt, A., Stewart, J., McGrath, P., Ross, D., & Quitkin, F. (1986). Effects of antidepressant medication on sexual functioning: A controlled study. *Journal of Clinical Psychopharmacology, 6,* 144–149.

Harrison, W., Stewart, J, Ehrhardt, A., & alAllali, A. (1985). A controlled study of the effects of antidepressants on sexual functioning. *Psychopharmacologic Bulletin, 21,* 85–88.

Hartung, C., & Widiger, T. (1998). Gender differences in the diagnosis of mental disorders: Conclusions and controversies of the DSM-IV. *Psychological Bulletin, 123,* 260–278.

Hastings, J., & Hamberger, K. (1997). Sociodemographic predictors of violence. *Psychiatric Clinics of North America, 20*(2), 323–335.

Hathaway, S., & McKinley, J. (1942). A multiphasic personality schedule (Minnesota): III. The measurement of symptomatic depression. *Journal of Psychology, 14,* 73–84.

Heifner, C. (1997). The male experience of depression. *Perspectives in Psychiatric Care, 33,* 10–18.

Hendren, R. (1990). Assessment and interviewing strategies for suicidal patients over the life cycle. In S. Blumenthal & D. Kupfer (Eds.), *Suicide over the life cycle: Risk factors, assessment, and treatment of suicidal patients* (pp. 235–252). Washington, DC: American Psychiatric Press.

Heppner, P. (1981). Counseling men in groups. *Personnel and Guidance Journal, 60,* 249–252.

Herman, J. (1992). *Trauma and recovery: The aftermath of violence.* New York: Basic Books.

Hersen, M., Bellack, A., Himmelhoch, J., & Thase, M. (1984). Effects of social skills training, amitriptyline, and psychotherapy in unipolar depressed women. *Behavior Therapy, 15,* 21–40.

Hoberman, H. (1990). Behavioral treatments for unipolar depression. In B. Wolman & G. Stricker (Eds.), *Depressive disorders: Facts, theories, and treatment methods* (pp. 310–342). New York: Wiley.

Hoberman, H., & Lewinsohn, P. (1985). The behavioral treatment of depression. In E. Beckham & W. Leber (Eds.) *Handbook of depression* (pp. 39–81). Homewood, IL: Dorsey Press.

Hollander, E., & McCarley, A. (1992). Yohimbine treatment of sexual side effects induced by serotonin reuptake blockers. *Journal of Clinical Psychiatry, 53,* 207–209.

Hollon, S., Shelton, R., & Davis, D. (1993). Cognitive therapy for depression: Conceptual issues and clinical efficacy. *Journal of Consulting and Clinical Psychology, 61,* 270–275.

Hoyt, D., Conger, R., Valde, J., & Weihs, K. (1997). Psychological distress and help seeking in rural America. *American Journal of Community Psychology, 25,* 449–470.

Hsu, J., & Shen, W. (1995). Male sexual side effects associated with antidepressants: A descriptive clinical study of 32 patients. *International Journal of Psychiatry in Medicine, 25,* 191–201.

Hunter, M. (1990). *Abused boys: The neglected victims of sexual abuse.* Lexington, MA: Lexington Books.

Isometsa, E., Heikkinen, M., Henriksson, M., Aro, H., Mantunnen, M., Kuoppasalmi, K., & Lonnquist, J. (1996). Suicide in non-major depressions. *Journal of Affective Disorders, 36,* 117–127.

Isometsa, E., Henriksson, M., Aro, H., Heikkinen, M., Kuoppasalmi, K., & Lonnquist, J. (1994). Suicide in major depression. *American Journal of Psychiatry, 151,* 530–536.

Itil, T., Hermann, W., & Blasucci, D. (1978). Male hormones in the treatment of depression: Effects of mesterolone. *Progress in Neuropsychopharmacology, 2,* 457–467.

Itil, T., Michael, S., Shapiro, D., & Itil, K. (1984). The effects of mesterolone, a male sex hormone, in depressed patients. *Methods and Findings in Experimental and Clinical Pharmacology, 6,* 331–337.

Jack, D. (1991). *Silencing the self: Women and depression.* Cambridge, MA: Harvard University Press.

Jackson, S. (1986). *Melancholy and depression.* New Haven: Yale University Press.

Jacobsen, F. (1992). Fluoxetine-induced sexual dysfunction and an open trial of yohimbine. *Journal of Clinical Psychopharmacology, 53,* 119–122.

Jacobson, E. (1954). Transference problems in the psychoanalytic treatment of severely depressed patients. *Journal of the American Psychoanalytic Association, 2,* 595–606.

Jacobson, N., & Addis, M. (1993). Research on couples and couple therapy: What do we know? Where are we going? *Journal of Consulting and Clinical Psychology, 61,* 85–93.

Jacobson, N., & Gurman, A. (1986). *Clinical handbook of marital therapy.* New York: Guilford.

Jarret, R., Eaves, G., Grannemann, B., & Rush, A. (1991). Clinical, cognitive, and demographic predictors of response to cognitive therapy for depression: A preliminary report. *Psychiatric Research, 37,* 245–260.

Jordan, J., Kaplan, A., Miller, J., Stiver, I., & Surrey, J. (Eds.). (1991). *Women's growth in connection.* New York: Guilford.

Kaelber, C., Moul, D., & Farmer, M. (1995). Epidemiology of depression. In E. Beckham & W. Leber (Eds.), *Handbook of depression* (pp. 3–35). New York: Guilford.

Kahn, A. (1990). Principles of psychotherapy with suicidal patients. In S. Blumenthal & D. Kupfer (Eds.), *Suicide over the life cycle: Risk factors, assessment, and treatment of suicidal patients* (pp. 441–468). Washington: American Psychiatric Press.

Kaplan, A. (1986). The "self-in-relation": Implications for depression in women. *Psychotherapy, 23,* 234–242.

Kaplan, H. (1977). Gender and depression: A sociological analysis of a conditional relationship. In W. Fann, I. Karacan, A. Pokorny, & R. Williams (Eds.), *Phenomenology and treatment of depression* (pp. 81–113). New York: Spectrum.

Kashani, J. H., Beck, N. C., Hoeper, E. W., Fallahi, C., Corcoran, C. M., McAllister, J. A., Rosenberg, T. K., & Reid, J. C. (1987). Psychiatric disorders in a community sample of adolescents. *American Journal of Psychiatry, 144,* 584–589.

Katon, W. (1987). The epidemiology of depression in medical care. *International Journal of Psychiatry in Medicine, 17,* 93–112.

Katon, W., Kleinman, A., & Rosen, G. (1982). Depression and somatization: A review. Part I. *The American Journal of Medicine, 72,* 127–135.

Kellner, R., Abbott, P., Winslow, W., & Pathak, D. (1989). Anxiety, depression, and somatization in DSM-III hypochondriasis. *Psychosomatics, 30,* 57–64.

Kelly, J., Murphy, D., Bahr, R., Kalichman, S., Morgan, M., Stevenson, Y., Koob, J., Brasfield, T., & Bernstein, B. (1993). Outcome of cognitive–behavioral and support group based therapy for depressed, HIV-infected persons. *American Journal of Psychiatry, 150,* 1679–1686.

Kendall, P., Hollon, S., Beck, A., Hammen, C., & Ingram, R. (1987). Issues and recommendations regarding use of the Beck Depression Inventory. *Cognitive Therapy and Research, 11,* 289–299.

Kendler, K., Neale, M., & Kessler, R. (1992). Major depression and generalized anxiety disorder: Same genes, (partly) different environments? *Archives of General Psychiatry, 49,* 716–722.

Kendler, K., & Prescott, C. (1999). A population-based twin study of lifetime major depression in men and women. *Archives of General Psychiatry, 56,* 39–44.

Kennedy, G., Metz, H., & Lowinger, R. (1995). Epidemiology and inferences regarding the etiology of late life suicide. In G. Kennedy (Ed.), *Suicide and depression in late life* (pp. 3–22). New York: Wiley.

Kernberg, O. F. (1985). *Internal world and external reality.* New York: Jason Aronson.

Kessler, R., Brown, R., & Browman, C. (1981). Sex differences in psychiatric help-seeking: Evidence from four large-scale surveys. *Journal of Health and Social Behavior, 22,* 49–64.

Kessler, R., & Magee, W. (1993). Childhood adversities and adult depression: Basic patterns of association in a U.S. national survey. *Psychological Medicine, 23,* 679–690.

Kessler, R., McGonagle, K., Nelson, C., Hughes, M., Swartz, M., & Blazer, D. (1994). Sex and depression in the National Comorbidity Survey. II: Cohort effects. *Journal of Affective Disorders, 30,* 15–26.

Kessler, R., McGonagle, K., Swartz, M., Blazer, D. G., & Nelson, C. B. (1993). Sex and depression in the National Comorbidity Survey: I. Lifetime prevalence, chronicity, and recurrence. *Journal of Affective Disorders, 29,* 85–96.

Kessler, R., McGonagle, K. A., Zhao, S., Nelson, C. B., Hughes, M., Eshelman, S., Wittchen, H. U., & Kendler, K. S. (1994). Lifetime and 12-month prevalence of

DSM-III-R psychiatric disorders in the United States: Results from the National Comorbidity Survey. *Archives of General Psychiatry, 51,* 8–19.

Khantzian, E. (1985). The self-medication hypothesis of addictive disorders. *American Journal of Psychiatry, 142,* 1259–1264.

Klein, M. (1940/1975). *Love, guilt and reparation.* New York: Delacorte Press.

Klein, M. (1959/1975). *Envy and gratitude and other works.* London, UK: Hogarth Press.

Klerman, G. (1989). The interpersonal model. In J. Mann (Ed.), *Models of depressive disorders: Psychological, biological, and genetic perspectives* (pp. 45–77). New York: Plenum.

Klerman, G., Weissman, M., Rounsaville, B., & Chevron, E. (1984). *Interpersonal psychotherapy of depression.* New York: Basic Books.

Kohut, H. (1977). *The restoration of the self.* New York: International Universities Press.

Kornstein, S. (1997). Gender differences in depression: Implications for treatment. *Journal of Clinical Psychiatry, 58* (supp. 15), 12–18.

Kornstein, S., Schatzberg, A., Yonkers, K., Thase, M., Keitner, G., Ryan, C., & Schlager, D. (1996). Gender differences in presentation of chronic major depression. *Psychopharmacology Bulletin, 31,* 711–718.

Kowalski, A., Stanley, R., Dennerstein, L., Burrows, G., & Maguire, K. (1985). The sexual side-effects of antidepressant medication: A double-blind comparison of two antidepressants in a non-psychiatric population. *British Journal of Psychiatry, 147,* 413–418.

Kraeplin, E. (1921). *Manic-depressive insanity and paranoia.* (R. M. Barclay & G. M. Robertson, Trans.). Edinburgh, UK: Livingstone.

Kraupl-Taylor, F. (1972). Loss of libido in depression (letter). *British Medical Journal, 1,* 305.

Krugman, S. (1995). Male development and the transformation of shame. In R. Levant & W. Pollack (Eds.), *A new psychology of men* (pp. 91–128). New York: Basic Books.

Labbate, L., Grimes, J., Hines, A., & Pollack, M. 1997. Buproprion treatment of serotonin reuptake antidepressant-associated sexual dysfunction. *Annals of Clinical Psychiatry, 9,* 241–245.

Labbate, L., & Pollack, M. (1994). Treatment of fluoxetine-induced sexual dysfunction with buproprion: A case study. *Annals of Clinical Psychiatry, 6,* 13–15.

Langhinrichsen-Rohling, J., Sanders, A., Crane, M., & Monson, C. (1998). Gender and history of suicidality: Are these factors related to U.S. college students' current suicidal thoughts, feelings, and actions? *Suicide and Life Threatening Behavior, 28,* 127–142.

Lauerma, H. (1996). Successful treatment of citalopram-induced anorgasmia by cyproheptadine. *Acta Psychiatrica Scandinavica, 93,* 69–70.

Lee, H., Song, D., Kim, C., & Choi, H. (1996). An open trial of fluoxetine in the treatment of premature ejaculation. *Journal of Clinical Psychopharmacology, 16,* 379–382.

Lerner, H. (1980). Internal prohibitions against female anger. *American Journal of Psychoanalysis, 40,* 137–147.

Lesperance, F., Frasure-Smith, N., & Talajic, M. (1996). Major depression before and after myocardial infarction: Its nature and consequences. *Psychosomatic Medicine, 58,* 99–110.

Lesse, S. (1983). *Masked depression.* New York: Jason Aronson.

Lesser, I. (1985). Current concepts in psychiatry: Alexithymia. *New England Journal of Medicine, 312,* 690–692.

Levant, R. F. (1995). Toward the reconstruction of masculinity. In R. Levant & W. Pollack (Eds.), *A new psychology of men* (pp. 229–251). New York: Basic Books.

Levant, R. F. (1996). The new psychology of men. *Professional Psychology: Research and Practice, 27,* 259–265.

Levant, R., & Pollack, W. (Eds.). (1995). *A new psychology of men.* New York: Basic Books.

Levinson, D., Darrow, C., Klein, E., Levinson, M., & McKee, B. (1978). *The seasons of a man's life.* New York: Knopf.

Levit, D. (1991). Gender differences in ego defenses in adolescence: Sex roles as one way to understand the differences. *Journal of Abnormal and Social Psychology, 61,* 992–999.

Levitt, A., & Joffe, R. (1988). Total and free testosterone in depressed men. *Acta Psychiatrica Scandinavica, 77,* 346–348.

Lewinsohn, P., & Gotlib, I. (1995). Behavioral theory and treatment of depression. In E. Becker & W. Leber (Eds.), *Handbook of depression* (pp. 352–375). New York: Guilford.

Li, G. (1995). The interaction effect of bereavement and sex on the risk of suicide in the elderly: An historical cohort study. *Social Science Medicine, 40,* 825–828.

Lindemann, E. (1944). Symptomology and management of acute grief. *American Journal of Psychiatry, 101,* 101–148.

Lisak, D. (1994). The psychological impact of sexual abuse: Content analysis of interviews with male survivors. *Journal of Traumatic Stress, 7,* 525–548.

Lisak, D. (1998). Confronting and treating empathic disconnection in violent men. In W. Pollack & R. Levant (Eds.), *New psychotherapy for men* (pp. 214–238). New York: John Wiley and Sons.

Lombardi, K. L. (1990). Depressive states and somatic symptoms. In B. Wolman & G. Stricker (Eds.), *Depressive disorders: Facts, theories, and treatment methods.* New York: Wiley.

Lowen, A. (1972). *Depression and the body.* New York: Penguin Books.

Lowen, A. (1975). *Bioenergetics.* New York: Penguin Books.

Loewenthal, K., Goldblatt, V., Gorton, T., Lubitsch, G., Bickness, H., Fellowes, D., & Sowden, A. (1995). Gender and depression in Anglo-Jewry. *Psychological Medicine, 25,* 1051–1063.

Luborsky, L., & Crits-Christoph, P. (1990). *Understanding transference: The core conflictual relationship theme method.* New York: Basic Books.

Maclean, N. (1992). *Young men and fire.* Chicago: University of Chicago Press.

Maffeo, P., Ford, T., & Lavin, P. (1990). Gender differences in depression in an employment setting. *Journal of Personality Assessment, 55,* 249–262.

Magni, G. (1987). On the relationship between chronic pain and depression when there is no organic lesion. *Pain, 31,* 1–21.

Maier, W., Lichtermann, D., & Merikangas, K. (1993). Epidemiology and genetics of affective disorders: Recent developments. In H. Hippius & C. Stefanis (Eds.), *Research in mood disorders* (pp. 1–16). Seattle: Hogrefe and Huber.

Maltsberger, J. (1986). *Suicide risk: The formulation of clinical judgment.* New York: New York University Press.

Mann, J. (Ed.). (1989). *Models of depressive disorders: Psychological, biological and genetic perspectives.* New York: Plenum.

Manson, S. (1995). Culture and major depression: Current challenges in the diagnosis of mood disorders. *The Psychiatric Clinics of North America, 18,* 487–501.

Maris, R. (1997). Social and familial risk factors in suicidal behavior. *Psychiatric Clinics of North America, 20*(30), 519–550.

Martin, J., & Dean, L. (1993). Effects of AIDS-related bereavement and HIV-related illness on psychological distress among gay men: A 7-year longitudinal study, 1985–1991. *Journal of Consulting and Clinical Psychology, 61,* 94–103.

Mason, J., Giller, E., & Kosten, T. (1988). Serum testosterone differences between patients with schizophrenia and those with affective disorders. *Biological Psychiatry, 23,* 357–366.

Mazur, A. (1995). Biosocial models of deviant behavior among male army veterans. *Biological Psychiatry, 41,* 271–293.

McCormick, S., Olin, J., & Brotman, A. (1990). Reversal of fluoxetine-induced anorgasmia by cyproheptadine in two patients. *Journal of Clinical Psychiatry, 51,* 383–384.

McGrath, E., Keita, G., Strickland, B., & Russo, N. (1990). *Women and depression: Risk factor and treatment issues.* Washington, DC: American Psychological Association.

McRoberts, C., Burlingame, G., & Hoag, M. (1998). Comparative efficacy of individual and group psychotherapy: A meta-analytic perspective. *Group Dynamics, 2,* 101–117.

Melamed, S., Kushnir, T., Strauss, E., & Vigiser, D. (1997). Negative association between reported life events and cardiovascular disease risk factors in employed men: The Cordis Study. *Journal of Psychosomatic Research, 43,* 247–258.

Mendels, J., Camera, A., & Sikes, C. (1995). Sertraline treatment for premature ejaculation. *Journal of Clinical Psychopharmacology, 15,* 341–346.

Merikangas, K., Prusoff, B., Kupfer, D., & Frank, E. (1985). Marital adjustment in major depression. *Journal of Affective Disorders, 9,* 5–11.

Merikangas, K., Risch, N., & Weissman, M. (1994). Co-morbidity and co-transmission of alcoholism, anxiety, and depression. *Psychological Medicine, 24,* 69–80.

Meth, R., & Pasick, R. (1990). *Men in therapy: The challenge of change.* New York: Guilford.

Michael, A., & Herrod, J. (1997). Citalopram-induced decreased libido (letter). *British Journal of Psychiatry, 171,* 90.

Monteiro, W., Noshirvani, H., Marks, I., & Lelliott, P. (1987). Anorgasmia from cloimpramine in obsessive–compulsive disorder: A controlled clinical trial. *British Journal of Psychiatry, 151,* 107–112.

Montejo, A., Llorce, G., & Izquierdo, J. (1996, May). *Sexual dysfunction with SSRIs: A comparative analysis.* Paper presented at the American Psychiatric Association 149th Annual Meeting., New York.

Moscicki, E. (1997). Identification of suicide risk factors using epidemiologic studies. *Psychiatric Clinics of North American, 20*(3), 499–517.

Motto, J., & Bostrom, A. (1997). Gender differences in completed suicide. *Archives of Suicide Research, 3,* 235–252.

Murphy, G. (1998). Why women are less likely than men to commit suicide. *Comprehensive Psychiatry, 39,* 165–175.

Murphy, J. (1995). What happens to depressed men? *Harvard Review of Psychiatry, 3,* 47–49.

Murphy, J, Olivier, D., Monson, R., Sobol, A., & Leighton, A. (1988). Incidence of depression and anxiety: The Stirling County Study. *American Journal of Public Health, 78,* 534–540.

Murphy, J., Sobol, A., Neff, R., Olivier, D., & Leighton, A. (1984). Stability of prevalence: Depression and anxiety disorders. *Archives of General Psychiatry, 41,* 990–997.

National Center for Health Statistics: Vital Statistics of the United States. (1987). Deaths for selected causes, Tables 290, 292. Rockville, MD: National Center for Health Statistics.

Neill, J. (1991). Penile anesthesia associated with fluoxetine use (letter). *American Journal of Psychiatry, 148,* 1603.

Newman, C., & Beck A. (1990). Cognitive therapy of affective disorders. In B. Wolman & G. Stricker (Eds.), *Depressive disorders: Facts, theories, and treatment methods* (pp. 343–367). New York: Wiley.

Nofziger, E., Thase, M., Reynolds, C., Frank, E., Jennings, R., Garamoni, G., Fasiczka, A., & Kupfer, D. (1993). Sexual function in depressed men. *Archives of General Psychiatry, 50,* 24–30.

Nolan, R., & Willson, V. (1994). Gender and depression in an undergraduate population. *Psychological Reports, 75,* 1327–1330.

Nolen-Hoeksema, S. (1987). Sex differences in unipolar depression: Evidence and theory. *Psychological Bulletin, 101,* 259–282.

Nolen-Hoeksema, S. (1990). *Sex differences in depression.* Stanford, CA: Stanford University Press.

Nolen-Hoeksema, S. (1991). Responses to depression and their effects on the duration of depressive episodes. *Journal of Abnormal Psychology, 100,* 569–582.

Nolen-Hoeksema, S. (1995). Epidemiology and theories of gender differences in unipolar depression. In M. V. Seeman (Ed.), *Gender and psychopathology* (pp. 63–87). Washington, DC: American Psychiatric Press.

Nolen-Hoeksema, S., & Girgus, J. S. (1994). The emergence of gender differences in depression during adolescence. *Psychological Bulletin, 115,* 424–443.

Nolen-Hoeksema, S., McBride, A., & Larson, J. (1997). Rumination and psychological distress among bereaved partners. *Journal of Personality and Social Psychology, 72,* 855–862.

Nolen-Hoeksema, S., Marrow, J., & Fredrickson, B. (1993). Response styles and the duration of episodes of depressed mood. *Journal of Abnormal Psychology, 102,* 20–28.

Nolen-Hoeksema, S., Parker, L., & Larson, J. (1994). Ruminative coping with depressed mood following loss. *Journal of Personality and Social Psychology, 67,* 92–104.

Norden, M. (1994). Buspirone treatment of sexual dysfunction associated with selective serotonin re-uptake inhibitors. *Depression, 2,* 109–112.

Nurnberg, H., & Levine, P. (1987). Spontaneous remission of MAOI-induced anorgasmia. *American Journal of Psychiatry, 144,* 805–807.

Oei, T., & Shuttlewood, G. (1997). Comparison of specific and nonspecific factors in a group cognitive therapy for depression. *Journal of Behavior Therapy and Experimental Psychiatry, 28,* 221–231.

O'Farrell, T., & Murphy, C. (1995). Marital violence before and after alcoholism treatment. *Journal of Consulting and Clinical Psychology, 63,* 256–262.

Oliver, S., & Toner, B. (1990). The influence of gender role typing on the expression of depressive symptoms. *Sex Roles, 22,* 775–790.

O'Neil, J. M. (1981). Patterns of gender role conflict and strain: Sexism and fear of femininity in men's lives. *Personnel and Guidance Journal, 60,* 203–210.

O'Neil, J. M., Good, G. E., & Holmes, S. (1995). Fifteen years of theory and research on men's gender role conflict: New paradigms for empirical research. In R. F. Levant & W. S. Pollack (Eds.), *A new psychology of men* (pp. 164–206). New York: Basic Books.

O'Neil, J., Helms, B., Gable, R., David, L., & Wrightsman, L, (1986). Gender role conflict scale: College men's fear of femininity. *Sex Roles, 14,* 335–350.

Oquendo, M., Malone, K., Ellis, S., Sackeim, H., & Mann, J. (1999). Inadequacy of antidepressant treatment for patients with major depression who are at risk for suicidal behavior. *American Journal of Psychiatry, 156,* 190–194.

Osgood, N., & Thielman, S. (1990). Geriatric suicidal behavior: Assessment and treatment. In S. Blumenthal & D. Kupfer (Eds.), *Suicide over the life cycle: Risk factors, assessment and treatment of suicidal patients* (pp. 341–379). Washington DC: American Psychiatric Press.

Osherson, S. (1986). *Finding our fathers: The unfinished business of manhood.* New York: Free Press.

Osherson, S., & Krugman, S. (1990). Men, shame, and psychotherapy. *Psychotherapy, 27,* 327–339.

Oxman, T., Rosenberg, S., Schnurr, P., & Tucker, G. (1985). Linguistic dimensions of affect and thought in somatization disorder. *American Journal of Psychiatry, 142,* 1150–1155.

Page, S., & Bennesch, S. (1993). Gender and reporting differences in measures of depression. *Canadian Journal of Behavioral Science, 25,* 579–589.

Pan, H., Neidig, P., & O'Leary, D. (1994). Predicting mild and severe husband to wife physical aggression. *Journal of Consulting and Clinical Psychology, 62,* 975–981.

Paolino, T., & McCrady, B. (Eds.). (1978). *Marriage and marital therapy.* New York: Brunner-Mazel.

Parkes, C., Benjamin, B., & Fitzgerald, R. (1969). Broken heart: A statistical study of increased mortality among widowers. *British Medical Journal, 1,* 740–743.

Patten, S. (1991). The loss of a parent during childhood as a risk factor for depression. *Canadian Journal of Psychiatry, 36,* 706–711.

Patterson, W. (1993). Fluoxetine-induced sexual dysfunction (letter). *Journal of Clinical Psychiatry, 54,* 71.

Persons, J. (1998). Indications for psychotherapy in the treatment of depression. *Psychiatric Annals, 28,* 80–83.

Peterson, A., & Halstead, T. (1998). Group cognitive behavior therapy for depression in a community setting: A clinical replication series. *Behavior Therapy, 29,* 3–18.

Peterson, C., & Seligman, M. (1984). Causal explanations as a risk factor for depression: Theory and evidence. *Psychological Review, 91,* 347–374.

Philpot, C. L., Brooks, G. R., Lusterman, D., & Nutt, R. L. (1997). *Bridging separate gender worlds.* Washington, DC: American Psychological Association.

Physician's desk reference. (1999). Montvale, NJ: Medical Economics.

Pichot, P., & Hassan, J. (1973). Masked depression and depressive equivalents: Problems of definition and diagnosis. In P. Kielholz (Ed.), *Masked depression* (pp. 61–81). Berne, Switzerland: Hans Huber Publisher.

Pipher, M. (1994). *Reviving Ophelia: Saving the selves of adolescent girls.* New York: Ballantine Books.

Pleck, J. H. (1981). *The myth of masculinity.* Cambridge, MA: Massachusetts Institute of Technology Press.

Pleck, J. H. (1995). The gender role strain paradigm: An update. In R. F. Levant & W. S. Pollack (Eds.), *A new psychology of men* (pp. 11–32). New York: Basic Books.

Pleck, J., & Sawyer, J. (1974). *Men and masculinity.* New Jersey: Prentice-Hall.

Plutchik, R. (1995). Outward and inward directed aggressiveness: The interaction between violence and suicidality. *Pharmacopsychiatry, 28* (Supp. 2), 47–57.

Pollack, W. (1990). Men's development and psychotherapy: A psychoanalytic perspective. *Psychotherapy, 27,* 316–321.

Pollack, W. S. (1992). Should men treat women? Dilemmas for the male psychotherapist: Psychoanalytic and developmental perspectives. *Ethics and Behavior, 2,* 39–49.

Pollack, W. (1995a). Deconstructing dis-identification: Rethinking psychoanalytic concepts of male development. *Psychoanalysis and Psychotherapy, 12,* 30–45.

Pollack, W. (1995b). No man is an island: Toward a new psychoanalytic psychology of men. In R. F. Levant & W. S. Pollack (Eds.), *A new psychology of men* (pp. 33–67). New York: Basic Books.

Pollack, W. (1998a). Mourning, melancholia, and masculinity: Recognizing and treating depression in men. In W. Pollack & R. Levant (Eds.), *New psychotherapy for men* (pp. 147–166). New York: Wiley.

Pollack, W. (1998b). *Real boys: Rescuing our sons from the myths of boyhood.* New York: Random House.

Pollack, W. S., & Levant, R. (Eds.). (1998). *New psychotherapy for men.* New York: Wiley.

Pollner, M. (1998). The effects of interviewer gender in mental health interviews. *Journal of Nervous and Mental Disease, 186,* 369–373.

Powell, B., Penick, E., Nickel, E., Liskow, B., Riesenmy, K., Campion, S., & Brown, S. (1992). Outcomes of co-morbid alcoholic men: A 1-year follow-up. *Alcohol Clinical and Experimental Research, 16,* 131–138.

Price, J., & Grunhaus, L. (1990). Treatment of clomipramine-induced anorgasmia with yohimbine: A case report. *Journal of Clinical Psychiatry, 51,* 32–33.

Pritchard, C. (1996). New patterns of suicide by age and gender in the United Kingdom and the Western World 1974–1992: An indicator of social change? *Social Psychiatry and Psychiatric Epidemiology, 31,* 227–234.

Rabinowitz, F., & Cochran, S. (1987) Counseling men in groups. In M. Scher, M. Stevens, G. Good, & G. Eichenfield (Eds.), *Handbook of counseling and psychotherapy with men* (pp. 51–67). Beverly Hills, CA: Sage.

Rabinowitz, F., & Cochran, S. (1994). *Man alive: A primer of men's issues.* Pacific Grove, CA: Brooks-Cole.

Rabkin, J., Rabkin, R., & Wagner, G. (1995). Testosterone replacement therapy in HIV illness. *General Hospital Psychiatry, 17,* 37–42.

Rabkin, J., Wagner, G., & Rabkin, R. (1996). Treatment of depression in HIV+ men: Literature review and report of an ongoing study of testosterone replacement therapy. *Annals of Behavioral Medicine, 18,* 24–29.

Radloff, L. (1977). The CES-D Scale: A new self-report depression scale for research in the general population. *Applied Psychological Measurement, 1,* 385–401.

Rado, S. (1928). The problem of melancholia. *International Journal of Psychoanalysis, 9,* 420–438.

Rado, S. (1951). Psychodynamics of depression from the etiologic point of view. *Psychosomatic Medicine, 13,* 51–55.

Real, T. (1997). *I don't want to talk about it: Overcoming the legacy of male depression.* New York: Fireside.

Reiger, D. A., Boyd, J. H., Burke, J. D., Rae, D. S., Myers, J. K., Kramer, M., Robins, L. N., George, L. K., Karno, M., & Locke, B. Z. (1988). One-month prevalence of mental disorders in the United States: Based on five Epidemiologic Catchment Area sites. *Archives of General Psychiatry, 45,* 977–986.

Reiger, D., Farmer, M., Rae, D., Locke, B., Keith, S., Judd, L., & Goodwin, F. (1990). Co-morbidity of mental disorders with alcohol and other drug abuse: Results from the Epidemiological Catchment Area (ECA) study. *Journal of the American Medical Association, 264,* 2511–2518.

Reimherr, F., Chouinard, G., Cohn, C., Cole, J., Itil, T., LaPierre, Y., Masco, H., & Mendels, J. (1990). Antidepressant efficacy of sertraline: A double-blind, placebo- and amitryityline-controlled multicenter comparison study in outpatients with major depression. *Journal of Clinical Psychiatry, 51* (supplement B), 18–27.

Rich, C., Young, D., & Fowler, R. (1986). San Diego suicide study: 1. Young vs. old subjects. *Archives of General Psychiatry, 43,* 577–582.

Riley, A., & Riley, E. (1986). Cyproheptadine and antidepressant-induced anorgasmia. *British Journal of Psychiatry, 148,* 217–218.

Ritter, A. J., & Cole, M. J. (1992). Men's issues: Gender role conflict and substance abuse. *Drug and Alcohol Review, 11,* 163–167.

Robins, L., Helzer, J., Cottler, L., & Goldring, E. (1989). *The diagnostic interview schedule–Version III-R.* St. Louis, MO: Washington University.

Robins, L., Helzer, J., Croughan, J., & Ratcliff, K. (1981). National Institute of Mental Health Diagnostic Interview Schedule: Its history, characteristics, and validity. *Archives of General Psychiatry, 38,* 381–389.

Robins, L., & Reiger, D. (1991). *Psychiatric disorders in America.* New York: Free Press.

Robins, L., Wing, J., Wittchen, H., Helzer, J., Babor, T., Burke, J., Farmer, A., Jablenski, A., Pickens, R., Reiger, D., Sartorius, N., & Towle, L. (1988). The Composite International Diagnostic Interview: An epidemiologic instrument suitable for use in conjunction with different diagnostic systems and in different cultures. *Archives of General Psychiatry, 45,* 1069–1077.

Robinson, L., Berman, J., & Neimeyer, R. (1990). Psychotherapy for the treatment of depression: A comprehensive review of controlled outcome research. *Psychological Bulletin, 108,* 30–49.

Roose, S., Dalack, G., & Woodring, S. (1991). Death, depression, and heart disease. *Journal of Clinical Psychiatry, 52* (Supp.), 34–39.

Rosenbaum, A., & O'Leary, K. (1986). The treatment of marital violence. In N. Jacobson & A. Gurman (Eds.), *Clinical handbook of marital therapy* (pp. 385–405). New York: Guilford.

Rounsaville, B., Klerman, G., Weissman, M., & Chevron, E. (1985). Short-term interpersonal psychotherapy (IPT) for depression. In E. Beckham & W. Leber (Eds.) *Handbook of depression* (pp. 124–150). Homewood, IL: Dorsey Press.

Rowe, M., Fleming, M., Barry, K., Manwell, L., & Kropp, S. (1995). Correlates of depression in primary care. *Journal of Family Practice, 41,* 551–558.

Roy, A. (1981). Vulnerability factors and depression in men. *British Journal of Psychiatry, 138,* 75–77.

Roy, A. (1987). Five risk factors for depression. *British Journal of Psychiatry, 150,* 536–541.

Roy, A., & Linnoila, M. (1986). Alcoholism and suicide. In R. Maris (Ed.), *Biology of suicide* (pp. 162–191). New York: Guilford.

Rubin, L. (1983). *Intimate strangers.* New York: Harper & Row.

Rubin, R., Poland, R., & Lesser, I. (1989). Neuroendocrine aspects of primary endogenous depression: VIII: Pituitary–gonadal axis activity in male patients and matched control subjects. *Psychoneuroendocrinology, 14,* 217–229.

Rupprecht, R., Rupprecht, C., Rupprecht, M., Noder, M., & Schwarz, W. (1988). Different reactivity of the hypothalamic–pituitary–gonadal axis in depression and normal controls. *Pharmacopsychiatry, 21,* 438–439.

Sachar, E., Halpern, F., Rosenfeld, R., Galligher, T., & Hellman, L. (1973). Plasma and urinary testosterone levels in depressed men. *Archives of General Psychiatry, 28,* 15–18.

Schaefer, A., Brown, J., Watson, C., Plemel, D., DeMotts, J., Howard, J., Petrik, N., Balleweg, B., & Anderson, D. (1985). Comparison of the validities of the Beck, Zung, and MMPI Depression Scales. *Journal of Consulting and Clinical Psychology, 53,* 415–418.

Scher, M. (1990). Effect of gender role incongruities on men's experience as clients in psychotherapy. *Psychotherapy, 27,* 322–326.

Scher, M., Stevens, M., Good, G., & Eichenfield, G. (Eds.). (1987). *The handbook of counseling and psychotherapy with men.* Newbury Park, CA: Sage.

Segraves, R. (1987). Bethanecol reversal of imipramine-induced ejaculatory dysfunction (letter). *American Journal of Psychiatry, 144,* 1243.

Segraves, R. (1993). Treatment-emergent sexual dysfunction in affective disorder: A review and management strategies. *Journal of clinical Psychiatry, 11,* 57–60.

Segraves, R. (1994). Treatment of drug-induced anorgasmia (letter). *British Journal of Psychiatry, 165,* 554.

Segraves, R. (1998). Antidepressant-induced sexual dysfunction. *Journal of Clinical Psychaitry, 59* (supplement 4), 48–54.

Seidman, S., & Rabkin, J. (1998). Testosterone replacement therapy for hypogonadal men with SSRI-refractory depression. *Journal of Affective Disorders, 48,* 157–161.

Seidman, S., & Walsh, B. (1999). Testosterone and depression in aging men. *American Journal of Geriatric Psychiatry, 7,* 18–33.

Seligman, M. (1975). *Helplessness: On depression, development, and death.* San Francisco: Freeman.

Seller, R., Blascovich, J., & Lenkei, E. (1981). Influence of stereotypes in the diagnosis of depression by family practice residents. *Journal of Family Practice, 12,* 849–854.

Sevy, S., Mendlewicz, J., & Mendelbaum, K. (1995). Genetic research in bipolar illness. In E. Becker & W. Leber (Eds.), *Handbook of depression* (pp. 203–212). New York: Guilford.

Shaw, B., Vallis, M., & McCabe, S. (1985). The assessment of the severity and symptom patterns in depression. In E. Beckham & W. Leber (Eds.) *Handbook of depression* (pp. 372–407). Homewood, IL: The Dorsey Press.

Sholomskas, D. (1990). Interviewing methods. In B. Wolman & G. Stricker (Eds.), *Depressive disorders: Facts, theories, and treatment methods* (pp. 231–247). New York: Wiley.

Shrivastava, R., Shrivastava, S., & Overweg, N. (1995). Amantadine in the treatment of sexual dysfunction associated with selective serotonin reuptake inhibitors. *Journal of Clinical Psychopharmacology, 15,* 83–84.

Silverman, C. (1968). *The epidemiology of depression.* Baltimore: Johns Hopkins Press.

Simpson, H. B., Nee, J. C., & Endicott, J. (1997). First-episode major depression: Few sex-differences in course. *Archives of General Psychiatry, 54,* 633–639.

Slipp, S. (1996). *Healing the gender wars: Therapy with men and couples.* New York: Jason Aronson.

Snyder, S. (1980). *Biological aspects of mental disorder.* New York: Oxford University Press.

Solomon, K., & Levy, N. (Eds.), (1982). *Men in transition: Theory and therapy.* New York: Plenum.

Sommers-Flanagan, J., & Sommers-Flanagan, R. (1995). Intake interviewing with suicidal patients: A systematic approach. *Professional Psychology, 26,* 41–47.

Sotsky, S., Glass, D., Shea, M., Pilkonis, P., Collins, J., Elkin, I., Watkins, J., Imber, S., Leber, W., Moyer, J., & Oliveri, M. (1991). Patient predictors of response to psychotherapy and pharmacotherapy: Findings in the NIMH Treatment of Depression Collaborative Research Program. *American Journal of Psychiatry, 148,* 997–1008.

Sovner, R. (1984). Treatment of tricyclic antidepressant-induced orgasmic inhibition with cyproheptadine (letter). *Journal of Clinical Psychiatry, 4,* 169.

Spitz, R. (1951). The psychogenic diseases of infancy. *Psychoanalytic Study of the Child, 6,* 255–275.

Spitz, R., & Wolf, K. M. (1946). Anaclitic depression. *Psychoanalytic Study of the Child, 2,* 313–342.

Spitzer, R., Williams, J., Gibbon, M., & First, M. (1990). *User's guide for the Structured Clinical Interview for DSM-R-III.* Washington, DC: American Psychiatric Press.

Stack, S. (1998). Gender, marriage, and suicide acceptability: A comparative analysis. *Sex Roles, 38,* 501–520.

Steele, T., & Howell, E. (1986). Cyproheptadine for imipramine-induced anorgasmia. *Journal of Clinical Psyhcopharmacology, 6,* 326–327.

Steiger, A., von Bardeleben, U., Wiedemann, K., & Holsboer, F. (1991). Sleep EEG and nocturnal secretion of testosterone and cortisol in patients with major endogenous depression during acute phase and after remission. *Journal of Psychiatric Research, 25,* 169–177.

Stein, T. (1982). Men's groups. In K. Solomon & N. Levy (Eds.), *Men in transition: Theory and therapy.* New York: Plenum.

Sternbach, H. (1998). Age-associated testosterone decline in men: Clinical issues for psychiatry. *American Journal of Psychiatry, 155,* 1310–1318.

Stoudemire, A., Kahn, M., Brown, J., Linfors, E., & Houpt, J. (1985). Masked depression in a combined medical–psychiatric unit. *Psychosomatics, 26,* 221–228.

Strauss, W., & Howe, N. (1991). *Generations: History of America's future, 1584–2069.* New York: William Morrow.

Stravynski, A., Verreault, R., Gaudette, G., & Langlois, R. (1994). The treatment of depression with group behavioral–cognitive therapy and imipramine. *Canadian Journal of Psychiatry, 39,* 387–390.

Stroebe, M. S. (1998). New directions in bereavement research: Exploration of gender differences, *Palliative Medicine, 12,* 5–12.

Stroebe, W., & Stroebe, M. S. (1987). *Bereavement and health: The psychological and physical consequences of partner loss.* Cambridge, UK: Cambridge University Press.

Styron, W. (1990). *Darkness visible. A memoir of madness.* New York: Random House.

Sutkin, L. C., & Good, G. (1987). Therapy with men in health-settings. In M. Scher, M. Stevens, G. Good, & G. Eichenfield (Eds.), *Handbook of counseling and psychotherapy with men* (pp. 372–387). Newbury Park, CA: Sage.

Swartz, H., & Markowitz, J. (1998). Interpersonal psychotherapy for the treatment of depression in HIV-positive men and women. In J. Markowitz (Ed.), *Interpersonal psychotherapy. Review of psychiatry* (pp. 129–155). Washington, DC: American Psychiatric Press.

Takeuchi, D., Chung, R., Lin, K., Shen, H., Kurasake, K., Chun, C., & Sue, S. (1998). Lifetime and twelve-month prevalence rates of major depressive episodes and dysthymia among Chinese Americans in Los Angeles. *American Journal of Psychiatry, 155,* 1407–1414.

Thase, M., Greenhouse, J., Frank, E., Reynolds, C., Pilkonis, P., Hurley, K., Grochocinski, V., & Kupfer, D. (1997). Treatment of major depression with psychotherapy or psychotherapy–pharmacotherapy combinations. *Archives of General Psychiatry, 34,* 1009–1015.

Thase, M., Reynolds, C., Frank, E., Simons, A., McGeary, R., Fasiczka, A., Garamoni, G., Jennings, R., & Kupfer, D. (1994a). Do depressed men and women respond similarly to cognitive behavior therapy? *American Journal of Psychiatry, 151,* 500–505.

Thase, M., Reynolds, C., Frank, E., Simons, A., Garamoni, G., McGeary, J., Harden, T., Fasiczka, A., & Gahalane, J. (1994b). Response to cognitive–behavioral therapy in chronic depression. *Journal of Psychotherapy Practice and Research, 3,* 204–214.

Thoits, P. (1987). Gender and marital status differences in control and distress: Common stress versus unique stress explanations. *Journal of Health and Social Behavior, 28,* 7–22.

Thompson, J., Ware, M., & Blashfield, R. (1990). Psychotropic medication and priapism: A comprehensive review. *Journal of Clinical Psychiatry, 51,* 430–433.

Tsuang, M., Simpson, J., & Fleming, J. (1992). Epidemiology of suicide. *International Reivew of Psychiatry, 4,* 117–129.

Tyson, P. (1982). The role of the father in gender identity, urethral eroticism, and phallic narcissism. In S. Cath, A. Gurwitt, & J. Ross (Eds.), *On fathers: Observations and reflections* (pp. 175–187). Boston: Little, Brown.

Tyson, P. (1986). Male gender identity: Early developmental roots. *Psychoanalytic Review, 73,* 405–425.

Umberson, D., Wortman, C., & Kessler, R. (1992). Widowhood and depression: Explaining long term gender differences in vulnerability. *Journal of Health and Social Behavior, 33,* 10–24.

Unden, F., Ljunggren, J., Beck-Friis, J., Kjellman, B., & Wetterberg, L. (1988). Hypothalamic–pituitary–gonadal axis in major depressive disorders. *Acta Psychiatrica Scandinavica, 78,* 138–146.

Van Houdenhove, B., Vestraeten, D., Onghena, P., & de Cuyper, H. (1992). Chronic idiopathic pain, mianserin and masked depression. *Psychotherapy and Psychosomatics, 58,* 46–53.

Vessey, J., & Howard, K. (1993). Who seeks psychotherapy? *Psychotherapy, 30,* 546–553.

Vogel, W., Klaiber, E., & Broverman, D. (1978). Roles of gonadal steroid hormones in psychiatric depression in men and women. *Progress in Neuropsychopharmacology and Biological Psychiatry, 2,* 487–503.

Vogel, w., Klaiber, E., & Broverman, D. (1985). A comparison of the antidepressant effects of a synthetic androgen (mesterolone) and amitriptyline in depressed men. *Journal of Clinical Psychiatry, 46,* 6–8.

Vredenburg, K., Krames, L., & Flett, G. (1986). Sex differences in the clinical expression of depression. *Sex Roles, 14,* 37–48.

Wagner, G., & Rabkin, J. (1998). Testosterone therapy for clinical symptoms of hypogonadism in eugonadal men with AIDS. *International Journal of STD and AIDS, 9,* 41–44.

Wagner, G., Rabkin, J., & Rabkin, R. (1996). A comparative analysis of standard and alternative antidepressants in the treatment of human immunodeficiency virus patients. *Comprehensive Psychiatry, 37,* 402–408.

Wagner, G., Rabkin, J., & Rabkin, R. (1998). Exercise as a mediator of psychological and nutritional effects of testosterone therapy in HIV+men. *Medicine and Science in Sports and Exercise, 30,* 811–817.

Waldinger, M., Hengeveld, M., & Zwinderman, A. (1994). Paroxetine treatment of premature ejaculation: A double-blind randomized, placebo-controlled study. *American Journal of Psychiatry, 151,* 1377–1379.

Walker, P., Cole, P., & Gardner, E. (1993). Improvement in fluoxetine-associated sexual dysfunction in patients switched to buproprion. *Journal of Clinical Psychiatry, 54,* 459–465.

Wallace, J., & Pfohl, B. (1995). Age-related differences in the symptomatic expression of major depression. *Journal of Nervous and Mental Disease, 183,* 99–102.

Warren, L. (1983). Male intolerance of depression: A review with implications for psychotherapy. *Clinical Psychology Review, 3,* 147–156.

Weiss, I., Nagel, C., & Aronson, M. (1986). Applicability of depression scales to the old person. *Journal of the American Geriatrics Society, 34,* 215–218.

Weissman, M., Bruce, M., Leaf, P., Florio, L., & Holzer, C. (1991). Affective disorders. In L. Robins & D. Reiger (Eds.), *Psychiatric disorders in America* (pp. 53–80). New York: Free Press.

Weissman, M., Gammon, G., John, K., Merikangas, K., Warner, V., Prusoff, B., & Sholomskas, D. (1987). Children of depressed parents: Increased psychopathology and early onset of major depression. *Archives of General Psychiatry, 44,* 847–853.

Weissman, M., & Markowitz, J. (1994). Interpersonal psychotherapy: Current status. *Archives of General Psychiatry, 51,* 599–606.

Wesner, R., & Winokur, G. (1990). Genetic and family studies of affective disorders. In B. Wolman & G. Stricker (Eds.), *Depressive disorders: Facts, theories, and treatment methods* (pp. 203–228). New York: Wiley.

Wexler, B., Mason, J., & Giller, E. (1989). Possible subtypes of affective disorder by differences in cerebral laterality and testosterone. *Archives of General Psychiatry, 46,* 429–433.

Whybrow, P. (1997). *A mood apart.* New York: Harper-Collins.

Wilhelm, K., & Parker, G. (1989). Is sex necessarily a risk factor to depression? *Psychological Medicine, 19,* 401–413.

Williamson, M. (1987). Sex differences in depression symptoms among adult family medicine patients. *Journal of Family Practice, 25,* 591–594.

Winnicott, D. W. (1936/1978). *Through paediatrics to psychoanalysis.* London, UK: Hogarth Press.

Winnicott, D. W. (1960/1965). *The maturational processes and the facilitating environment.* New York: International University Press.

Winokur, G. (1972). Depression spectrum disease: Description and family study. *Comprehensive Psychiatry, 13,* 3–8.

Winokur, G. (1979). Unipolar depression: Is it divisible into autonomous subtypes? *Archives of General Psychiatry, 36,* 47–52.

Winokur, G. (1991). *Mania and depression.* Baltimore: Johns Hopkins University Press.

Winokur, G. (1997). All roads lead to depression: Clinically homogeneous, etiologically heterogeneous. *Journal of Affective Disorders, 45,* 97–108.

Winokur, G., Behar, D., & Van Valkenburg, C. (1978). Is a familial definition of depression both feasible and valid? *Journal of Nervous and Mental Disease, 166,* 764–768.

Wolman, B., & Stricker, G. (Eds.). (1990). *Depressive disorders: Facts, theories, and treatment methods.* New York: Wiley.

Wong, M. (1978). Males in transition and the self-help group. *The Counseling Psychologist, 7,* 46–50.

Wortman, C. B., & Silver, R. C. (1989). The myths of coping with loss. *Journal of Consulting and Clinical Psychology, 57,* 349–357.

Wu, X., & DeMaris, A. (1996). Gender and marital status differences in depression: The effects of chronic strains. *Sex Roles, 34,* 299–319.

Yalom, I. D. (1980). *Existential psychotherapy.* New York: Basic.

Yesavage, J., Davidson, J., Widrow, L., & Berger, P. (1985). Plasma testosterone levels, depression, sexuality, and age. *Biological Psychiatry, 20,* 222–225.

Young, M., fogg, L., Scheftner, W., & Fawcett, J. (1994). Interactions of risk factors in predicting suicide. *American Journal of Psychiatry, 151,* 434–435.

Young, M., Scheftner, W., Fawcett, J., & Klerman, G. (1990). Gender differences in the clinical features of unipolar major depressive disorder. *Journal of Nervous and Mental disease, 178,* 200–203.

Zahner, G., Hsieh, C., & Fleming, J. (1995). Introduction to epidemiologic research methods. In M. Tsuang, M. Tohen, & G. Zahner (Eds.), *Textbook in psychiatric epidemiology* (pp. 23–53). New York: Wiley-Liss.

Zisook, S., Peterkin, J., Goggin, K., Sledge, P., Atkinson, J., & Grant, I. (1998). Treatment of major depression in HIV-seropositive men. *Journal of Clinical Psychiatry, 59,* 217–224.

Zlotnick, C., Elkin, I., & Shea, M. (1998). Does the gender of a patient or the gender of a therapist affect the treatment of patients with major depression? *Journal of Consulting and Clnincal Psychology, 66,* 655–659.

Zlotnick, C., Shea, M., Pilkonis, P., Elkin, I., & Ryan, C. (1996). Gender, type of treatment, dysfunctional attitudes, social support, life events, and depressive symptoms over naturalistic follow-up. *American Journal of Psychiatry, 153,* 1021–1027.

Zung, W. (1965). A self-rating depression scale. *Archives of General Psychiatry, 13,* 508–516.

Index